The Changeling

The autobiography of

MURRY HOPE

By the same author

The Changeling

The autobiography of

MURRY HOPE

LIGHT PUBLISHING

At the College of Psychic Studies

LONDON
First published in 1999 by
LIGHT PUBLISHING
At the College of Psychic Studies
16 Queensberry Place
London SW7 2EB

British Library Cataloguing in Publication Data.
A catalogue record for this book is available from the
British Library.

ISBN 0 903336 31 6

The aim of LIGHT PUBLISHING at the College of Psychic
Studies is to explore all aspects of spiritual and psychic knowledge.

The views expressed in all publications by LIGHT
PUBLISHING at the College of Psychic Studies are those of the
author, and do not necessarily reflect the views of the College of
Psychic Studies.

Typeset, printed and bound in Great Britain
by Whitstable Litho, Whitstable, Kent.

Cover by Chris Andrews

I dedicate this book to all those loved ones, and dear and loyal friends, who have stood by me over the last seven years and helped me during my hour of need.

CONTENTS

ACKNOWLEDGMENTS

My gratitude and thanks to my cousin, Paul Henri Thomelin, for his dedicated and unstinting work on the genealogy of our family; to those of my friends who have patiently, and diplomatically, waded through pages of my manuscripts; to Trish Miller, for the daunting task of correcting my erring grammar and generally knocking the work into shape; to Leppi Publications who kindly allowed use of their photography of my Russian Grandfather; and to my Publishers, LIGHT Publishing at The College of Psychic Studies, for allowing me to express my true self within the context of these pages.

Introduction

There was a belief in ancient times that on rare occasions, when a mother took her first sleep following the birth of a child, the fairies, gods, immortals, angels, earth spirits, etc., surreptitiously exchanged the infant for one of their own kind. Such beings were referred to as 'changelings'. In some versions of the tale the mother, upon waking, feeling the child to be alien, rejected it immediately, while in others the natural father and mother are slain by enemies, and the infant is saved by a serving woman, who flees with it to the woods, where it is raised by her kinsfolk – who just happen to be childless! In this environment it is schooled from infancy in the ways of the ordinary people, and stays therein until it receives 'the call' to its true destiny – a fact inevitably understood by its foster parents, who bid it farewell with all their love. As these children matured, they were seen as being 'odd', or different in some indefinable way, and because they were also observed to possess strange or unusual gifts, they were often greatly feared. Strangely enough, I was destined to act out this role to a 'T', although sometimes unconsciously, as were those to whom fell the task of fostering me. Such characters from the past as Merlin, Magician to the Court of King Arthur, Thomas the Rhymer, and Alexander the Great, are often cited as alien changelings, and there have doubtless been others, whose lives and deeds are unsung.

As Carl Jung discovered, no tradition or myth is without its reality at one level or another, so what we are really dealing with is not a direct body-for-body exchange, but rather *the ensoulment of that body by a non-hominid spirit, essence, psyche, 'energy field', or whatever term might be appropriate to either individual belief or collective credo.* Then who or what are these beings that have entered human bodies, but whose essences are not of the hominid ilk, and why have they elected to be born here? I cannot speak for those of the past, but there are a few things that I can make quite clear concerning my own case: I am NOT an 'alien' in the popularly understood meaning of the word. I have never been a Martian, Pleiadian, little green man with a T.V. aerial on my head, 'grey', or any fictional-type character from Star-Trek or similar entertainment scenarios. It is not beyond the realms of possibility that such beings do exist, albeit in some parallel, if not immediate, Universe; but then, there have been aliens incarnate in human bodies from time immemorial, although it is only in recent years that these have been viewed in terms of 'space people'. Considering the comparatively short period in the evolution of this planet that the hominid species has been around, perhaps human beings themselves are aliens, Gaia's only 'real' family being the plants, animals, and elemental or devic spirits, by whose good offices our Earth came to be what it is.

As a proponent of the 'field theory', I view what is commonly referred to as the soul or spirit in terms of a field of active particles begging organisation, which undergoes exposure to mass/matter in certain periods during its search for knowledge/information, thus increasing its band-width. Or, to put it in simple terms, as we learn and experience, so the soul 'ages', references to 'old souls', 'young souls', etc., being in general use in popular esoteric parlance. Another analogy could be a shattered hologram, each fragment of which contains an exact copy, albeit somewhat ill-defined, of the original picture. One may employ any number of terms to describe these fragments, which are distributed over vast periods of time, appropriate semantics being designated by prevailing scientific and metaphysical schools of belief. In the light of this concept, it is possible to access the data-banks of a more advanced fragment (commonly referred to as the 'higher self'), in order to obtain help or information. Some of the terms employed in standard metaphysical use are, however, inappropriate to the expression of broader, less defined abstractions, and can therefore prove misleading in that they generate quasi-religious analogies. In modern paraphysics, it is generally accepted that the body exists within the 'field', and not vice versa, several leading scientists and paraphysicists, notably Dr. Rupert Sheldrake and Professor Peter Stewart, having already committed themselves to this belief in print.

In order to avoid speculation as to my origins, I wish to state that my essence – the term I have elected to use to describe my soul/field – is of devic origin. For the benefit of those who may read this book who have no prior esoteric knowledge: there are many, many life forms, within this and other universes, which do not necessarily need to enter physical bodies as we know them, but commence their life cycles as minute particles which eventually accrue to create mass. ALL SUCH LIFE FORMS, FROM THE TINIEST CREDIBLE PARTICLE TO THE GREATEST CONCEIVABLE UNIVERSE, HAVE A CONSCIOUSNESS. Awareness, however, (or 'soul-age', to use a popular term), only develops via the various avenues of experience associated with both the individual field and the group species through which it has evolved, its band-width expanding proportionately at each stage.

Angelic/devic beings are an entirely different life form from homo sapiens. They commence their life cycles as spirits of the five elements: Fire, Air, Water, Earth and Time (yes, there is a fifth element!), each of these being a force in itself. These five forces align with the four great energy sources accepted by science: the Strong Nuclear – Fire; the Weak Nuclear – Water; Electromagnetism – Air; and Gravity – Earth. The fifth element, Time, is still under consideration by scientists, some of whom have accepted its potential as the co-ordinating Force, while others are still debating the subject, and seeking physical proof for same. The Ancients accorded names to the four recognised elements: The Spirits of Fire were known as Salamanders, those of Air – Sylphs, those of Water – Ondines, and those of Earth – Gnomes.

As each elemental essence evolves, it acquires its two-fold, three-fold, four-fold and eventually five-fold nature, and once it has mastered all five elemental qualities it will assume its rightful role in the angelic kingdoms. (For full details, see Chapter 21). Although, during each of these stages we interact with mass in one form or another, five-fold devas only enter physical bodies on very rare occasions, and for specific reasons, two examples being (1) in the Observer Mode, (as in my own case) to record, for the data-banks of our kind, major evolutionary changes; and (2) to effect genetic mutations, as in the Atlantean episode, about which I shall be writing later. Perhaps the ensuing chapters will give my readers some idea of our kind and our purpose.

I commenced my evolutionary cycle as a particle of the Force that scientists will come to know as Time, and, as a Time Essence, I am also closely affiliated to the Salamanders, or Fire devas. As such, in my native state my energies would be expressed via the Fifth, or reconciling Force, which is Time, the manifestation of matter/mass being contingent upon the slowing-down of Time. But then, I have covered that side of my knowledge in other books.

As a Time Essence I have always had the ability to 'view' other periods of time, which facility landed me in hot water during my schooldays, as those readers who are brave enough to tackle the forthcoming pages will find, to their amusement! To put the lid on the many who claim to have known me in Egypt, India, Rome, France, or wherever: prior to my first and only previous incarnation on this planet, which was in Atlantis, when I was united with my devic family (see Chapter 13), I did have one other physical life, as a Paschat (Lion person), which experience I needed in order to become accustomed to wearing a material form. Not possessing the required software in my youth, however, it took me some years to recall the Paschat episode, about which I shall be writing in detail in Chapter 19.

There is one point that needs to be clarified at this juncture:

the fact that I was born with a non-hominid soul in no way implies that I am any better or worse than anyone else. The pre-birth agenda designates that one may never use powers which, although they may be common practice in one's natural environment, would either appear phenomenal here on Earth, or render one an advantage over those among whom one has been sent for some special purpose, which, in my own case, as I have already stated, amounts to the role of observer – nothing more sinister! Also, hominid essences have many advantages over me, which will become obvious as this narrative proceeds. While on Earth I am able to explore various scenarios of human life, via both the genes that my soma has inherited and the hominid group-soul to whose data-banks those genes afford me access.

My critics will doubtless say that this is the story of a weird woman, who believes herself to be some peculiar sort of alien. I DO NOT BELIEVE – I HAVE KNOWN, SINCE BIRTH AND BEFORE. The word 'belief' implies an element of doubt. Jung was once asked if he believed in God. 'No, I do not believe', he replied. There was an icy silence before he continued, 'I KNOW'. Devic I may be, but I have never shared humankind's belief in some supreme creator 'in its own image and likeness'. Pure cosmic racism! Homo-sapiens is by no means the only 'thinking' life-form in this Universe. There are many of equal status, and others that are considerably more advanced, both spiritually and technologically, as hominids will learn to their chagrin in years to come. These beings may not always be visible to the five acknowledged senses, since many of them exist in parallel universes of faster (higher) frequencies than the one we view in our night skies. As a result, their fields (souls/essences) often carry a highly radioactive charge which, in the normal course of events, can induce imbalances in the human body. Any changeling whose ensouling 'field' hails from a frequency which is in some way incompatible with the hominid soma – and the endocrine system in particular – is faced with a pretty rough passage through life, females in particular tending to be sterile. So, while that changeling may appear to display what are sometimes seen as special gifts, the price to be paid overall is far higher than those meagre advantages that many observers might envy.

There is one other matter which begs clarification and that is the subject of freewill, or freedom of choice. There is an obnoxious heresy doing the rounds at the moment which states that Earth is the only planet of choice – balderdash (I would employ a stronger expletive if I did not consider that it might cause offence to some sensitive soul). As explained above, prior to coming to this planet I experienced my one and only previous life in the worlds of physical matter as a Paschat (Lion Person) in the Sirius System – hence my overpowering affinity with all felines. I can assure my readers that we all had freewill/choice, as did our hominid-type neighbours from the other inhabited planets in our solar system. As a being who has travelled not only to the ends of this Universe but also to many others, I have never yet encountered any life-forms that do not have freewill.

In analysis, however, the concept of freewill would appear to be incongruous if viewed in the light of the limitations that are inevitably imposed upon its expression. Such factors as the overall evolution of the home planet, environmental conditions, genetics, cerebral hardware, and other somatic considerations, need to be taken into account, in addition to the soul-age/field band-width of the individual at each given stage along the path towards full cosmic, conscious awareness. But in spite of all these apparent anomalies, the whole evolutionary process, in all its aspects, is contingent upon the expression of freewill to some degree or other, all life-forms effecting that option in their choice between order/chaos, construction/destruction, kindness/cruelty, etc., in accordance with the limitations imposed by the boundaries of each level through which they pass on their evolutionary journey. I hesitate to use the terms 'good' and 'evil', since moral attitudes inevitably change as one progresses. As a devic spirit, I have always been able to choose between using the energies of my kind in either a positive (constructive) or negative (destructive) way.

However, there are subtle variations of the 'choice' theme. For example, those essences or souls that are still bound to their respective 'collective' (group soul) do not necessarily choose their bodies as is popularly supposed. Rather, they are subconsciously drawn to situations which either allow them to gain the experiences necessary for field expansion, or simply to return to where they were before, and where they therefore feel comfortable. Only individuated souls/essences can effect this specific choice, and these can be easily identified by their attitude towards other species.

Renowned geneticist Richard Dawking may lay the blame for what we 'are' fairly and squarely on our genes, but, like attracting like, dysfunctional genes (I hesitate to use the word 'bad') are more than likely to attract a dysfunctional essence that is passing through a retrogressive stage in its evolvement. Besides, genes cannot express themselves without the intervention of the life-force supplied by the field (soul/ essence), and when this force withdraws, as in death, those genes also die with the body. I have always viewed my body as a separate entity from 'myself' – a collection of genes brought together through the evolutionary process of matter/ mass. Sometimes we clash, I overwork it, and it protests by producing an illness. Most times we get on well together, although it is frequently frustrated by the train of events to which it is subjected in order to allow me to fulfil what I came here to do. I view genes as a separate life-form which work in concert with the elements of matter and the soul/essence, and whose growth and self-expression are dependent upon the interplay between both. As I will be dropping a genetic bomb on the reincarnation theme in Chapter 4, a temporary halt on the subject seems appropriate.

Over the ensuing pages I hope to explain, and to bring some understanding of, the difficulties encountered by an alien soul in an earthly body: the problems of adaption, rejection, how one deals with physical discomforts such as intense pain resulting from cruelty/abuse, etc., and, even more deadly, mental cruelty. There are also a few difficulties in learning to programme that computer known as the human brain: in the constant errors that one makes, from which one inevitably learns the hard way; in coping with the human condition 'per se' while anxiously counting the years to one's eventual freedom from this hominid encapsulation, and the ecstasy to be experienced when one is again reunited with one's own kind.

One of the problems facing me in the ensuing chapters is that I am (for my sins) able to access the mental data-banks of the sceptics, and to anticipate their reactions. There will inevitably be the usual collection of psychologists, psychiatrists, physicians and geneticists, who will find convenient explanations within their disciplines for such peculiarities of character, (the word compensatory springs to mind!) as will become obvious as this narrative proceeds: so what does one do if one is all too aware of the standard professional answers? To facilitate the task in hand, why not pre-empt a few of these? And what better than a psychiatrist's assessment of my personality, etc., to start with?

I have always classified myself as belonging to the 'Anxious Personality' type, with, perhaps, a slight dash of the 'Obsessional'. However, in the 1970's, a friend of mine was employed as private secretary to a psychiatrist of note, who had devised a simple test for personality analysis, a test which was also designed to highlight any mental disorders, dormant or otherwise. As a favour, she asked if he would apply this test to a friend of hers, to which he agreed, and said document, which covered several pages of personal questions, was passed to me, to be returned later for analysis. Here is the summary:

> 'Mentally well-balanced, intelligent, articulate, with a strong   desire for a tranquil and peaceful state of harmony, but disposed to somatize when under stress. Exercises initiative in overcoming obstacles and difficulties. Holds, or wishes to achieve, a position of authority in which control can be exerted over events. Circumstances, however, may force compromise.'

'Delights in the tasteful, the gracious and the sensitive, but maintains an attitude of critical appraisal. Keeps a strict and watchful control on emotions and emotional relationships, which are unemotionally jettisoned if judged to be of no further use. Will accept so much in a relationship, but nothing beyond a certain point. Needs to know where she stands.'

'Needs to protect herself against her tendency to be too trusting, as she finds it liable to be misunderstood and exploited by others. Is inevitably forced into a position of compromise in order to keep the peace.'

So, dear reader, you may cry 'rubbish' after the first few chapters (if you can stay with it for that long), dismiss it as a psychological quirk or attention-seeking outlet in my personality, suggest that I should have taken up sci-fi writing, or recognise the truth in the light of my essence.

As to the physical side (in case my readers have already started building a picture of someone with horns and a tail), after a catscan at Gloucester Hospital in 1982 as a result of a fall, the officiating physician commented that I had one of the most perfectly formed brains he had ever seen in a scan. (Dear me, no strange bumps or Spock-like ears, although I was once observed by a dermatologist to have a strong green pigment in my skin). However, what physicians have observed during my periods of hospitalisation are an abnormally low body temperature, slow heart-beat/respiratory rates, an intolerance to cold and darkness, and highly sensitive central and autonomic nervous systems. My physical co-ordination is poor, however, my peripheral vision highly suspect, and our psychiatrist friend was correct in his statement that the body takes the rap for the mind. Oh, yes, and here 'is' an unusual one: I adore radioactivity. In fact, a long session of X-rays leaves me on top of the world, totally revitalised and recharged. But then, we devas are highly radioactive anyway. The genetics I shall be dealing with in Chapter 4, my cousin, a dedicated amateur genealogist, having traced our family tree back to the ninth century A.D. and earlier.

Of course, all this proves nothing, and I am still acutely aware that a lot of what I shall write will be classified under one or other category of mental illness or alienation. After browsing through DSM-111-R (Diagnostic and Statistical Manual of Mental Disorders) of the American Psychiatric Association, I arrived at the conclusion that everyone is viewed by the psychiatric fraternity as one or another form of 'fruitcake'; so, hopefully (?), they will add 'changeling' to their 567-page analysis of human faults, failings, foibles and weaknesses. I therefore intend to forego the angst, dodge the inevitable brickbats, and proceed in the safe knowledge that our generation's science fiction will inevitably end up as some future generation's science fact.

But to return to my own situation in the here and now. An alien field, such as I am, carries an entirely different evolutionary programme from that of the standard hominid. Therefore, when it takes on a hominid body there are many clashes, resulting in problems both psychological and physical. As far as I am concerned, however, please dismiss any preconceptions of 'weirdos' – where I came from there were no such things. Weirdos are trying to make some kind of social statement: I am not. At a recent lecture I was accused by several New Agers of being 'square' – do me a favour – I am positively *cubic*! Although this is my second time here, so I have already been indoctrinated to a degree into hominid brain processes, society in those long-gone times was so vastly removed from that of today as to render this time round a 'first' all over again.

Having read the foregoing, I do not doubt that many social misfits will hasten to classify themselves as changelings. But in so doing they both err and show themselves in their true light, because a changeling is duty-bound to 'fit in' as much as possible in order to explore in depth the psychology of the group-soul/field of the body into which it has incarnated. Misfitting would prevent this, especially in earlier years of the life in question. If a changeling intends to 'come out', the confessions will inevitably appear either in later life for teaching purposes, or nearing the end of that existence, when the task in hand has been completed. Obvious differences inevitably giving rise to controversies, the changeling also endeavours to keep a low profile, and to appear as normal as possible by human standards until his/her work is completed.

For many years, spiritualistic, metaphysical or occult semantics were the only vehicles available for the expression of exalted cosmic principles. In recent times, however, several orthodox disciplines have mercifully opened their doors by providing terminology more pertinent to the truth, and more easily accepted by the sceptical. Science has, in fact, been my liberator in that it has supplied me with appropriate cerebral software through which to express, in more acceptable terms, that which I have known and experienced over the past 68 years. I am therefore indebted to such stalwarts as Doctors Rupert Sheldrake, John Gribbin, Fred Alan Wolf, David Bohm,

and Professor Stephen Hawking among others, for giving me
the wherewithal to skim the alternating waves of doubt and
inspiration on the surfboard of my own innate, if limited,
understanding. I also owe a considerable debt to Professor
Peter Stewart, who introduced me to the 'field theory',
without which I would have been denied the ability to express
much of the material contained in the following chapters, and
to the term 'pananimist' – a person who acknowledges the life
force in ALL things, both animate and inanimate.

It is unfortunate that certain legitimate terms sometimes
carry dark connotations, the word 'occult' being an example.
Any dictionary will tell you that it simply means 'hidden', its
use in astronomy never seeming to give offence to anyone in
the scientific or rational fields of thinking. Likewise with the
word 'magic', which derives from the words *MOG, MEGH,
MAGH,* which, in the very ancient languages of Pehlvi and
Zend signify 'priest', 'wise' and 'excellent'. But since many of
those who read this book are probably more familiar with
those semantics generally employed among the majority of
adherents to metaphysical beliefs, I would like to define my
use of certain terms that could prove either frightening or
offensive to some, especially when I come to Chapter 21,
wherein I deal with the works of St.Thomas Aquinas, who,
according to historical sources, was an occultist of some
repute. Commensurate with my present understanding, the
genuine occultist (or magician) aspires to negotiate and
control forces of a cosmic or paranormal nature by the use of
mind-power or ritual; the psychic/medium/channeller
presumes to be manipulated by essences or intelligences
external to the purely physical; the mystic seeks to imbibe and

merge his/her consciousness with both the manifest and unmanifest through prayer, contemplation and observation. Of course, it can be argued that all three categories of person could equally be using their specific areas of expertise to contact less desirable energies, and the Universe is not, I can assure you, short of these, as my later discourse on the subject of angels will show. However, for those readers who demand a more scientific approach, an explanation of the above is given in terms of modern physics, in Chapter 13.

It would, however, be remiss of me if I failed to mention the cult of Shamanism, which has undergone a revival in recent years. Shamans are often referred to in the 'wounded healer' context, ancient initiatory rites having demanded both physical and mental suffering on the part of the aspirant before he/she was deemed ready to enter general practice. Shamans often work with the spirits of the elements, animals, plants, trees and nature generally, and may also be seen to employ one or any of the aforementioned metaphysical practices in the pursuit of their calling.

But to return to my own tale, which is, perhaps, more tragedy than comedy, since it tells of years of suffering in an alien body which I have slowly learned to control and of the mental pain I have endured in my efforts to conform. In fact, my life to date has been a strange journey of discovery – vague, fleeting memories of odysseys through time – to a frequency from which one can access any of many universes. The amalgam of personalities which constitutes the person I am today took years to discover, isolate and accommodate. However, playing by such unfamiliar and uncomfortable rules can be tedious in the extreme, although my previous life as a

Paschat afforded me a sort of animal cunning which has helped to see me through. Paschats were known throughout this neck of the Universal woods for their orderly existence and fair play, and, together with that branch of the angelic kingdoms known as Seraphim, they share the task of keeping Law and Order (equilibrium) in this Universe.

So let the story commence – at the beginning of this, my present life.

BIRTH CHART

NAME __MURRY HOPE__

NUMBER _____

HOUSE SYSTEM __PLACIDUS__

	D.	M.	Y.
Birth date	17	9	29
Birth place	Westcliffe-on-Sea		
Latitude	51	32	N
Longitude		43	E

TIME	H.	M.	s.	
Birth time as given	6	00	00	p.m.
Zone standard *E—W+				
Summer (or double) time * —	1	00	00	
G.M.T.	5	00	00	p.m.
G.M.T. date : :				

	H.	M.	S.
Sid. time noon G.M.T.	11	43	44
Interval *TO/FROM noon p.m.+	5	00	00
Result	16	43	44
Acceleration on interval p.m.+			50
Sid. time at Greenwich at birth	16	44	34
Longitude equivalent *E+W—		2	52
LOCAL SID. TIME AT BIRTH	16	47	26
Subtract 24 hrs. if necessary —			

* Delete whichever is not required.

SOUTHERN LATITUDES:
ADD 12 HOURS AND
REVERSE SIGNS.

Ruling Planet ♆	Positive 6	Triplicities:
Ruler's House 1	Negative 4	Fire 3 + MC
Rising Planet	Angular ♀ ♃	Earth 2
Mutual Reception		Air 3 + ASC
		Water 2
		Quadruplicities:
		Cardinal 4
		Fixed 1
		Mutable 5

PLANET		DEC.	ASPECTS									
			☉	☽	☿	♀	♂	♃	♄	♅	♆	♇
SUN	☉				⊻	⊻		□ʷ	☍ᵃ		⊻	⊼
MOON	☽							□	Q	⊻	☌	△ʷ
MERCURY	☿					✶	☌	△	✶		∠	□
VENUS	♀						✶	✶	△	△	☌ʷ	⊻
MARS	♂							△	✶	☍	∠	□
JUPITER	♃								☍	✶		⊻
SATURN	♄										△	⊼
URANUS	♅										⊼ʷ	
NEPTUNE	♆											⊼
PLUTO	♇											
Asc.	Asc.	⊼		△	☍	△	△	✶	✶ʷ		⊼
M.C.	M.C.		□	✶	·	△	☍		△	·	⊼

PROGRESSED DATA

NOON POSITIONS _____ Prog.   D. M. Y.

CORRESPOND TO _____ Noon Date

P ☉ _____ P ♀ _____ P ♄ _____

P ☽ _____ P ♂ _____ P Asc. _____

P ☿ _____ P ♃ _____ P M.C. _____

CHAPTER 1

At the Beginning

Once upon a time – I make no apologies for the old-hat start, and those readers who manage to make it to the last page will see why – in a small seaside town called Westcliff-on-Sea, in the County of Essex, in south-east England, a heavily pregnant woman drove herself to the local nursing home, where it had been arranged for her to give birth to her child. Her contractions had already started, but there was no-one available at the time to take her. Her husband, Beresford Charles Hope, although a mere forty-seven years of age, was in the final stages of cancer and his life was rapidly nearing its end. Although the Hopes already had a beautiful two-year old daughter named Berrie, he had desperately wanted a son and was pinning his dying hopes on the arrival of a male child, whom he planned to call Jack, to be followed by the family name of Murry. But the Hand of Fate had one last, bitter blow in store for the dying man; at six o'clock BST on 17th September 1929, his wife, Violet, gave birth to another daughter, a strange-looking infant with a shock of red hair. Poor Beresford was totally distraught when he heard the news, his chances of ever having a son being well and truly over. An air of doom overshadowed the whole household, and it was latterly remarked among his staff and friends that the shock of what he saw as failure was the final nail in his coffin. He died shortly after.

Although both parents had hoped for a son, they had, as a precaution, considered Yasmin as a possible girl's name. In due deference to Beresford's insistence on the name Jack, however, the newborn baby was named Jacqueline Murry. And so the unwanted and unwelcome changeling caught her first glimpse of her new environment: a world that was to prove the most severe testing ground yet in her evolutionary journey.

Whether it was due to the double trauma of giving birth and losing her husband under such sad and tragic circumstances, or whether she simply felt uncomfortable with the baby, one will never know. What we do know is that Violet wanted nothing to do with it from birth and promptly handed it over to their Nanny, Nurse Rhoda Adams, who also looked after Berrie. The Hopes had sufficient finances to keep a staff which included, as well as a Nanny, a cook-housekeeper and a maid, the two former being related.

Very shortly after Beresford's burial, Violet suddenly vanished, leaving the baffled staff to cope as best they could. In today's world, the double trauma of birth and death would be dealt with psychiatrically: post-natal depression, perhaps, combined with shock. But in those times there were no such services available, even for money, and what my Nanny described as 'a sort of numbness and disbelief' befell the household. Friends of Beresford's eventually came to their aid, the house was duly sold, and Nanny and her sister, Fan, took the two children to the home of their relatives who owned a property at 151, Westcombe Hill, Blackheath.

As time passed and there was still no sign of Violet, many feared the worst. Berrie was eventually put up for adoption, and the couple in question, who already had children of their own, would have also taken Jacqueline, were it not for the fact that she was a sickly child who needed constant, professional nursing, and was, at the time, receiving prolonged treatment for a renal problem at Greenwich Cottage Hospital. Besides, Nanny and her family had taken a shine to the baby and were considering giving her a home among their own kind.

How much do I remember of all this? Of the actual birth I have no recollection. Sensations, perhaps, but I was somehow shielded from the excruciating pain of being born into an alien world. Maybe this was something I effected for myself, or perhaps my kindly spiritual kindred lent a helping hand. My first actual memory, however, was very clear indeed. I could not have been more than two months old when I recall being outside my body and watching Nanny holding the small form that I was destined to be stuck with for the ensuing years. I remember, quite clearly, thinking to myself, 'Oh heck, what have I been landed with? And it's female as well', which didn't please me at all, as I seemed to be all too aware that, in the climate of opinion prevalent in those times, women were denied the freedom of expression and the available options that they have today. And then what I can only describe as a mood of resignation took over, and I Thought, 'Oh, well, there is nothing I can do about it now, so I had better get back in there, make haste with whatever I have to do, and get the job over and done with'. Strangely enough, this sort of acceptance has stayed with me throughout my life, and my friends often laugh when they suggest that I take a break or a holiday and I reply, 'Sorry, I simply have to get on with the job in hand. Can't relax until it is all tied up and finished.' What I am trying to say is that I was aware of being an alien changeling from the very beginning, although it was some years before I could find a hominid name to describe the species to which I really belonged. I was subconsciously, if not consciously, aware that I had entered a pre-programmed body which carried the Atlanto/Siriun gene, and that, as the energy of Time slowly allowed my awareness to develop, genetic memory and field memory would slowly merge to create the whole picture: but such realisations took many years to unfold.

The next six, wonderful years, spent with Nanny and her family, were among the most precious times in the life that was later to afford me so much pain and suffering. And so the story, momentarily a happy one (for me, anyway), begins. As an infant I hovered precariously between the fuzzy worlds of non-locality and the hominid body I had taken on. It was a slow and tedious process. Nanny remarked later that I was always asleep. In fact she stated quite categorically that I was the easiest baby she had ever handled, and most certainly the quietest.

Nanny had been in service since qualifying in her early years. Many were the tales she told me of the numerous families she had worked for, places she had travelled to, and tokens of appreciation rendered to her when she left to take up the next appointment. These frequently came in the form of watches: she had a large box of beautiful specimens, each of which was inscribed 'To Nurse Adams, in gratitude' (or similar), from Lady Cecily Barnet, Lady Game (whose two sons she nursed, David, killed in WWI, and Philip, later head of the Metropolitan Police), and many others whose names now escape me.

The residents of 151, Westcombe Hill included Nanny's sister, Fan, (Frances, probably, but I never heard her referred to as anything other than Fan), who had also been in service with my father, and to whom I gave the name 'Blue Granny' (as contrasting with her other sister, Eliza, who lived in Wimbledon, and whom I knew as 'White Granny'). This had nothing whatsoever to do with their skin colour, but rather their aprons! Blue Granny, who had been a professional cook-housekeeper until she retired, always wore a blue and white striped apron, while White Granny always seemed to sport a sort of black and white flowered overall. Even as a small child I hated the colour black, so 'white' it had to be. Blue Granny's husband was grandfather 'Elf' to me (Alfred, no doubt) and their surname was Wellard. Also in residence at 151 was their son, Alan, an electrical engineer who worked at a place called Siemans (I'm not sure how to spell that one), which Nanny told me was 'just down the road'.

The house itself was a shrine to Victoriana. The entrance passage was tiled in terracotta, white (well, it was once, I suppose) and black. The facing staircase featured some rather threadbare carpet, secured by brass rods which were lovingly treated with Brasso every Friday. But the 'front room' was the *pièce de résistance*. Antimacassars and aspidistras went without saying, gracing the heavy, mahogany furniture with the essence of the time-warp it represented. Brown chenille curtains decorated with bobbles embraced the bay window, which sported a seat that was obviously designed for people whose rears were less endowed than those of the current residents. I fitted into it comfortably, however, and would delight in watching the traffic labouring up the hill to the top, where there was a pub called 'The Standard' and a cinema called 'The Roxy'. There were also a lot of steamrollers around in those times, or so it seemed to me, as I was petrified of them. They used to puff extra hard up the last bit, their drivers enjoying a quiet Woodbine when no-one was looking. Strangely enough, I was frightened of any form of machinery, especially of an electrical nature, and it was many years before a psychologist, who specialised in researching alien phenomena, was able to explain why. (ref. final page of Chapter 13).

Nanny's front room housed many other antiquities, some of which would doubtless fetch a fair price in today's world. There was an ancient harmonium which both Nanny and Blue Granny played at certain times of the year, these being birthdays, Easter and Christmas. The Wellards were a numerous family and I came to know them all as 'uncles' and 'aunts'. There was Uncle Charlie and Aunt Maud, Uncle Bert and Aunt Beck, and Uncle Alan, to name but a few. They, too, had children, some of whom will feature in the next chapter to illustrate the wonderful world of instinctive psychology with which Nanny was so highly conversant, and which she saw fit to bestow upon me from a very early age.

Backing onto the front room was the sort of 'middle room' which usually faced either the garden or back yard in houses of this kind. Further on along the passage was the door which led to the kitchen and scullery. An old-fashioned type of range dominated the kitchen and kept the place permanently warm. Above it hung two very twee pictures of pretty little girls being guarded by tall, white-winged angels. Nanny would often gaze at it and remark, 'Only the good die young. You know, Jack, it doesn't pay to get too fond of anyone, because God gets jealous and takes them away from you'. Nanny had never married, and I have often wondered which soldier or sailor had been her beloved in earlier wars, never to return to claim his true love.

Washing was frequently to be seen hanging on a line suspended above the old range, 'airing', as Nanny would say. This was the room we all ate in, except on Sunday afternoon, when tea was taken in the front room, on a fancy tablecloth with posh china. The food served at this Sunday ritual never varied. It consisted of shrimps, winkles and any other shell-fish in season, followed by home-made cakes and scones, and lots of cups of tea. Incidentally, I was always known as 'Jack', never 'Jackie' or 'Jacqueline'.

In the scullery there was a gas stove, a deep, brown sink, an old-style 'copper' for washing and lots of storage cupboards. The main food cupboard, however, was under the stairs. It was very cold in there, as the floor was stone, and there was a further flight of stairs leading from it down to the coal-cellar, which was filled via a hole in the pavement outside the house. I recall with clarity how Nanny and Blue Granny used to take their washing out of the copper with a pair of wooden tongs, rinse it, and run it through the mangle. Blue Granny would feed the items through, while Nanny laboriously turned the great handle. Beyond the scullery was a downstairs loo, and then a door leading out into what seemed to me at the time to be a very large garden. Doubtless it was not as large or as broad as I might describe, although, to a small child, it certainly seemed that way.

Now to the next storey. The landing at the top of the first flight of stairs featured two doors, one of which led to the bathroom, and the other to Nanny's and my bedroom. The bathroom was yet another monument to the reign of Queen Victoria, with its mahogany fittings and enormously deep bath (the taps of which took the strength of an ox to turn on and off), and a loo which flushed noisily at the pull of a massive chain, which for a long time was well beyond my reach. Many was the time when poor old Nanny was obliged to climb the stairs to do the deed for me.

From this landing, another short flight of stairs led to Alan's room on the left, and Blue Granny and Grandfather Elf's room directly ahead, the latter being obviously the main bedroom as it was situated in the front of the house. Beyond all this was a further flight of stairs, which led to an attic. This attic so fascinated me that one day I crawled up the stairs, opened the door, and peered in. It was full of junk, but there was one object that really frightened me, although I cannot think why. This was a huge tuba, which, I was later told, Grandfather Elf's brother used to play before he died. Perhaps the spirit of this old tuba player still haunted his instrument? One will never know, but I was sufficiently scared of it to beat a hasty retreat down the perilously narrow flight of stairs to the safety of my bedroom. I recall at a later date Nanny saying to me 'Jack, would you like to help me to clear a few things out of the attic?' I think she was somewhat puzzled when I told her that I had it in mind at that moment to clean the stair rods.

This was an excuse I often used when I wanted to dodge out of some odious task. Cooking, for example, is something I have hated since childhood, and when Nanny asked me if I would like to help her make a cake, as she frequently did, those old stair-rods inevitably raised their weary heads to protect me from what I viewed at the time as a fate worse than death. She soon got the message, and ended up letting me off that particular chore, although she did once add 'You'll have to face up to it one day, Jack!'

The sensations I underwent as a child were strange, to say the least. I have often asked other people if they ever felt similarly, but have so far drawn a blank. For example, I recall feeling like a disembodied entity or energy-field, my present body being nothing more than a sort of space-suit, the visor of which I peered through suspiciously, cautiously, oft times wondering exactly what I had let myself in for. And my dreams – now there is a strange thing. From babyhood I always dreamed as an adult, and never as either a male or a female, but rather as some androgynous sort of being to whom the male-female concept was totally alien. Psychologists will doubtless have an explanation for the latter, but as to the former, I have never come across anyone else who experienced as an adult in dreams when they were a mere baby. But then, I am not a psychologist.

As I grew older, I used my dreamtime to explore the myriad alternatives of hominid experience, both male and female, in worlds parallel to the one we live in at present. In fact the hominid male-female complex has proved to be one of the hardest things for me to understand. As a child I simply could not compute the difference, which frequently landed me in hot water as I grew older. Strangely enough, today's feminist lobby seem to dislike me, although I cannot understand why. But then, that is hominid logic (or lack of it, by my devic standards!). I can also recall being fully cognisant of my dreams, although I lacked the appropriate terms of reference to explain what I had seen, express what I knew, and effect an appropriate interpretation. Such cerebral software had to be gathered over the ensuing years in the school of human life. Later, however, and with Nanny's help, I was able to overcome this difficulty and to give her some idea as to what I had 'seen' during my nightly travels through time.

The sheer frustration of being a child caused me to long for adulthood. I had little, if anything, in common with other children. I could not stand dolls, or anything feminine for that matter, preferring soft toys, and anything mechanical – which I would assemble with a dexterity incompatible with my age. This has lasted all through my life, cars in particular, and fast, sporty ones at that, being among my favourite things. I also adore flying. Looking at the frustrations endured by my small body in those times is reminiscent of having a comprehensive computer programme without the appropriate code essential to access its data-banks.

Later in my life, people have often suggested that the lack of a natural father and mother could have caused emotional damage to my psyche. Rubbish! All my physical parents did was to provide me with the body. After that, those who had elected to take on the task of guiding that body to the next stage took over. To this day I have no feeling whatsoever for my deceased biological parents, and, even when I did meet up with my mother a few years later, she was like a stranger to me, and one I did not particularly like.

As a small child living with Nanny and her family, I would describe myself as singularly unprepossessing, with reddish hair, slanted eyes and an overall goblin-like appearance. From the earliest times I suffered from poor co-ordination, which once evoked from Nanny the remark, 'You know, Jack, you're a clever kid, but by God you're cack-handed!' My sister, on the other hand (whom I saw for the first time, albeit only briefly, when she was about six), was stunningly beautiful, with long, dark curls and violet eyes, like my mother. My father had been grey-eyed and blond. In Nanny's kitchen there was a high, ladder-backed chair, over which a somewhat elderly mirror was precariously suspended. As soon as I could crawl, I mounted the ladder-back steps and peered curiously into the mirror. The sight which confronted me produced a wail of horror! Nanny came dashing in to see what was wrong. 'I'm a monkey, Nanny,' I bawled. 'I don't want to be a monkey, can't I be like I used to?' 'And what might that be?', Nanny questioned, comfortingly. I recall thinking hard and then pointing to Blue Granny's tabby cat, Tiger. 'Like that', I said. Nanny explained that this was a cat, and that I was a little girl. I was inconsolable, however, and refusing all comfort from Nanny, withdrew to a corner to cry the shock out of my system. Strangely enough, it was not until much later in my life, when the full memory of my experience among the Paschats came flooding back to me, that I was able to substantiate and account for this strange behaviour.

But back to my life with Nanny. To this day I can recall every detail of the bedroom we shared. There was one window which overlooked the back garden. My bed was nearest that window, while Nanny's was against the wall on the other (house) side of the room. To my right, at an angle to the back wall, there was an old dressing-table (which later came into my possession when I was in my twenties). On the wall directly facing Nanny's and my beds there was a washstand with the usual old-fashioned jug and basin. I can recall it being decorated with large, pink roses. Then there was the fireplace, in which Nanny would make a small fire during the very cold winter nights, or if I was ever very ill. On the other side of the fireplace was the matching wardrobe to the dressing table. It had a mirror on the outside of the door, into which I would occasionally peer – with disgust at what I saw. This usually resulted in my squeezing myself into the small space between the wardrobe and the wall as though to hide from the 'me' I had just had the misfortune to face. Under the bed was what Nanny used to call the 'jeremiah', or jerry for short. The bathroom being next door, Nanny had no use for such an article, but she did not like me wandering about in the night when I was very small, in case I took a tumble down the stairs. I recall this particular jerry because it was an ornamental china affair with an 'eye' in the bottom. I asked Nanny what the eye was doing there. She replied, 'To see that you do your business properly, young lady'. I often sat by that bedroom window and watched Grandfather Elf doing the garden. When the weather was warm enough I was allowed out there to play – something I seldom ever did, however, preferring the company of adults.

As a child I could not stand other children. I saw them as being cruel, unfeeling and, worst of all, NOISY! I have never been able to tolerate noise, at any stage of my life. I was also a natural pananimist, seeing the life-force in all things, even teddy bears, soft toys, etc., so to watch a child pulling a leg off its toy bear would produce floods of tears from me – tears of pain for the suffering bear. This sensitivity even extended to cartoons. On one occasion Nanny took me to see a film at the Roxy. She loved Ginger Rogers and Fred Astaire films, and so did I. But in this particular programme there was a cartoon featuring the Three Stooges, who, at one point in the plot, jumped into some wet concrete which was then seen to harden, entrapping them. I could not have been more than three or four years old at the time, but that night I cried pitifully. When Nanny asked me what was wrong, I told her that by then the concrete would have hardened around those poor men's legs and crushed their bones, and they would never be able to walk again! She explained to me that it was all a kind of joke, but I made it quite clear to her that from then on I wanted to see adult films only, those made specially for children proving more than I could handle. To this day I cannot watch a film in which any form of torture is featured, even if it is in context with the story, or with correct historical facts. When I was three years old I was taken suddenly ill with appendicitis. Before the doctor could get there and arrange for the ambulance, the appendix had burst, and peritonitis set in. I was rushed to Greenwich Cottage Hospital, where I was operated on with alacrity. The strange thing about this incident is that I can recall all of this happening, but I could feel nothing, although my body was crying out so I knew it was hurting. I can also recall in detail, and from outside my body, watching the surgeon as he went deftly about his business. Then nothing, until I was returned to the corner bed

in the small ward, where Nanny and her relatives all trooped
in to see me. I can even remember the nurse lifting me out of
bed to take me to the bathroom, and the visit from the
surgeon, an elderly man with grey hair, on the day I was to be
discharged. 'What is your first name?', he asked me.
'Jacqueline', I replied. Whereupon he took an indelible pencil
from his pocket, exposed my large scar, and wrote my name
gently across it. 'There you are, Jacqueline', he said. 'It's all
over and done with, and now you can go home.'

I have reached the conclusion that from babyhood I must
have scanned the brain I was stuck with and searched the
genetic data-banks of my body for potential, also noting
obvious character deficiencies. I fear it didn't add up to much,
however, not because it lacked talent, but because physical
rather than mental stamina was observed to be in short
supply. But then, only one tiny fragment of the whole 'me' was
connected to that body at the time, although a little more has
subsequently seeped through from the reservoir of my whole
field-consciousness. In the next chapter I will tell of my
burgeoning psychic powers, although in truth these were not
'psychic' as such, but more concerned with time-travel. To all
but a few this subtle difference will not be obvious, so I will try
to approach it in a general, and hopefully more easily
understood, manner.

CHAPTER 2

'Always Know Where You Are'!

'Always know where you are, Jack'. This was Nanny's constant message to me. To her, stability was all-important. She had been raised in stable conditions, within a stable family, in a stable world. She also had the commonsense – nay, intuition – to know that her strange, elfin-like little charge would also need to hang on to the stability she had known in former existences. Nanny was a natural psychologist. During those early years she taught me more about the nature of people, and how they ticked, than I could ever have learned from a text-book. For example, she would always cue me in when we were about to make one of our regular visits to her numerous relatives. 'Now this afternoon, Jack, we're going to see Uncle Joe and Aunt Maud. If they offer you a penny, take it. She's as tight as a duck's arse, and they are better off than any of us. They can afford their own place, and they have that expensive cat (a Siamese, apparently), so they won't miss a penny! Of course, I took whatever was on offer, be it a chocolate bar, penny, or on one occasion (my birthday), a sixpence!

Aunt Maud and Uncle Joe had three daughters: May, Grace

and Ena. May was, unfortunately, dying from T.B., while Grace suffered from some debilitating bladder problem which necessitated her paying constant visits to the loo. So, when Grace was allowed to take me to the pictures on one occasion, Nanny warned me to make sure that we had seats near to the 'Ladies'. Ena was the youngest, and the prettiest. One day Nanny said to me: 'Maud and Joe's Ena is going out with a young man this evening. She's got a pair of real leather gloves, like ladies wear, so she'll look very smart in her new coat'. I think I murmured something like 'Very nice', but that was all. After a pause, Nanny added that she hoped they wouldn't get up to any hankey-pankey. Being unfamiliar with that expression, I asked what it meant. 'Something that grown-ups get up to when they shouldn't. You'll find out all about that when you get older. But take a word of advice from an old lady – I'd sooner have a nice hot cup of tea any day'. Experiences over the ensuing years have afforded me every good reason to concur.

Much of Nanny's early nursing time had been spent overseas, in South Africa in particular, where she went with an ambassadorial family. She was comparatively old when she came into service with my father. Hazarding a guess, I would say she must have been in her mid to late fifties then, and certainly that age or more when he died. Therefore, to me she was of the same age-group as Blue Granny and White Granny, although I subsequently learned that she was the youngest of the three, and therefore the baby of that family.

Which leads me into the next observation. I have no recollection of either Blue Granny or Grandfather Elf dying, and rather suspect that when such events took place I was whisked away to stay with White Granny and her husband, Grandfather Tom, who lived with their daughter, Winifred, in Wimbledon. Win, as she was known, had a twin brother, Walter, Wal for short, who, along with his rather bossy wife, Ada, would visit us from time to time. One of these dear people was destined to play a major role in my future by taking over where Nanny left off at her death in the latter part of WWII.

When I returned from my first stay at White Granny's house, Grandfather Elf had 'gone to heaven', or so Blue Granny told me. It could not have been more than a year later when I was next packed off to White Granny, and returned to find Blue Granny gone to join her beloved husband. That left just Nanny, Alan and myself at 151, Westcombe Hill.

To return to Nanny's homespun psychology: when taking me to visit Aunt Beck and Uncle Bert, Nanny cautioned me, 'If they offer you a penny, put it back in the tin on the mantlepiece when no-one is looking. The poor souls don't have a bean between them, and young Bert (their son) can't get work because of his bad eyesight. And if they offer you a bar of chocolate, tell them I've said you mustn't eat between meals, but thank you very much anyway.'

Among Nanny's numerous friends was one Mrs Tree, a tall, raw-boned woman whose dark hair was turning iron-grey, and who always wore a dark blue dress. Nanny cautioned that as Mrs Tree couldn't stand children, I would have to stay in the back room when she came. And besides, she was a communist. I asked what a communist was. 'Oh, someone who believes everyone should be equal, and no-one should have more money, or more anything for that matter, than anyone else; which, of course, is rubbish, because it doesn't work. You see, Jack, if you get ten men in a row and give them all five pounds, in six months' time one will have turned that five into a hundred, another will have made fifty out of it, and so forth, but one or two will have blown it on beer and cigarettes, and be back on the dole'. I pondered on her words and decided they made sense. However, Nanny must have adjudged that it was time for Mrs Tree and me to meet, so here is how she arranged it: Mrs Tree, she told me, did not like the King because he didn't talk to working people, whereas the Prince of Wales went down the pits and talked to the miners, and they with coal-dust all over them to boot, therefore she liked him. So she primed me beforehand to say all the right things.

Mrs Tree duly arrived, and I was allowed to go into the front room to meet her. I recall shaking her hand timidly, and when she asked what I had to say for myself, I replied, 'Wasn't it nice of the Prince of Wales to visit those poor, hard-working coal-miners down in the pits? Don't you think the King ought to do that, too?' Mrs Tree sat up with a start, and her face lit up like a beacon. 'Good God, Rhoda', she exclaimed, 'the child's got common sense. She'll go a long way. If I'm still around when she's older, I'll take her along to Party Headquarters'. Whereupon I was presented with a shiny silver sixpence and allowed to stay in the room for a short while, at Nanny's instigation, while they talked. I was, however, cautioned to make an excuse to return to my room before I said something that might let the cat out of the bag!

Nanny had decided to take my initial education into her own very capable hands. So, as soon as my funny little paws were capable of holding a piece of chalk, she bought me a small blackboard and easel, and taught me to write my name. Within a week I could write – albeit somewhat shakily – Jacqueline Hope, 151, Westcombe Hill, Blackheath, London S.E.3. 'Now, you write that down for the policeman if you ever get lost, Jack.' She told me. I never did get lost, but from then on I started to share her daily newspaper, the News Chronicle. She would read passages out to me until I was able to recognise the words for myself. By the age of four I could read almost anything outside of the technical, and by six I could cope with the classics. I recall the first Christmas after I had just mastered the art of reading. Nanny offered to buy me a book of my choice as a present. There were several on display in the children's department of the large store to which she regularly took me for a 'look round'. These were mainly fairy-tales, the brothers Grimm, Hans Andersen, and so forth. I surprised her by choosing The Pied Piper of Hamelin, which she found strange. I had no idea why I chose it until I read the text – it was about a group of children who were enticed by a magic piper to embark on a journey to another world – a kinder place, into which one could disappear, well away from the harshness of everyday hominid existence.

Just as I am today, Nanny was a creature of set habits, one of which embraced the ritual of visiting Lewisham market every Saturday to see what was going cheap, and to collect our ocean fare for Sunday high tea. One used to be able to buy a pint or two of shrimps, whelks, winkles, or whatever, for a song in those days, although, of course, earnings were proportionately low. Both Nanny and I were partial to a nice crab, and she knew exactly how to buy just the right one.

When we got home she would show me how to remove the 'dead man', the name she had for the poisonous pieces. I loved these Saturday shopping escapades, and used to look forward to them with much anticipation. The same went for our annual summer visit to Ramsgate, where we always stayed with Mrs Odell, one of those archetypal 'thirties' English landladies.

I would often run errands for Nanny, usually to the shop round the corner, which was only a stone's throw away. However – and here is one for the psychologists – I was always frightened of dogs, to the extent that I would circumnavigate a whole block rather than face one. Although I have now rationalised it, this fear has stayed with me to this day; a dog's bark inevitably giving rise to an instantaneous adrenalin peak.

Christmas time was always greeted with enthusiasm by the Wellards. There was the usual Christmas fare, and lots, lots more. On Boxing Day they would all gather in the front room for a sing-song and a glass of port. This was when either Nanny or Blue Granny played the harmonium, and the old Victorian songs were religiously done to death, as were the current Music Hall hits, many of which were more than slightly naughty! So as not to make me feel left-out, while the grown-ups savoured their port I was given a similar glass, containing some coloured juice drink, made to look as much as possible like that enjoyed by the adults. Being the only child present on these occasions, I enjoyed all the attention, but bedtime was bedtime, and I was duly marched upstairs for the usual ablutions and beddybyes. One small but significant ritual attached to the latter involved Nanny putting me to bed at a regular time each evening and not coming back into our bedroom until she, too, was ready to hit the sack. I used to peep through the bedclothes and watch her unwind her long hair, which she normally kept tightly bound into a bun. When she turned down the sheets in readiness for the night, she would always say, 'Are you asleep, Jack?', to which I would reply, 'Yes, Nanny'. And that was my signal to depart to the Land of Nod.

Nanny's family were anything but rich, but in spite of this they never went short of the essentials of life, plus some pretty good extras. The understairs larder was always hung with hams, sides of beef and the likes, and at Christmas there was the inevitable turkey and pudding, which Nanny and Blue Granny delighted in making. She also liked to go to the pictures, and I always accompanied her. It was mostly the Roxy that we visited, although there were times when we ventured down to Greenwich or Lewisham to see something special.

As an example of the way simple things would please me, Nanny would say, 'If you are a good girl, I will take you to see the twenty-four hour clock at Greenwich Observatory'. Obviously the sight of the clock was interesting, as I seemed to have a subconscious fascination with time, but I had already seen it several times before, so the highlight of that visit usually lay in the penny ice, of the 'Stop Me And Buy One' variety, that inevitably accompanied that particular jaunt.

In addition to our weekly visits to the Roxy, Nanny also allowed me to listen to the wireless (as radio was called in those days). However, the best programmes always seemed to come after my bedtime, these being thrillers, detective yarns, spooky tales and adult adventure stories. There was one exception, a 'Children's Hour' serial entitled 'Prowlers of the Deep', which was really creepy. I used to look forward eagerly to each episode and can recall the theme music to this day.

Nanny would often come out with some rather 'fruity' sayings, especially if she had forgotten temporarily that I was in the room. On one occasion, when a relative had upset her she exclaimed loudly, 'The trouble with your Uncle Charlie is that he doesn't know which way his arse hangs!' But suddenly noticing the presence of my small form, she added hastily, 'Now you didn't hear that one, girl, alright?' In fact, there were lots of 'you didn't hear that one' over the years, which always amused me.

One day Nanny told me that Uncle Tom, White Granny's husband, had gone to heaven to be with Blue Granny and Grandfather Elf, which left White Granny on her own. Her daughter, Win, would look after her, however, so she would not need Nanny's help. Win could play the piano and used to take students for lessons. She was also a skilled seamstress. The next piece of news from this camp was that Win had met a gentleman, and they were going to be married. His name was Charlie Beacon and he was a widower with three sons. He lived at 15, Spencer Place, a council house in the village of Sandridge, some three miles from St.Albans, and was prepared to give White Granny a good home there.

Charlie's eldest son, Eric, lived at home with his father. His second son, Ron, was an officer in the Merchant Navy, and there was Ken, who was still a teenager. In time, White Granny moved in with the Beacons, and Nanny and I went to Sandridge to pay them a visit. This was my first experience of country life, and I loved it. Milk was collected from Lady

Saltmarsh's prize herd – a stone's throw away from Spencer Place – fresh mushrooms were always available in the surrounding fields, and everyone seemed to live on the fat of the land. I always swore than one day I would also live in a similar environment, but little did I guess just how that wish was to come true.

Charlie Beacon was a highly skilled artisan. Like his father, old George Beacon, who lived across the way, he had spent most of his life travelling the length and breadth of the country, visiting stately homes to repair valued furniture, or to make similar pieces to match existing ones. The Beacons reckoned they could produce a Chippendale that was unrecognisable to an expert. Charlie had two sisters, Kit and Elsie, and a brother, Frank, who was a professional forester on the Cliveden Estate, which in those days belonged to the Astor family. Both his sisters had married comfortably, and the whole family paid each other regular visits. White Granny and Win seemed very happy at 15, Spencer Place, Sandridge, although there was a major upset when Ken died, at seventeen, of pneumonia. Nanny and I attended the funeral, along with other family members. However, I had a strange premonition on that first visit – it was as though I could see myself there, in the place that was ultimately to become my next, truly secure home – one which I remember to this day with warm gratitude and thanks.

CHAPTER 3

Open, Sesame!

I had often heard Nanny talking about something called 'church', but in a somewhat derogatory manner. One Sunday she happened to mention that a lady she knew would not be calling as arranged, because there was something special on at church. 'Nanny, what is church?' I enquired. She rubbed her chin and pulled a wry face before informing me that churches were nasty, dark, cold, damp places where some people went on Sundays to see who had the best hat, which prompted me to ask why they bothered to go. 'Well', said Nanny, taking a deep breath and looking heavenwards, 'Probably because they think that is the best place to worship God'. 'But what is God?' I persisted, 'And why do they have to worship it?' She looked at me with an expression akin to a mixture of sympathy and resignation before continuing: 'People all over the world have their own beliefs about God. Some think there are many gods, and some insist that there is only one, that being *their* god, so they fight wars about it, and torture and kill each other.' 'But Nanny, you know just *everything*, so which god do you like best, and does it have a church?' And this is the story she told me.

Many years before her family moved to London, which was seen as the best place to obtain good positions in service, the Adams lived in a small village in the Derbyshire hills. In that village there was a 'wise woman', who could heal sick people and animals, knew all about the secrets of the earth and growing things, and could read the future. It was therefore the custom for families to take their children to her when they were six years old, when she would advise the parents as to the career that would best afford them comfortable avenues of expression, and accord with their natural gifts. I hand over to Nanny:

'When I was six years old, my mother and father took me to see the Wise Woman. She felt the back of my head, looked at the palms of my hands, drew up a round chart on some paper, then closed her eyes and stayed silent for what seemed to me like an hour. Then she spoke: "This little girl will live in the houses of great ladies, where she will be well treated. She will look after their children, and will travel many thousands of miles across the sea with them in a big ship." 'As I had always been afraid of water and boats of any kind, I protested that I didn't want to go over the water, couldn't stand water, hated it... and stamped my foot indignantly. Whereupon my mother gave me a clip across the ear and told me I would do as the lady said, whether I liked it or not, and that was the end of it.'

'As I grew older, of course, I chose a career in nursing', Nanny continued, 'and after completing my initial hospital training and receiving the qualifications I had studied for, I decided to specialise in the care of children. For a while I worked at a children's hospital where I learned about what is called 'pediatrics'. And then, having good experience and qualifications behind me, I set out to be a private Nanny. I never looked back. And as for that dreaded trip across the sea, I was nursing the children of a gentleman who was appointed to a senior ambassadorial position in South Africa, so naturally I went with the family. After that there were other trips by water, which I never really enjoyed, but they went with the job. So, you see, Jack, the Wise Woman was right. What we need is more Wise Women and less churches.'

I was somewhat puzzled. 'Then why don't people train to be Wise Women, and are there also Wise Men?' 'There used to be both in olden times, but the Churches persecuted them and took their lives. Now I mustn't tell you any more about this, or I shall get upset, and we don't want that, do we? When you are older you will make up your own mind, but perhaps I could make a suggestion: Why don't you train to be a Wise Woman?' I asked if there was a school one could go to for that. She replied that there was, and that it was called The School of Life, whereupon she closed the conversation abruptly by pretending to remember an urgent chore that needed attending to.

I now know why none of Nanny's family ever seemed to go to church, although she later explained to me that in order to appear 'respectable' they usually went, albeit under social pressure, for 'hatches, matches and dispatches'. I frequently heard them grumbling about something called 'hypocrisy', however.

From the very earliest days I was with Nanny, she always went to great lengths to emphasise the necessity for security and order. In the chaos/order debate, Nanny was definitely

Order, and that, I decided, was what I wanted to be. But I learned later, to my chagrin, that the comfort of order was not always the best of life's teachers, especially for a changeling. I think it was the late Dion Fortune who felt that elementals were amoral. As far as single elementals are concerned, of course, she was correct, for unless the four-fold nature at least has been attained to, such souls/essences have no points of reference via which to define the chaos/order or, in hominid terms, evil/good divide, and they therefore follow a purely instinctive path. So being a deva does not mean that one is all-wise; or wise at all, for that matter.

Once five-fold, however, which elevates them to the angelic kingdoms, it is a different matter. Perhaps there was an absence of four or five-fold devas around in Dion's day, these only tending to appear prior to the onset of vast changes – as chroniclers, perhaps, as in my own case. But with space-time opening up, people will have to accustom themselves to the presence of devas, as they will need our co-operation when they come to deal with physical aliens from other spheres.

Another question that has been put to me since I started this book is, 'Why should female changelings be sterile?' The reason is that the radioactive field frequencies of four or five-fold devas, being totally incompatible with the human endocrine and chakric systems, can cause chaos, particularly in those chakras which relate to the reproductive organs. However, a single ondine, for example, or an ondine/gnome double, might possibly be able to negotiate this difficulty, and produce progeny – water, as an element, being so closely related to both human psychology and physiology. In my own case, my strong fire/time energies were not only responsible for my sterility, but also served as an intense irritant to the two lower chakras and their related endocrines, (the Svadisthana in particular), resulting in renal/urinary tract problems which commenced at birth and have stayed with me all my life.

The Nature/Nurture debate in sociology and psychology inevitably rears its Cerberian head when the question arises as to the cause of the various psychoses that are prone to manifest as people make their way through the labyrinth of life. Do these result from their genes, (nature), the programming influence of their 'fields' or soul/essences, or are they solely attributable to their upbringing (nurture)? As someone whose initial start in life was precarious, to say the least, I feel I am in some position to put the weight of my experience behind this one, and state, categorically, that I favour Nature. This is because, having worked in both the children's and education departments of two local council authorities, and subsequently in counselling, I have met people who have been raised in the most appalling conditions, but who have subsequently risen in the arts, sciences or humanities to make considerable contributions to society. Many of these have, like myself, never enjoyed a normal family life, known a mother or father, or savoured those small but meaningful luxuries that many of us can look back on with warmth and happiness. Equally, I have known others who have had loving parents/family lives and excellent educations, but ended up drugged to the hilt in some filthy squat. Those hoary old sociological excuses such as 'their mother didn't breast feed them', or, 'they were never hugged enough' don't cut any ice with me. Both the soul/age (field bandwidth) and the genes will express themselves, regardless of what children have for breakfast, or whether they are read bedtime stories and hugged for twelve hours a day. My Nanny seldom hugged me, but I adored her. She also smacked me when I was naughty, but I was, at some deep level, grateful to her for her putting me right, and preparing me adequately for the rat-race into which I would embark upon reaching maturity.

The title of this chapter is an expression borrowed from the old fairy tale "Ali Baba and the Forty Thieves" (Arabian Nights). It was between the ages of five and six that my 'sesame' started to open; or, as some might prefer, my somewhat unusual gifts (or curses, as viewed from the downside) commenced to manifest. As I have explained previously, in my dreams I could escape into a world in which I seemed to know my way around, and could therefore exercise a degree of control. They were also related to my burgeoning psychology. For example, the event that occurred in one dream, which I can remember with absolute clarity to this day, seemed to take place while I was visiting White Granny and Win in Wimbledon. I was walking with Win down a long road of terraced houses which had low walls separating their front-gardens from the pavement. There was a lovely tabby cat on the wall of one house, and, as I could never resist cats, I stopped to stroke it. Suddenly I heard a dreaded steamroller coming along the road behind me. I looked for Win, but she had obviously not noticed my absence, and was a long way ahead, well out of hailing distance. I recall being filled with fear, and suddenly waking.

With my present knowledge of psychology, interpreting this dream in a five-year-old seems simple enough. Win was my 'prop', and sooner or later, as I matured, that prop would be removed, and I would be exposed to the thing I feared the most: the insecurity of chaos, as represented by the steamroller. But what of the cat? Now we go back to my Paschat life, or maybe even to my present existence, where my beloved cats represent for me the orderliness and 'family' feeling that I have never had since Nanny and Win passed over. I have always associated cats with security, although, in recent years, I have been obliged to accept the fact that even they sometimes need to roam free and end their lives in a manner appropriate to their wishes, and that this might not always be in front of the fire in old age, or at the vet's when they can no longer cope.

The dreams started to become more interesting. I found I could 'fly' through the atmosphere and assume a position from which I could observe various goings-on. On one such occasion I found myself suspended above a high mountain, on the top of which was a sort of terrace. There was a seat on this terrace, and an attractive woman was seated thereon, swinging her legs in an easy-going sort of way. I noted that she was talking to a man. I could even hear what they were saying. She said to him, 'Dance for me, go on, there is nobody about'. The man seemed somewhat embarrassed, but, as he was obviously flattered by the woman's attentions, he performed what I can only describe as a little jig. She clapped her hands in applause, and laughed gaily. Then I 'flew' away. The picture, however, stayed in my mind upon waking, and I related it to Nanny, who asked me what the man looked like. I thought for a moment. 'He was dressed like a soldier but with black boots. And he had a funny sign on his sleeve. Oh yes, and he had a funny little moustache'. 'Can you draw me the sign?' Nanny asked, and passed me a scrap of paper. I drew what I later came to know as a swastika. Some days later the picture of Adolf Hitler appeared in our newspaper, and Nanny asked me if this was the man I had dreamed about. I replied that it was; but nothing more was said.

There was a corollary to this, but it was not effected until the nineteen-seventies, when I was sitting watching television with my ex-husband. Some film footage of Hitler's private life had become available, one section of which showed, to the last detail, the exact scene I had witnessed all those years before. I recognised the lady immediately: it was Unity Mitford, sister-in-law of the British Fascist, Oswald Mosley. And the location – the Eagle's Nest at Berchtesgaden.

I subsequently had several similar dreams while I was with Nanny. In one, which I can still recall, I was hovering above a scene of utter destruction. The air itself seemed to be alight and people were rushing towards a river, trying to get into the water, away from the flames. The horror was indescribable. I woke in a distressed state and told Nanny what I had seen. She managed to calm me, and I eventually went back to sleep. From the descriptions later given by the Japanese, I knew I had witnessed the effects of the first atomic bomb on Hiroshima. So, you see, my 'gift', if you can call it such, is not one of clairvoyance or psychism, but of *time travel*. Perhaps, in sleep, I surf the internet of human consciousness in order to gather together as many strands of human experience, past, present and future, as I am able to compute, including wars and the interplay of destructive forces.

In recent years people have often asked me to travel back

in time for them, to look up this or that. Strangely enough, I would much rather tackle the future. Humanity does not have a particularly good track-record, and viewing those long-gone days often presents nothing more enlightening than the torture and deprivation that marked the age or period in question. I recall being dragged into an old castle by my American ex-husband, who was, as are most Americans, fascinated by such edifices. I experienced a feeling of unease upon entering the building, and when we reached a certain place I was forced to flee outside, where I was thoroughly sick. I had heard the screams of agony, and witnessed, momentarily, a scene of brutality beyond description. Later I heard what had actually taken place there. It was just as I had *seen*.

Even as a child, and in the safe confines of Nanny's loving care, I found this life a strange one to negotiate. Living in many worlds simultaneously, and negotiating the tortuous path between the 'reality' of the present and other dimensions with which I was more familiar, and within which I felt more comfortable, was never easy. Neither was coming to terms with that computer known as the human brain, and accepting the limitations of the human body. Somehow, in Atlantis, it was much easier. I seem to have used a different area of my brain in those times. Also, I was with others of my own kind, and therefore not alone. *De profundis clamavi ad Te, Domine!* (Out of the depths do I cry unto Thee, oh Lord.)

But to return for one moment to life with Nanny. As I had always been something of a physical weakling, Nanny tended to cosset me. One instance stands out in my mind. It was 1935, the year of the Royal Jubilee. A street party had been arranged, and all the local children were given red, white and blue paper dresses for the girls, and similarly coloured tops for the boys. I was also given one, but Nanny refused to let me wear it. 'You will catch your death of cold in that thing', she remonstrated. 'No, my girl, you stay indoors where you will be warm, and safe from infection'. And so I never attended said party. Most children would have shown resentment at this, but somehow it did not seem to worry me, especially as I was allowed to stay up late – well, to eight o'clock – to listen to a thriller on the wireless. However, all Nanny's care and attention was shortly to be thrown to the wind. The next events destined to take place in my life heralded a period of misery, anxiety, and that chaos and insecurity that I feared so much. Here is how it all started.

I must have been coming up seven years old when Nanny had a letter, which seemed to worry her immensely, followed a few days later by a visitor. It was my mother, who had returned from – goodness knows where. She had married again (a man of Austrian/Jewish origin named George Zoller), and had two small children. She told Nanny that she felt it her duty to try and take me back. Berrie she could not have, as she had been legally adopted, and the family in question would not hear of it. From the moment I set eyes on her I disliked her. Agreed, she was a very beautiful woman, but she lacked the depth of character that made Nanny the strong and understanding person she was. However, after much debate it was agreed to allow me to stay with them for a short time to see how I fitted in. A week or so later I reluctantly bid Blackheath a sad farewell and was taken to an address at Wells Street in London, where my mother and her new husband had an apartment.

One of the children was a toddler, the other a babe in arms. As previously explained, I have always hated children, and therefore had no intention of either playing with them or making friends. After all, what had we in common? I was used to the company of sensible adults, who treated me with the kind of respect I always preferred to those 'cuddles' every child is expected to enjoy. I recall thinking to myself 'what am I doing here? I don't belong'. It was on one of those confusing days that I had what was possibly my first 'psychic' experience.

The bathroom, which was down a short flight of steps from the main living quarters, was one of those cavernous, hollow-sounding sorts of rooms, decorated in the inevitable green and cream of the period. I stumbled down those steps en route to the loo, and carefully shut the door behind me. For a moment I paused, taking stock of the unfriendly surroundings, but then I sensed a sudden change in the psychic atmosphere as a voice behind spoke my name, 'Jacqueline', as clearly as the voices I heard in that everyday existence we call the present. Somehow I dared not look round, but stood quite still, as though riveted to the spot, and answered 'yes'. 'Listen for me again', it replied. Suddenly the atmosphere assumed a normality, and I was back in the real world of despair, confusion and loneliness. It was years before I heard that voice again, and came to know that it belonged to the Angelic Being who had been my father, both in Atlantis and with the Paschats.

But back to the reality of the time. There being a Lord Mayor's Show about a week after my arrival, it was suggested that we all go to join the thronging crowds, eager for a peep at the pomp and finery of the occasion. But I was already pining for Nanny, and for the comfort and security of 151, Westcombe Hill. I devised a ruse to get me back there.

From an early age I always knew that I had a strange ability to produce symptoms of illness in my physical body, should the circumstances so require. During the short period at Wells Street I had a repetitive dream. There was a glass pyramid and I was trying to climb up it, but as soon as I got so far, I found myself sliding down again. And then, one night, I actually made the top. The next morning I was taken seriously ill and rushed to the Royal Middlesex Hospital, which, I recall clearly, was 'just across the road'. I have since consulted the London A to Z, and found this to be so. I rather gather I had diptheria, and it was touch and go for a while. However, it served its purpose beautifully. My mother's husband felt that he could not have his children exposed to such a virulent illness, and my mother wanted nothing to do with nursing a sickly child, all of which resulted in their arranging for me to be returned to Nanny as soon as I was discharged from hospital. Hooray! But that, sadly, was but a brief respite. The worst was still to come.

CHAPTER 4

The Downward Spiral

The close affinity I had with Nanny was, I am sure, quite different from the sort of relationship one has with a blood relative, or even an adoptive parent. In the light of my present knowledge, I am aware that Nanny had played a similar role in the Old Country, a term I use with affection when speaking or writing of Atlantis. We were bound as much in the past as in the present.

Nanny was logical and orderly. My mother, I was later to find out to my extreme cost, was quite the opposite. She was feckless, totally irresponsible, and, in my book of logical (if somewhat unsentimental) rules, should never have had children in the first place; although her last two did stand by her until the end. Prior to meeting my father she had been married to a French-Canadian soldier by the name of Charles Bujold. It appears that during the 1914/1918 war, wounded servicemen who were able to get up and about were often invited to the family home, Charles Bujold being one such soldier, and a friendship developed between him and my mother. When he was fully recovered, they courted and eventually married, after which they went to live in Canada, where their son, Royden, was born. It seems, however, that both Charles and Royden died, the former possibly from his wounds, and the latter – well, we shall never know, the secret surrounding Royden's death, if it was a secret as such, having died with my mother.

According to what we were led to believe, my mother was one of a family of three sisters and a brother, born to Walter Edward Murray Williams, a former businessman who latterly took a commission in the Devonshire Regiment, and his wife, Constance Carlotta, an Irish opera singer of some repute. The Williams had four children, we were told: Norah Constance, Gladys Mary, Violet Constance and Walter Hugh. For many years this pretence continued until research undertaken by my cousin, Paul, a dedicated genealogist, highlighted a rather more interesting, and decidedly different, story: only two of said children were actually Walter and Carlotta's. The other two had possibly been born to his sister, Zetta, and surreptitiously incorporated into her brother's family in order to avoid scandal, such being the practice among their class in those days. And herewith commences the tale of my mother's real father. My mother, however, rather pre-empted the discovery by disclosing to me, in one vulnerable moment, that she recalled living in Russia as a child, and travelling in a troika.

Walter Williams had three sisters, Rosetta (Zetta), Edith and Augusta; all three of whom graced the drawing rooms of the European high society of their day. Zetta, however, moved in even higher circles, being a frequent guest at the Court of Emperor Franz Josef himself. A wealthy woman in her own right, she travelled extensively, accompanied by an entourage of servants, and kept apartments and houses in several European capitals. One supposes that in modern parlance she would be accorded the somewhat undignified title of 'courtesan', but for all that she had a brilliant mind; a woman ahead of her time, who both spoke and wrote in at least five languages. Some of her letters are still to hand in the collection of memorabilia that my cousin has lovingly preserved. These include cards denoting her position at table at high banquets, requests for the next dance at state balls, and so forth.

It being the custom in those times for a respected member of the family to embrace any 'little mistakes' that might occur along the line, grandfather Williams and his wife nobly stepped in to support his sister's predicament. My cousin Paul's mother, Norah, appears to have been one such 'mistake'. The other was my mother, whose father's identity is revealed below.

Before she died in Australia in 1972, my mother felt that I should know the truth about her real father, Alexei Romanov, a member of the Russian royal family, so she wrote a poignant letter which arrived while I was on tour with the opera company (see chapters 15 & 16). I recall sharing the information with my closest friend, Jill Ashby, who not only remembered the contents of the letter in detail, but also filled me in more recently on a strange (and related) incident which took place while we were later on tour.

But to return to my mother's letter. It appeared that Constance Carlotta had preserved a photograph of Alexei, given to her by her late sister-in-law, which she had kept to show her adopted daughter before she died, just as my mother perpetuated the truth by passing the information on to me.

Sadly, after her death the picture was destroyed, along with other memorabilia, its significance having been totally missed. Fortunately, a photograph of Alexei surfaced in a privately published work about the Romanov dynasty, just in time for inclusion in this book.

Strangely enough, it was also at the last moment, during one of my rare telephone conversations with my step-sister, Wendy, in Australia, that it occurred to me to ask her if our parent had ever disclosed to her, or her sister, any data regarding her Russian past. It seemed that Violet had indeed often discussed her early life in Moscow, with holidays at a large estate in the north, and that there were several other flashes of memory pertaining to her Russian origin, details of which Wendy was pleased to pass on to me.

Additional information that has recently emerged confirms that she came to the U.K. to take up residence with the Williams family at the age of 8, and this, when matched against intimate personal details exchanged in correspondence between Zetta and her sister-in-law, Constance Carlotta, tends to confirm beyond doubt that my biological grandfather was the Grand Duke Alexei Alexandrovitch (1850-1908), fourth son of Tsar Alexander II, and uncle to the last Tsar, Nicholas II, who met his death at the hands of the revolutionaries. In fact it was Constance who actually introduced Zetta to the man who was to become her lover and the father of her child, my mother. Both Zetta and Alexei were born in the same year.

An interesting genetic corollary also surfaced when I was recently studying Slavonic beliefs. The Slavonic religious pantheon combined animism, pantheism and polytheism

(Professor Stewart's 'pananimism', to which I myself am a devoted adherent), and, in spite of the prevailing State religion, an acknowledgement of the existence of the fairy folk, nature spirits and the spirits of the elements. The concept of the overall influence of great angelic forces was also commonly accepted. Spiritualism was first introduced into Russia by travelling dignitaries, who were able to observe manifestations of psychic phenomena and acquaint themselves with the works of Alain Kardec (the French exponent of Spiritualism). Members of the professions and aristocracy were first to embrace it, but it was in the reign of Alexander II (my great-grandfather) that he and members of his family became devoted adherents. Lewis Spence tells us:

'Chief among the distinguished devotees of the subject was Prince Wittgenstein, aide-de-camp and trusted friend of Alexander II, who not only avowed his beliefs openly but arranged for various mediums to give séances before the Emperor, one of these being the well-known D.D. Home. So impressed was the Tsar that, it was said, from that time onwards he consulted mediums and their prophetic powers as to the advisability or otherwise of any contemplated change or step in his life, doubtless driven to such dependence on mediums by the uncertain conditions under which occupancy of the Russian throne seemed to exist.' (*An Encyclopaedia of Occultism*, p.343).

So, you see, my psychic gifts and beliefs are well entrenched in my genetic inheritance. The Romanovs carried the A positive blood group (as I do myself) and, according to a recent report in the daily press, members of the Romanov dynasty can also be identified by bone and skull features, which, as I shall shortly relate, were identified in my anatomy by the late Dr. Charlotte Wolfe.

As to the aforementioned incident which Jill only recently related to me, this occurred while she and I were partaking of a short repast at a café in Brussels. Sitting across from us at another table were two older people: a man of obvious foreign origin and a very smartly-dressed and amply-bejewelled woman of eastern European appearance. When I left Jill for a short visit to the ladies' cloakroom, the woman approached Jill and asked her who I was. When she explained that I was a soprano appearing with a visiting opera company, the woman replied, 'I did not ask you *what* she was, but *who* she was.' Being aware of my Russian origins, Jill's first thought was 'KGB', so she closed like a clam, at which moment I emerged from my ablutions. But, as the woman returned to her companion, Jill noticed her nodding her head in a 'yes, yes' fashion, after which they both smiled, as though satisfied, and left. In fact, Jill was so worried in case I was followed, that she kept a close eye on me for the rest of the tour!

But these good folk, whoever they were, were not the only ones to tie me in with Russian ancestry.

In the nineteen sixties I was privileged to be granted an audience – afternoon tea, in fact – with the celebrated psychiatrist Dr. Charlotte Wolfe. Dr. Wolfe had been a student of both Sigmund Freud and Ernst Kretschmer, the latter having specialised in the analysis of physiognomy as related to the psychology of the individual. Dr.Wolfe's many years of observation of the human form had served to acquaint her with racial physiognomy to the extent that she could render an accurate description of a person's genetic background from his or her face and bone structure. During our light repast I saw her eyeing me intently. Subsequently she asked to see my hands. 'I gather you are acquainted with your genetic background?' she questioned. I told her that I had some idea, but that, in the light of her expertise in the subject, any input she could make would be greatly appreciated. She said, unhesitatingly, 'Dominantly Russo-Boyar, with, I would say, a German connection somewhere along the line – the Russian genetic influence is so evident in the cheekbones and the cranial structure'. (The Boyars were the old Russian aristocracy who were abolished by Peter the Great during efforts to modernise and unify the country. Many of them later intermarried with members of the German and other eastern European royal families.) Since then I have met many Russians who have asked me if my family originated in *their* country, and friends of mine who have photographs of me on their mantlepiece, and who frequently offer lodging to visiting Russian musicians and singers, are always being asked if their friend is Russian. In the case of one lady singer, the resemblance was so close that we could have been sisters!

As to my father, during the brief period I knew my mother I had little, if any, opportunity to enquire as to his background, or the kind of man he was. Nanny and her family always referred to him as 'a gentleman in the true meaning of the word, and an exemplary employer'. Like his father, Edwin Hope (an artist of some repute, who also edited a 'gentlemen's magazine' entitled 'Pearson's Weekly'), Beresford received a public school education and was something of a man-about-town, always immaculately dressed, and sporting an appropriate buttonhole. However, much of this being pure hearsay, it would be irreverent of me to offer anything in the nature of a character reference. What we do know is that he was a businessman, which seems to be confirmed by the fact that he is entered on my birth certificate as 'toy manufacturer'. We also know that, like my mother, he had been married previously, the marriage having broken up somewhat acrimoniously. When I returned to Nanny in my early teens, I recall asking her how a man like my father could have tolerated my mother. She shrugged, thought about it for a moment, and then replied, 'I remember Fan (Blue Granny) mentioning how she once asked Mr. Hope why his wife showed no interest whatsoever in either the culinary arrangements or the running of the household generally. He replied that he had chosen his wife as a loving and beautiful companion, not an unpaid domestic'. Blue Granny was, it seemed, somewhat peeved by this remark.

My father had three sisters, the eldest of whom Nanny described as being somewhat snobbish. The second in age was an international beauty of her time, who travelled extensively, and eventually married a wealthy Greek by the name of Jaudonopoulo (I may have spelled this incorrectly as I have only Nanny's pronunciation to go on). The youngest, who seems to have been the brainy one, read medicine (quite an achievement for a woman in those times), and went into general practice. As my father was 47 when he died in 1929 and was the youngest in the family, these ladies will all have long since departed, so we have no way of checking the facts.

The clan Hope is believed to have originated north of the Border, in the Galashiels area. In the singular absence of precise records relating to my paternal grandfather's origins, my guess is that he was probably one of those illegitimate children to whom the natural father, although making no admission of parentage, afforded a public school education, after which said offspring were left to their own devices. Both my father's and my paternal grandfather's appearance (from photographs) suggest a Scandinavian origin, numbers of the Vikings having settled in that area of Scotland. However, I could be wrong.

During the last few years, my cousin Paul has spent a great deal of time and money researching the family history on my mother's (and his mother's) side. So, for those among my readers who, along with Richard Dawking, might be inclined to blame genetic lineage for my idiosyncratic beliefs, here are a few of the known facts, although, regrettably, lack of access to the relevant records precludes me from verifying my mother's Russian connection. For the earliest information, Paul is indebted to Francis Jones of the 'Wales Herald of Arms Extraordinary', who supplied details of Elystan Glodrudd (born circa. 980 A.D.), ruler of the territory once known as Rhwng Gwy ag Hafren, which was situated in mid-Wales. Elystan, of the 'Shining Fame', founded the 5th Royal Tribe of Wales. In other words he was a King, and the fact that his descendants enjoyed similar status is borne out by entries in the early historical chronicles of Wales. The names of Bevan, Williams and that branch known as the 'Ladder Lloyds', feature strongly throughout the history of our family. The early 19th century historian, Samuel Merrick, traces the family back to Owain Grynedd, Prince of North Wales.

Skipping to the 16th century: an ancestor, Sir Rhys ap

Griffith, K.G., a descendant of the Lord Rhys of Dynevor, married Catherine Howard, daughter of the 2nd Duke of Norfolk, thus creating the Welsh/English alliance which was to make itself felt genetically in the ensuing years. In February 1998, Paul wrote to the present Duke of Norfolk's Librarian at Arundel Castle, who confirmed the above, and also added further details of that side of the family's history, which have helped Paul to trace the line back, via the Plantagenets, to Eleanor of Aquitaine, wife of Henry II, and earlier. As to the Welsh branch of the family, Briana Lloyd, daughter of Sage Lloyd of Ffosybleiddied, Groom of the Bedchamber of James II, was my great, great, great, great grandmother! However, the family tree in its entirety, although meticulously researched, is far too long and complicated to feature in a work of this kind, although it is, of course, along with photographs of the Williams seat at Penycoed, available for viewing should anyone feel inclined to challenge our claims.

A recent article in the national press highlighted the fact that pioneering research undertaken at Cambridge University by Erik Keverne and Azim Surani has found that genes inherited from the maternal side play the dominant role in the development of the thinking part of the brain, whereas those from the father shape the regions associated with primitive instincts, emotions, aggressions and eating. Every child inherits two sets of genes from each parent. Most of the time these behave in the same way, whichever side they come from, but a few, known as 'imprinted genes', work only if they come from the mother, while others are activated only if they are paternal.

This seems an appropriate point at which to deliver the

genetic bombshell promised in the Introduction. Many so-termed past-life memories are, it would seem, nothing more than brief glimpses into the data-banks of ancestral genes. I have had proof of this myself, and soon learned to distinguish between genetic flashbacks and genuine field (soul) recall of experiences in other periods of time, either on Earth or elsewhere in the Cosmos. Think about it.

So much for the past. Now let us return to the sad and dire events which took place in my eighth year. To pick up the story where I left off: after returning to Nanny following my episode in hospital, life once again assumed a degree of normality. My seventh birthday passed happily, and, for a time, peace reigned. I was enjoying life at the local school, my reading expertise serving to give me the edge over later beginners. The months ticked happily past, and then 'the' letter arrived. I recognised the writing straight away and was overcome by a strange foreboding. My mother and her husband had purchased a property in Southall, and, now that their own children were out of the baby stage, it was felt that I should once again be given a chance to become one of 'their' family. It was a tearful little girl whom Nanny handed over to the Zollers on that damp, autumn day. Why did they have to do this to me? I was so happy with Nanny, and I hated them.

The house at Southall was nothing special, but at least it had enough space for me to have my own room. The nearest junior school was some distance away, so I had a long walk there and back. The children at the school in Blackheath had been a fairly decent crowd, and I had been well looked after by two older nieces and a nephew of Nanny's, who kept an eye on me. The Southall school, however, offered no such kindnesses, and, for the first time in my life, I was exposed to the rougher element.

Life at 344, Lady Margaret Road started as purgatory and finished as hell. George Zoller's sister owned a local bakery, and she would regularly send a variety of delicious cakes and pastries for the children. The two Zoller children always had first choice. I had what was left, or what they didn't like. My mother had absolutely no idea of how to bring up children. When she became bored I was turned out on to the street, or the canal bank in this instance, to 'make my own fun'. Neither did she ever care if I was hurt. On one occasion I was on a swing in the local playground. I have never been able to swing high, or, in fact, to tolerate the G-Force in even a simple thing like a fast roundabout. When exposed to this force I inevitably pass out. Nanny knew this and monitored it with care. On the occasion in question, however, I was swinging gently when a crowd of rough boys came up behind, and sent the swing rushing forward. I was catapulted off, and hit my head badly as I fell. In fact I was unconscious, but no one seemed to care, and, as I was told later, they simply walked away laughing, in the belief that I was putting it on. When I finally came round I staggered 'home'. My mother made no attempt to care for my wound, neither did she take me to a doctor or hospital when I was obviously suffering from concussion. She simply took the little girls out to get some chips, after saying that a few chips would cheer me up! There were numerous other incidents. And then after my eighth birthday, things finally came to a head.

Nanny, Win and their families used to send me parcels containing small items of clothing and other goodies, which were promptly taken from me by George and given to his children. My mother protested, and the rows began. These got worse and worse, and ended in violence. Strangely enough I do not recall actually being beaten up, although I know that my mother suffered physical abuse on my account. Perhaps I was also subjected to the fist and belt, but if so my mind has blanked it out, even to this day. As the weeks sped by, the strife escalated into an all-out battle between George and his children and my mother and me.

One scene which I do remember with absolute clarity involved George locking himself in the kitchen, with me, threatening violence, and refusing to let my mother in. They were screaming at each other, and in desperation she took a brick and smashed the glass on the outside kitchen door. Reaching in through the broken glass, she unlocked the door and freed me. There was blood all over the place. The next bit is a blank.

These scenes must have been more frequent and intense than I realised at the time, as the neighbours reported them to the NSPCC. An inspector came to visit, as did some officials from the children's department of the local council. By the strangest of coincidences, later in my life I actually worked for that very council, and was able to view the records in question. The decision was made that I should be sent away, as my presence was obviously the cause of considerable disharmony in the family.

George's sister, Rene, she of the cake-shop, was well-heeled but childless, and had taken a shine to me from the word 'go'. In the circumstances she offered to adopt me, and to afford me the good education that my burgeoning intellect was seen to deserve. But George, being my official guardian, squashed that one. If anyone was to have Aunt Rene's money it was *his* children, and not the child of another man. It was also discovered that my father had been a Freemason, a fact which would have merited me a place at a Masonic school. Again George Zoller put his foot down: if his children could not have that education, then neither could I.

By this time the case had come to Court and a Court order was placed for me to be removed from the Zoller household on grounds of safety. Of the options available, Zoller accepted a Catholic convent, which was little more than an orphanage, a home for abandoned children of the variety that usually end up as pathetic little bundles on the doorsteps of churches. The prior requisite for acceptance was that I be baptised, so I was carted off to the local Catholic church, St.Anselm's in Southall, for the deed to be done. Strangely enough I had nightmares about that church for years after. In later, adult terms, I can only liken my predicament to that of a missionary who had been captured by hostile natives, and forced, under threat of torture, to take part in their rituals. And yet I knew, inwardly, that rebellion would be a waste of energy. It paid to go along with the system. It was less hassle. And so an air of resignation overtook me when I found myself incarcerated within the bleak walls of Nazareth House, Hammersmith, Mother Convent of an Order known as The Sisters of Nazareth. The great nightmare of chaotic experience had begun, and the black-clad nuns, those minions of Set, Lucifer, or whatever name each credo may accord to such energies, were now in command. And yet, beyond those threatening structures, the throbbing pulse of 1930's London beat to the norm of the time, doubtless oblivious of that pocket of captivity which housed such unwanted specimens of human childhood as this poor changeling.

The next chapter describes the blackboard jungle into which I had been pitched, head first. And yet, out of evil inevitably cometh good, my eighteen months at Hammersmith serving to teach me how to survive in a hostile environment, and to emerge wiser for the experience.

CHAPTER 5

Enter the 'Spooks'

There was a short driveway from the gates of the convent to the main buildings, which housed not only the children but also the nuns and some old people. A pathway led therefrom to the playground, on the other side of which was a set of double doors through which we passed into a small hallway. To the left was the changing room, and to the right the refectory – into which I was unceremoniously ushered. Rows of children of various ages were seated at long tables, many of their necks bent sideways to get a good look at the newcomer. Seated in a raised chair at the top of the room was the head nun, Sister Mary of Lourdes, who, I was later to learn, was known to the children (behind her back, of course) as 'Fish'. She was short, stocky and elderly, with a somewhat pinched face and small, beady eyes. Having dismissed my escort somewhat curtly, she led me to a table where a group of children were obviously waiting for food to be served, and pointed to a vacant seat. 'Sit there for now, and we'll find a more appropriate place for you tomorrow. 'Whereupon she returned to her 'throne'.

Jungle story No.1 coming up! None of the other children

spoke to me, but they all giggled slyly, which had the effect of making me feel uncomfortable, to say the least. An older girl, who had obviously been doing the rounds of other tables, then arrived on the scene with a pan of hard-boiled eggs and a basket containing what Nanny would have described as 'doorsteps' of greased bread. The routine seemed to be to hold one's tin plate out so that the server could drop her fare somewhat ceremoniously thereon.

Having had no food for some hours, I was about to engage in the consumption of said offerings when one of the girls leaned across the table and said to me, 'Sister has just indicated that she wants to see you'. 'Where do I go, and to which sister?' I asked, innocently. 'The old one up there', she replied, pointing to the 'throne' at the top of the refectory. The rest of them sniggered ominously, so I should have guessed that some skulduggery was afoot. Not wishing to create an impression of insubordination on my first day, I made my way to where Sister Mary of Lourdes was seated. 'You wanted to see me, sister?' I asked, innocently. 'What are you talking about, girl? I did no such thing. Now return to your seat immediately,' she answered, somewhat crossly.

I recall almost crawling back to my allotted chair. By now, I suppose my readers have all but guessed what had happened: my egg and bread had done a disappearing act. Being both hungry and angry, I remonstrated with the other girls, who replied by causing a degree of noise, which brought Sister M. hurrying down to the table to enquire what was wrong. Putting on a great act of being hard-done-by, the lead girl said that I had already eaten my humble fare, and was simply trying it on to get a second helping. Whereupon Sister

M. called me a greedy little pig, gave me a sharp clip round the ear and sent me to wait outside, supperless. Message received and understood. This was jungle life *par excellence*, and I needed to assume the rôle of the leonine cub if I was to survive.

Following this dubious repast, I was escorted to the wardrobe room to be kitted out with the green and navy convent uniform. I was also given a number – 167 – which henceforth featured above my bedspace and on all the labels of my clothes.

After a few days I soon caught on as to what was required of me, both by the other girls and by the staff, and so I settled down into the routine of hard labour and cruelty which was the price paid by all of us for not being blessed with parents who cared whether we were dead or alive.

The schooling was good, if strict, and, being somewhat brighter than most, I slowly ingratiated myself into the good books of the teacher-nuns. Also, I had the advantage of being better-read, and better acquainted with the outside world, than many of the children. Some of them had been there since they were babies and were therefore totally unfamiliar with life beyond those high, ominous walls. I used to tell them about films I had seen, adventure stories I had listened to on the wireless, the dancing of Astaire and Rogers, and many more of the wonders 'outside'. Slowly I made friends and life became bearable, especially after the sister in charge of the choir discovered that I had a good singing voice. I was soon included in the choir – something I thoroughly enjoyed.

Incidentally, I have decided to use initials only when referring to those nuns who employed violence. I would estimate them to be in their thirties or forties at the time, and thus undoubtedly passed on by now, but I have no wish to cause embarrassment to any surviving relatives.

One incident landed me in hot water. We had been given a history lesson covering the Tudor period. While noting what had been said, I somehow felt that we were not being told the whole truth, so, in a quiet moment, I shot back in time and took a few notes, observing events as my consciousness slowly returned through the years to the present. What I witnessed made for good writing, and, for a short while anyway, I felt quite pleased with myself. But such elation was short-lived. After reading our papers, Sister N. called me up in front of the class: 'By whose authority did you go out of bounds to the senior library?' she asked, icily. I protested that I did not know where that was. By now she was fuming. 'You wicked girl: first you go out of bounds to collect information ahead of my teaching, and then you compound this impudence with lies. I suppose you thought I would think you were clever. Well, here is your double punishment, first for cheating, and then for lying about it.' I was then introduced to her famous steel ruler – on my knuckles. The pain was excruciating, and I was unable to hold a pen for at least a week

We were all obliged to go to Mass every morning. The chapel was quite large, and I recall in particular the life-size statue of St. Peter which guarded its portals. Many years later I dreamed of that same statue, only the name inscribed underneath was 'Zeus'. One wonders from which pagan original it was copied. In addition to the children's choir, there was also a nuns' choir which would take over on special occasions. The first time I ever heard a real operatic soprano voice, other than on the wireless, was when Sister Aloysius sang the 'Adoro te Devote'. I was spellbound. It appeared that she had been an operatic soprano prior to sustaining a terrible personal loss, which had driven her to take the veil. The Order took good advantage of her talent, and people would often visit the chapel to hear her sing such delightful pieces as the Mozart 'Ave Verum', which I later sang with the junior choir. I recall thinking at the time how I would love to be an opera singer like Sister Aloysius, and I never once heard the 'Adoro te' without thinking of her.

It took me only weeks to learn the Mass in Latin – including the priest's part, and within months I was cantor. The nun who ran the choir was a strange mixture of dedication and suppressed violence (not always suppressed, as I found to my cost). Although beatings were the norm, as were knuckles attacked with a steel ruler until the fingers were twice their normal size, now and again Sister N. *really* cut loose, and everyone got out of her way. Unfortunately at that time I had not learned the drill. It all happened in the changing room one day, when one of the girls accidentally dropped something as Sister N. came into the room, her attention taken up by some documents she was perusing. Failing to see the dropped article, she tripped over it and fell heavily onto the floor. She quickly picked herself up, and, in a fit of violent anger, reached for the stick she always carried, which had fallen out of her sleeve. She lunged at the girl in question, who side-stepped hastily, leaving me to face the full brunt of the attack. Grabbing me by the back of my dress collar, she lashed out over and over again. The pain became so intense that I externalised, thus shutting out the agony, watching from outside my body as the small shell had all hell beaten out of it. Later in life, when I read about those poor soldiers who were obliged to build the Burma railway for the Japanese, and who carried on in spite of the pain, I knew exactly how they did it.

Finally her temper subsided, and she left the room without a word. The other girls immediately helped me up. Some of them had hidden unguents, given to them by visitors, which they kept for such occasions. These were immediately produced from the back of lockers, and I was cared for as best they knew how. My back and shoulders were black and blue for some time after, and sleep was difficult. But somehow, when faced with such overwhelming odds, one soldiers on, there being no way of escape. This was, apparently, no isolated incident. Sister N's violence was well-known.

Later, when we all went to compulsory confession, several of the girls told the priest about it. He was, it seemed, all too familiar with the scenario, but there was little he could do. One wondered how he felt when asked to give Sister N. absolution (assuming, of course, that she confessed to her misdeed). She was, I fear, a very sick woman, and for that reason alone I bore her no resentment.

This was to prove but one of many such incidents, but I had learned my lesson. Survival depended on getting well out of her way, keeping a low profile, and never getting 'involved'. Strangely enough, 'never get involved' was one of Nanny's constant warnings. How wise she was.

Needless to say, the one ambition all we girls shared was a desire to escape those ominous walls. So strong was this wish that when there was no-one in authority about, we would chant the following ditty:

'This day next week where shall I be,
Outside the gates of misery.
The gates will be opened and I shall be free:
Oh, how happy I shall be, singing –
Glory, glory, alleluia, Sister hit me with the ruler,
Sister chased me with her broomstick, and made me
    black and blue!'

In view of all this suppressed (and sometimes unsuppressed!) violence, it is little wonder that the place was riddled with poltergeist phenomena. The first I heard about this was the strange tale of Sister Gobinet's Missal. (I may have spelled the worthy sister's name incorrectly, but I never saw it in print). It appears that Sister Gobinet possessed strange powers over the Devil. So effective were these powers that the Devil took umbrage and stole her Missal, which he took down to his infernal regions to spite her. Sister Gobinet, however, had recourse to the angels, who rescued said book and restored it to its rightful owner. On its return, it was placed in a glass display case – complete with its singed pages and badly burned cover (caused, of course, by the fires below!) – to be seen as a lesson for all who might see fit to cross swords with Old Nick, and who might not have Sister Gobinet's angelic friends in tow to help out in such an emergency!

Tales of Sister Gobinet's adventures often dominated both classroom and playground. On one occasion, we were told (several of the older girls assuring us youngsters that they had actually seen this with their own two eyes), the devil manifested as a serpent in the toilets at the bottom of the playground, and Sister Gobinet's specialised talents were immediately called upon. She arrived armed with her special magical weapon – a large yard-broom – and, after lifting the metal lid, proceeded to sweep the offending serpent down the main drain. Even the priests, it seems, sought her aid for the riddance of unwelcome phenomena, all of which were judged to be the doings of His Infernal Majesty! In the light of my present knowledge, said nun was obviously blessed with the qualities of a natural exorcist. Later in my own life I was able to find out just how those worked.

The food overall was pretty ghastly, and mostly by permission of Heinz & Co. (as was then), who doubtless contributed it to the convent as a charitable act. But compared with the fare at my next port of call, in the north, it was The Ritz, and there was sufficient of it to keep body and soul together.

On my ninth birthday, which was in the September of that first year (1938), I was invited by Sister Mary of Lourdes to enter a raffle, with six other girls, for a box of chocolate money which some kind patron had donated. Sister's favourite among the very young ones was asked to pick a number from a hat, and whichever of us guessed it correctly got the chocs. When it came to my turn, I distinctly heard a spirit voice say to me 'seventeen', so that was what I said, and it proved to be the winning number. With a large box of chocolates all to myself, needless to say I suddenly acquired several new friends and they all had a share in the proceeds, which served to put my popularity rating up a few notches.

In time I was obliged to take my first Communion. As already explained, I found it less hassle to go along with the imposed religious system, so I duly carried out what was required of me with as much dignity as I could muster at the time. All the other first communicants in my group were much younger, and one of the perks of the day consisted of being allowed to play in a large hall called Nazareth, which contained, in addition to a fairly good-sized stage (upon which I was later destined to perform), a playroom with all sorts of toys.

Being past the toy stage, I was less than interested in the so-called 'treat' until I espied a small, silver aeroplane, large enough to seat a nine year old. When pedalled, it sported a moving propeller. I made a beeline for it, and had just seated myself comfortably, anticipating a good ride, when we were all called to attention. Father Savage, the priest who had officiated at our 'ceremony', had come to entertain us. I felt cheated, but nevertheless kept my eye on the aeroplane in the hope that he would get his religious business over and done, and allow us some more playtime. Sadly that was not to be, the worthy father having decided to relate the many experiences he had undergone as a missionary in Africa!

And so I never got back to my little silver plane, either on that or several other occasions when I was allowed into Nazareth. But my longing to fly persisted into adulthood until I finally took flying lessons. Being above the clouds in a jumbo-jet is my idea of bliss, well away from the sorrows of earthly existence. There I am greeted by my own kind, the air devas or sylphs, and their Queen, Paralda.

In addition to our school work, we children were also obliged to undertake all our own cleaning, washing, etc. The laundry work was carried out by the older girls (my turn came at the next convent), while we younger ones were required to attend to such chores as polishing the wooden floors. This was usually executed in long lines of up to twelve or more girls, all on their hands and knees, rubbing away from side to side in perfect rhythm. There were little songs we had to sing while we polished thus, one of which I recall quite clearly:

'Number twelve, number twelve, we are polishing
      twelve by twelve.
With a rum-tum tiddle and a rum-tum tee,
Jolly polishing girls are we.'

Beds also had to be stripped and stacked each morning, although this chore was somewhat easier at the Hammersmith convent than it was at Nazareth House, Heaton Park, Manchester, as readers will discover in the next chapter.

We were also committed to undergo retreats. I have often heard people I know speak in glowing terms of retreats they have been on, and the great spiritual upliftment they have derived therefrom. Not so myself, even in those childhood days. Our convent retreats usually consisted of several days' silence, during which we would be addressed by some visiting retreat priest. These came in a variety of shapes, sizes and temperaments. One such priest we had at Hammersmith was a Jesuit named Father Cary Elwes. Jesuits, we were always told, were the cream of the Church, and the best exorcists (aside from Sister Gobinet, one assumed?) to be had anywhere. A later story in my life will, I trust, serve to dismiss this myth once and for all.

In fact Father Cary Elwes turned out to be quite jolly and he did the best he could to keep us children entertained. One little story he told us has stayed with me. In the Litany of the Saints, which, in those times was inevitably spoken or sung in the traditional Latin, there is a series of statements which demand the response *'Libera nos Domine'* (Deliver us, O Lord). Father Cary Elwes told how he, as a little boy, would religiously answer these, until one day, when he went home to his mother for lunch, he found himself faced with a crisis of faith. The weather on that occasion was somewhat inclement to say the least, and he took his seat at the meal table to the accompaniment of thunder and lightning. When his mother served up a dish of fish and chips, he arose in horror and exclaimed, 'But, Mummy, I can't possibly eat that today, it's against the Church's teachings, and I would be committing a sin!' His mother, somewhat mystified, asked for an explanation. 'Well, in the Litany of the Saints it says distinctly "Liver on a stormy day".' The tale has often afforded me a smile.

There were, of course, situations in which we deliberately changed the words of hymns for a giggle. In one hymn there was the line 'The Banner, the Cross', for which we always sang 'Gertie Banner got lost', Gertrude Banner being one of the lesser-liked seniors; while our own words for the hymn for the Pope 'Full in the Panting Heart of Rome, Beneath the Apostle's Crowning Dome', are best not committed to print. Suffice it to say that they commenced with the line 'Full in the pantry there are buns, which Mother gives to the Holy Nuns'!

Meanwhile, the spooky manifestations continued, and Sister Gobinet's stature grew proportionately. One evening after school we were informed of a treat. A film had been made of the life of St. Teresa, the Little Flower, and it would befit us all to note how she stood up to the temptations of the Evil One. And so we were all seated in the darkness, and the story began.

Strangely enough, the dear Saint did not seem to spend much of her early life doing battle with Old Nick, but when it came to her death we were all in for a shock. In the darkened scenario she was shown lying on her deathbed, clasping a crucifix and praying softly. Then the camera swung to face the full-length, black (of course) curtained windows on the other side of the room, which slowly opened to reveal the Devil, dressed in matching black and complete with horns, cloven feet and a long, spiked tail! Taken by surprise, several of us nearly jumped out of out skins.

Our dormitories were quite long. My bed was about fourth from the door leading into the room and my friend Peggy Prendergast's bed was to the right of it. There were at least six more beds before the bathroom/toilet door at the bottom of the dorm, and nature obliged most of us to make the necessary trip at least once during the hours of darkness. That night, we carried out our essential visit in groups of about ten, each holding precariously on to the hand of the other, even through the door of the actual loo, which no-one dared close. The sheer idea of bumping into the kind of apparition that faced the dear Saint proved all too much for any of us.

The beatings and heavy workloads were punctuated by lighter moments. At Christmas time, for example, after attending Midnight Mass, we were allowed to visit the old people, who always gave us sweets, hankies, or some small religious trinket. We were also treated to the pantomime at the Kings Theatre, which, during the one Christmas I was resident at that convent, was Cinderella. As was (and still is, I gather) the custom, the comedian sang a little ditty, the words of which were displayed on a large screen so that the audience could all join in. Whether it was the words themselves, rather than that particular pantomime experience, that caused my ever-expanding data-banks to include such rubbish I may never know. However, on looking back, as I have been obliged to do for this book, I cannot help observing how certain scenes, the relevancy of which beg rationalisation, stand out clearly in one's mind. Twee as it was, that simple, everyday ditty often gave me hope during the darker moments which were to come:

'Always say, it's turned out nice again,
Shout hooray, it's turned out nice again.
Things look black, you've got the sack,
Try and learn this little knack!
Always say, it's turned out nice again, in sunshine
    or in rain.
If you don't get a lucky break, to worry is a big mistake,
Because in the morning when you wake,
You'll find it's turned out nice again!'

For all its faults, the Mother House of the Order of the Sisters of Nazareth was responsible for introducing me to the theatre, albeit in the form of a children's musical playlet entitled 'A Fairy Wedding'. Being slightly taller than the other girls, I was cast in the role of The Queen of Hearts, whose sole responsibility was to carry in the wedding cake which, according to the tale, she had carefully prepared for the occasion. All good, clean fun, and I can remember the whole darned thing, word for word.

And so the summer of 1939 passed, and we children went about our daily routines, oblivious to the gathering storm-clouds of war and to the impending dangers. I recall watching out of the dormitory window with Peggy as the barrage balloons made their first appearances over the skies of London. And then came that fateful third of September, after which we were gathered together, split up into small groups, and despatched to rural areas temporarily, until suitable places could be found for us in other, safer convents within the same Order.

CHAPTER 6

War, Work and Poltergeists

Since we were totally unaware of the impending horrors of an all-out war, the train journey from London to Devizes, which commenced on the Underground, was something of a thrill for us evacuees.

Our next train, an old-time puffer, took us to the Wiltshire town of Devizes. Apparently, arrangements had already been made with Catholic families in the area who would take us in. We were therefore organised into small groups, each with an adult to whom fell the task of knocking on appropriate doors to see which of us the inmates felt like accommodating. When we arrived at an attractive little lodge, which obviously belonged to a large estate, the lady of the house, a Mrs Giddings, came and looked us over. She chose me, but she also indicated that she could take a second girl. Not one of my own class volunteered, so it was left to a younger girl, from a group of juniors which was 'doing' the other side of the road, to take up the place. Her name was Nancy Newsome. Nancy and I tolerated each other for the few weeks we were destined to stay in residence there. We didn't actually fall out, but she was overheard telling her class that I was weird.

Mrs Giddings' husband worked for the owner of the Estate. However, we saw little of him as he was called up shortly after. She also had a son of seventeen named Joseph, and a daughter of nineteen named Mary (well, what do you expect from a good Catholic family!). Joseph worked at the local brewery, and Mary was employed at a confectioner's. These two had little time, if any, for us children.

The one vital experience I did undergo at Devizes was to renew my acquaintance with my own kind. We were only a short distance from open country and fields, and I would often visit those sweet meadows to replenish my energies. One in particular was on a slope and I delighted in lying down at the top and allowing myself to freewheel, roly-poly style, to the bottom. Those few weeks of comparative freedom served to help me through the bleak years that lay ahead. In moments of reverie I would return to that green hillock, and roll down it over and over again.

The school was only a few yards from Bessborough Lodge, that being the official title of the Giddings residence. One supposed that the estate to which it obviously belonged also incorporated the name 'Bessborough'. The mellow September and October days eventually gave way to the foggy mists of late autumn, which, with their ominous undertones of an impending winter, carried messages of the doom and destruction to follow. One morning we were called together at the schoolroom and told to have our clothing packed and ready to leave the next day. We were then split into groups of twenty, each under the direction of a nun or senior girl, and ferried off to those locations that were to be our homes for the next few years, the little group which included yours truly being destined to end up at Nazareth House, Heaton Park, Manchester.

On arrival, my first impression of the place was its coldness. It was nothing whatsoever like the convent at Hammersmith, being much more modern and spacious. I later learned that the main part of the building, which, as before, housed the nuns and a few old people, had originally been a privately owned mansion with several acres of grounds, that had been bequeathed to the Church upon the demise of the last resident. An extra wing had subsequently been added to accommodate children. This consisted of the dormitories and school quarters, which spanned three floors.

We twenty newcomers were dubbed 'the Hammersmith girls', and allotted a small dormitory all to ourselves which was well heated and quite cosy. Strangely enough I can remember the roll-call of twenty names to this day, commencing with Betty Doyle and ending with Eileen Callaghan (we were always lined up according to height). I was flanked on one side by Rosie Kitto and the other by Pat Nolan. There was one shock for which we were certainly not prepared. None of the Manchester girls (as distinct from the Hammersmith girls) ever wore shoes, except when they were taken outside the grounds, and occasionally to church. At all other times, even in midwinter, they went barefoot, which doubtless landed many a girl with arthritis problems in later life.

There was an explanation for this curious custom. A visiting priest, who had been a missionary on some tropical islands, noted how perfectly the children's feet were formed, which fact he emphasised to the nuns. With no heed whatsoever as to the climatic differences, they immediately withdrew all footwear, both in and out of doors, and we were subjected to both the pain of the winter cold on the one hand and the hard surface of playground and field on the other. It took months for our poor feet to acquire the necessary leather-like texture to cope with such appalling conditions. When I eventually left that terrible place it was months before I could walk in any form of shoe, even a soft sandal. But then life is, surely, one long learning experience, and the period from November 1939 to March 1944, which destiny had chosen for my incarceration at Nazareth House Heaton Park, was peppered with incidents obviously designated by the Fates to serve either as pointers to the future, or as lessons in human frailty. All in all, I was generously supplied with a fair selection of character-building material.

The grounds surrounding the convent were both extensive and attractive, and there was also quite a large lake which supported a generous mixture of aquatic wildlife. Legend had it that a small boy had been drowned therein, and that his velvet-clad ghost was often to be seen wandering along the bank, crying piteously. Several of the Manchester girls claimed to have seen it on more than one occasion.

Some of the fields had already been ploughed up by government order and planted with appropriate vegetables. These were to prove invaluable to us children over the ensuing years, although the farmer in question would have been horrified had he found out how much of his produce was destined to find its way to the dormitory.

The one good thing for which the school was noted was its choir, their particular expertise lying in the interpretation of plain chant. In fact, during the music festivals which took place regularly in the region during peace time, the Heaton Park girls always won the plain chant section hands down.

When we Hammersmith girls first arrived there, the head nun was Sister Erconwald, a tall, stately, well-spoken and obviously highly refined woman, about whom tales of tragedy abounded. These all amounted to the usual story of unrequited love, and the fact that she had come from the upper classes was acknowledged in that she was always referred to simply as 'Sister,' whereas her assistant, Sister T., merited the use of her full title. While 'Sister' reigned, all was quiet and well organised. She was a gentlewoman in every sense of the word, and I do not recall any violence taking place when she was around.

Whereas at Hammersmith all the teachers had been nuns, at this convent our tutors, aside from the Head Mistress were (mercifully) minus the veil. However, whether we were taught by lay teachers or nuns, the cane was always in evidence. One learned one's lessons or took the consequences. Strangely enough it seemed to work, even with those labelled 'backward'. Outside the classroom, however, violence was frequently in evidence, especially when Sister T. was around. In contrast to 'Sister', she was a short woman, with black eyebrows and the typical clear blue eyes of the Irish. She used to keep a cricket wicket-stump up one of her voluminous sleeves, and, although she had obviously not acquainted herself with Sister N.'s steel ruler, that wicket-stump was jolly painful when it met with either the palm of one's hands or the back of one's neck or shoulders. A psychologist would doubt-less have assessed her as a highly frustrated, angry and violent woman.

The educational system was a simple one. Each class was referred to as a 'Standard', these ranging from Standard 1 – Infants, 2, 3 and 4 – Juniors, and 5, 6, 7 and 7x – Seniors. The 'x' students being those who were ready to enter for School Certificate or Matriculation, which, in those days, were usually not taken until one was at least sixteen years old. Promotional examinations were held once a year, those students who passed being automatically elevated to the next Standard. This inevitably resulted in mixed age-groups at all levels, the slower learners finding themselves in the same Standard, along with those from the Standard below who had merited promotion. In my own case, by the age of 14 I had shot up to Standard 7x, at which point I was temporarily stuck, being too young to enter for either School Cert or Matric, and also being denied access to the educational material required for those exams. I was fortunate in that I could learn pretty well anything, although maths, geometry, anatomy and physiology and history were undoubtedly my best subjects. Art was my worst, with English a poor second – as those who have been brave enough to reach this point in my narrative will undoubtedly have concluded.

There was, of course, the same round of domestic chores that we had at Hammersmith. Floors had to be scrubbed and polished, the laundry attended to, and so forth. One particularly onerous task allotted to me and a girl named June Jacobs was the dreaded 'green passage'. This stretched from one end of the school building to the other, sloping all the way. It was composed of a green rubbery sort of material, the parts nearest the walls being plain green, followed by a white strip, while the centre part, which was most walked on, was mottled green/black/white. Every Saturday morning June and I would set our bucket, scrubbing brushes, clothes and kneelers at the top, and work our way down, a patch at a time. Sometime Sister T. would come up behind us, notice a small mark we had missed on the white line, and throw the bucket of water back over the lot so that we had to do it all again. Halfway down there was a door which led from the nursery onto this passage, which some of the four and five-year old residents would delight in opening just as we were working outside. Then they would deliberately make a mess on the spot we had just cleaned, which action was promptly met by whacks round the legs with our wet cloths! Incidentally, there were also some six or seven small boys in residence at the convent. They had their own dormitory and a special table in the refectory. Emphasis was always placed on the fact that boys were far superior to us girls, because they could become priests, whereas the best any of us could hope for in the spiritual stakes was to become a nun.

Unlike the tatty eating hall at Hammersmith, the Heaton Park refectory was an airy, well-appointed room which was graced by small, neat, four-seater tables, each of which displayed a glass vase of artificial flowers (except on high feast-days when these were replaced temporarily by the real thing). We were also taught, at Sister's instigation, no doubt, the correct way to set a table and the appropriate cutlery for certain dishes (not that we ever saw any of the latter, however). The food, in fact, was absolutely appalling. Breakfast often consisted of two hunks of bread spread with lard (or dripping if one was lucky), and the occasional egg was the treat of the week. We were also forced to eat raw tripe which smelled disgusting. Should any child fail to be seen consuming it, Sister T. would have her out on 'the front', where she would be made to eat it mouthful by mouthful, the quivering stick ominously indicating the ghastly alternative. One soon learned that the best way to cope was to comply, and vomit it up afterwards.

A somewhat unfortunate food ritual had developed over the years. This consisted of favours being repaid by either taking on unwanted food or parting with special treats. For example, as I was good at maths, I would often help out those less gifted in return for their egg, which came round usually once a month. Likewise they would dispose of my tripe, or any other dish that displeased my palate. The disaster area lay in our monthly dose of Epsom salts, 'debts' due involving hours of physical discomfort in the loo for some poor little souls. There was also much thieving of produce from the fields, this being passed around secretly among friends. Well, we really were *very* hungry!

At Christmas and Easter we had the treat of our lives – one sausage! Other than the tripe, that was the only meat we ever saw. And as for those 'doorsteps' of bread, when pulled apart they displayed long strings of smelly, sticky stuff (raw or unfermented yeast?). Needless to say, they tasted awful. Sometimes we were given roasted bones to chew on, the idea being that they would help our teeth.

Some months after our arrival, I and a girl named Kathleen went down with chicken pox. We were immediately placed in isolation in a strange room known as 'Mary Ann's Room' (I never found out who Mary Ann was). Sister T. was scathing about my spots in particular, calling me a dirty little girl, which, needless to say, annoyed me somewhat. After putting up with this for a couple of days I decided on a course of action. I have always been able to heal myself, so that night, upon leaving my body, I decided to do just that. The next morning, to Kathleen's amazement, my pustules had all but vanished, and when Sister T. came visiting, I proudly showed her my signs of rapid recovery. But was this appreciated? Far from it! She examined my body in amazement, and then backed away, crossing herself vigorously and exclaiming, "Tis not natural, 'tis the work of the devil!'. One couldn't win either way.

And now to the routine of the bath gown. As it was considered unseemly that any child should ever see the unclothed body of another, we were each issued with a gown, the routine being that we went into the loo to don it before presenting ourselves at the side of the bath. These gowns always covered as much of the body as possible. The weekly bath was supervised either by the nun herself or one of the senior girls. The routine entailed one of us being immersed in the water ahead of the other, who sat on the side. The side-sitter would scrub her own feet (or have them scrubbed for her if she were a junior), while the one seated in the water would have to keep her eyes shut while appropriate ablutions were applied to her body either side of the gown. After that she was covered by a towel and stepped out of the bath, leaving the water place available to the side-sitter. And so we all moved up to let the next one in. I cannot ever recall being properly washed in my private parts, neither were we ever allowed to effect that action for ourselves.

And now for the spooky bits. It could not have been as

much as a year after we had been there that Sister Erconwald
was taken ill. The doctor was called, at the instigation of Sister
Philip (who ran the kitchen but was also a trained nurse). I do
not recall 'Sister' ever being taken to hospital. She died in her
cell shortly after and her body was duly laid out in the chapel
so that we could mourn for her. I found this all very strange.
But scarcely had the dear lady gone to her heaven when she
was perceived, standing on the landing of the main staircase.
In fact, if one is to believe all the sightings claimed, her poor
soul was earthbound for quite some time.

She was not the only ghost to walk the corridors of this
strange habitat. There was the annual escapee, whose
footsteps could be heard descending the fire escape down the
side of our dormitories. As this apparition inevitably made its
presence felt on a certain date, we would wait that night with
bated breath, and listen for 'her'. And sure enough, there
would be the descending clip, clop, clip, clop down the metal
rungs of the fire-escape. The scene was in full view of the
dormitory window, so we could see for ourselves that there
was no-one there. And then, quite suddenly, there would be a
clatter, followed by a moan, and the phenomenon would
instantly cease. The story told to us was that one of the nuns,
tiring of the ways of the cloth, and with the aid of an outsider
who procured for her some appropriate clothing and a pair of
high-heeled shoes, fled down the metal steps. However, in her
haste to get away, she caught the heel of one of her shoes in the
ironwork, lost her balance, and was thrown to her death; the
lesson to be learned being the folly of trying to run away from
God, as the Devil would inevitably get you.

Following Sister Erconwald's demise, Sister T. took over,

assisted by a newcomer in the person of Sister Clare, a shy, retiring lady who managed to keep well in the background.

For all her violent moods, Sister T. did have one redeeming factor, a love of classical music, and opera in particular. Since she ran the choir, in addition to our plainsong we were also obliged to learn full operatic choruses. As any follower of the divine art knows, operatic choruses, by and large, were written for four voices; soprano, alto, tenor and bass, a fact which failed to daunt the good nun. She simply divided the altos into two sections, and allotted the bass line to those with the lowest voices. Ditto the sopranos and tenors, although the tenor line, being somewhat difficult in parts, was inevitably given to those among the sopranos whom she felt to be good musicians, yours truly being one such. Later in my life, when I was with the English National Opera, I used to sing the tenor line behind the men, just for giggles. One stalwart Welshman (Sadlers Wells, which ENO was originally called, used to be known in the business as 'Sadlers Welsh'), said to me 'How come you know our line, cariad?' When I told him, he laughed his head off.

But back to the ghosties. So far we have had the boy in the lake and Sister Erconwald. The next manifestations were to prove considerably more sinister. One of the Hammersmith girls underwent a series of poltergeist experiences, one of which I was able to witness first-hand. The first of these occurred just outside our dormitory in the wee, small hours.

By now, the older Hammersmith girls having left school and returned south, those of us remaining were moved to the main dormitory. It was often the practice for us to visit the bathroom in pairs, although a bucket was always supplied, just outside the dormitory door, for emergencies. As the bathroom itself, with its two loos, was some way along the corridor, most times we all had recourse to the bucket. On the occasion in question, said girl, let us call her Edna (not her real name), whose bed happened to be adjacent to mine, woke me to ask if I would accompany her along the passage. But the night was cold, and necessity failed to dictate my need to forsake my warm bed, so I politely refused. Having then tried Barbara, who occupied the next bed, and met with the same response, she obviously decided to risk it alone.

Poor Edna never got further than the door of the nun's cell, which was adjacent to our dormitory door. No sooner had she stepped on the red-tiled floor outside than she gave out a, piercing scream and rushed back into the dormitory. This alerted the nun, who came running out to see what was wrong. The lights went on and Edna's injuries were there for all to see. There were huge scratches down the side of her face and arm, of the kind usually inflicted by large animals, and she was bleeding profusely. An explanation was requested and this was her story.

As she left the dormitory door, she noticed something crouching in the corner between the door of the nun's cell and the small dormitory at the other side, which was locked and no longer in use. The 'thing' was considerably larger than a domestic cat and resembled more a medium-sized primate. Its eyes, she said, were like burning coals. Before she could escape it leapt at her, its huge claws effecting the wounds she now displayed. There were no animals anywhere in the building, such things as pets never being allowed in any circumstances. Having dismissed all rational explanations, the nun was forced to admit that some spookery was at work here. Edna was put into temporary isolation until her wounds healed, and a priest was called in to exorcise the spot in question. For some weeks we all walked around in terror, but slowly the memory of the incident faded away.

There were two main flights of stairs to the dormitories, a somewhat drab and well-worn one at the back of the building and a much grander affair at the front, which sported huge landings adorned with life-sized statues of the Holy Family. Spooks seldom favoured the back stairs, with one exception: the claw – which, legend had it, the devil decided to leave on a disused altar that had been unceremoniously dumped on the top landing – as a warning of some kind? Needless to say, the claw was no longer in evidence, but we were told with all sincerity that girls from the past had witnessed its presence, although we were never informed as to what actually happened to it. Strange!

During the days of the blitz on Manchester, and after we emerged from the cellars following the all-clear, we were able to watch the fires in the distance from our dormitory windows. Several of us used to plan what we would do if our building was hit; we would make for the city, claim to have lost our memories and our parents and ask to be taken in by some kindly families. It seemed a good idea at the time and a possible means of escape from our involuntary imprisonment.

At times some of us were required to carry out fire-watching duties, the routine being to alert the warden, a Mr. Screeton, who would then set about sorting it out with a bucket and stirrup pump. None of us liked patrolling the top passage, even in pairs, as it had a distinctly spooky atmosphere. But on to our next poltergeistly manifestation, which on this occasion took place downstairs for a change.

On one side of our changing-room there were some cupboards and a row of basins. Facing these were rows of hooks upon which we could hang our clothes, and on the other wall, opposite the door, there were two loos. It could not have been all that long after the scratching incident that I was in the process of washing my hands in one of the basins. The Head Girl, Georgina, was doing likewise beside me. Edna came into the room and engaged the basin beside Georgina's. We were all wearing short-sleeved dresses, so her arms, like ours, were in full view. After running the water for a second, she said, 'Oh, I should have gone in there first', pointing to the loo, the door of which was wide open, indicating its vacancy. So saying, she walked away from us, entered the loo and shut the door. The door had barely closed when she let out an ear-piercing scream and rushed out, her right arm extended in front of her. On it, printed in black, and I do mean *printed* and not scrawled, were the words: 'DEVILS – I HAVE COME TO TEMPT YOU'. Without thinking, Georgina grabbed Edna's arm and attempted to wash off the offending words. Try as she would, they refused to budge. Realising that she was up against something paranormal, fear gripped her, and she called Sister Clare who happened to be in the corridor outside. After a single glance at the phenomenon, the worthy nun sought immediate help from her superior, Sister T. who was soon upon the scene.

Sister T.'s reaction was similar to Georgina's. 'How dare you play such wicked tricks', she scolded, dragging the unfortunate girl to the basin by the collar of her frock, whereupon she applied the same treatment as Georgina. All this time I was standing watching. Edna was right-handed, and the dexterity required to produce such perfect printing in a few seconds would have taxed an accomplished sign-writer. Besides, both Georgina and I had watched her wash her hands less than a moment before and there had been no trace whatsoever of any writing. Sister T. then started to panic, the full realisation of what she was dealing with having suddenly dawned on her. She rushed Edna to her office and telephoned for a priest. One duly arrived, and the same procedure was applied, this time with holy water. The results were negative.

Finally she was taken in a car to Liverpool, never to return. Some months later, when I was sent back to Hammersmith prior to being handed over to Nanny, I met up with Edna once again. Needless to say, my first question was, 'Have you had any further spooky manifestations, and what happened when you were sent away?' She told me she had been taken in a car to Liverpool Cathedral, where the Bishop had prepared some holy oils. As he lifted the soaked pad to apply it to her 'writing', the words suddenly disappeared, in full view of all present, and before the oil had even touched her skin. She was then seen by a Jesuit priest, who told her that her unfortunate manifestations were due to the presence of a 'catalyst' among her former schoolmates who obviously possessed 'certain powers' which was why she was removed from that environment and returned to Hammersmith immediately. Since her return south, there had been no further problems, and, I gather, none since. Why do I feel guilty?

While on the subject of Liverpool Cathedral, the time approached for some of the older girls, myself included, to be confirmed, which ceremony was always undertaken by the Bishop himself. There were about eight of us, if I recall, all dressed in white, and well schooled to say the right things and answer correctly the questions put to us by the worthy cleric. I recall my question being 'What is holy oil?' The catechism answer being 'Oil of olives, mixed with balsam, and blessed by the Bishop on Holy Thursday' which, needless to say, I rattled off with alacrity. We were duly ushered to the altar rail to undergo our anointing. And then a strange thing happened.

As the Bishop leaned forward to anoint my forehead, the scene suddenly changed. I found myself temporarily in a time-warp. The architectural gloom of the Cathedral gave way to a different scenario – a place of stunning beauty, illuminated by a brilliant white light; and the person standing over me was not the Bishop, but a tall man with long, fair hair and slanted eyes. His robes were azure blue and white and encrusted with jewels, and his headgear was like nothing I had ever seen. But more meaningful to me than the splendour of his apparel and the bright light was the feeling of pure love that radiated from him to me. He leaned over and touched me on the forehead. I simply said 'Father'. And I knew it was he who had spoken to me in the bathroom at Wells Street, and whom I came to know later as Helio-Arcanophus – Chief High Priest of the Sun – but whose real, *family* name I shall be revealing in a later chapter.

Although the moment seemed to last for an eternity, only a second or so had passed in Earth time, and by then the Bishop had moved on to the next girl. I underwent a similar experience years later, when, as a member of an adult choir, I was obliged to meet the Cardinal and carry out the ritual of kissing his ring.

But coming down to Earth, and back to those iniquitous toilets in the old changing room, I recall a retreat priest (a rather boring, monotonous-voiced Franciscan) reminding us that God observes everything, even our most private actions and deeds. Bearing this in mind when attending to a subsequent call of nature, it suddenly struck me that He was watching me, even there! However, my rational mind immediately relieved me of the embarrassment by suggesting that if said Being created us in the first place, It must have been fully aware of the bodily functions of Its creation. I never gave the matter another thought.

While on the subject of loos, there was another set of them, about eight in number, right by the entrance to the two classrooms. Although none of us was allowed possessions of any kind, we somehow managed to accumulate the odd few pieces. Perhaps they came as Christmas gifts (we were allowed parcels from relatives), or they were traded for some culinary treat – which we did have occasionally, the odd egg being an example. Anyway, I had quite a small collection, including a silver chain with a small silver locket which housed a miniature silver rosary and a highly prized ten-shilling note – a present from relatives of my Nanny's who happened to live up north and who came to visit me during the last few months that I was there. The family, it seemed, had a whip-round, 10/- being the net result! In one of the above-mentioned toilets I discovered a loose brick which I carefully prized out. There was a small cavity behind, into which I secreted my much-valued cache, contained in a small, cotton bag that I had made from an old handkerchief. But when the time came for me to leave, it was all very sudden and I was never able to retrieve it. One cannot help wondering if, when those loos were later updated, a certain workman might have struck lucky?

One of the punishments meted out by those who fell foul of Sister T. was the dreaded 'standing on the front'. This involved standing on the front of the dormitory in the freezing cold, clad only in one's nightdress, with one's hands above one's head, after everyone else had gone to bed, while Sister T. read her 'Office'. Were those arms to drop for one second, her wicket would be firmly applied to them. As I was never one of her favourites, she would find any possible excuse to have me standing there. As the pain in my arms became unbearable at times, I devised a psychological method of coping with it. The wall facing me was covered with a reddish brown paint which had been 'smudged' to create a pattern. Within this pattern I made out the picture of a hermit sitting in his cell. I would project my consciousness into that of the hermit, and thus escape into his cell and his pain-free world. It always worked. Without this escape route I do not think I could have endured the pain of such torture.

Sister T. was a firm believer in hard work being good for the soul, and so, for a time, I was given charge of the scullery which involved a considerable amount of heavy-duty stuff. However, after some months of this, my soma started to feel the ill effects, so once again I was obliged to use my powers to extricate myself. While seated one evening in Sister Clare's needlework class, the sheer exhaustion of my work began to bear down on me so I took the only way out and temporarily vacated my body. Unable to bring me round, Sister Clare promptly sent for Sister Philip, who called the doctor. I was carried to sick quarters where, on Dr. Cowan's advice, I was allowed a week of complete rest. When I returned to normal duties I found, to my delight, that I had been relieved of that dreadful scullery chore.

Although the respite advised by the doctor lasted a few weeks, upon reaching the age of fourteen I was obliged to take my turn in the laundry. The conditions there were primitive in the extreme and we had to wear clogs to stop our feet becoming sore through constant exposure to wet, concrete floors. My allotted task was the washing of some 100 underwear items, using an old-fashioned type washboard anchored in a huge tub. All very tiring, although there was a perk that went with washhouse duties, in that we were allowed to get to the bathroom before anyone else and thus were able to indulge ourselves in the unhurried use of the hot water system.

There were also many other jobs we were obliged to carry out, knitting our own jumpers and making our own skirts being two more personal examples. We also covered hangers for a local department store, knitted berets, and produced many other small artefacts for industry or the war effort.

Once a month we were given tests at school to see who would come top of the class, the fortunate pupil being rewarded by the princely sum of half a crown and a day in Manchester with one of the 'situation girls' (those who had left and were working for their living). However, as I inevitably won these, after four months Sister T. decided the idea was not such a good one and stopped them forthwith. On one occasion, I used my half a crown (which was a fortune for a school-girl in those days) to purchase a small, silver ring which I prized highly. Sister T., however, upon espying this ornament, promptly relieved me of it on the grounds that it could 'cause pride and conceit – the ways of the devil'. But I did manage to get it back in the end, as my readers will shortly see.

Among the many superstitions which predominated among the girls in our school, the 'white pigeon' certainly took top billing. It went like this: the roof of our dormitory being in full view of the playground, if a white pigeon was observed to be stationary about the area of one's bed, one would leave the next day. It never failed to work. And so it was that several of us were taking our short break in the playground on that cold day in late February when someone shouted, 'Look, there's a white pigeon, and it's right over Hope's bed'. (We were never allowed to use Christian names, nor were we ever addressed by them). Sure enough, there was the white bird, perched approximately over the spot occupied by my bed. And I knew that my time of freedom had finally arrived.

CHAPTER 7

Freedom At Last!

Our daily routine consisted of being awakened at 6 a.m. by Sister Amyria, an elderly nun to whom the task fell of sounding the morning Angelus. At the last of the first three bells Sister T. would open her cell window and announce 'The Angel of the Lord Declared unto Mary', to which we were obliged to answer, 'And she conceived by the Holy Ghost'. Sometimes she would make this announcement in Latin, *'Angelus Domini Nuntiavit Mariae'*, so it always paid to be prepared either way – *'Et concepit de Spiritu Sancto'*. And, since Sister T. knew every voice in that dormitory, it was God help anyone she did not hear effect the appropriate response. We then had to stack our beds and report to the bathroom for our morning ablutions, after which we were required to get dressed and line up on our knees in the passage for morning prayers. Mass in the chapel followed and then we would make our way, in the usual double line, to the refectory for breakfast.

On the morning following the white pigeon sighting, when Sister T. and Sister Clare entered we all awaited the usual ritual; *'Benedicamus Domino'*, she would say, to which we would chorus our reply, *'Deo Gratias'*. She would then motion us to be seated. On this particular morning, however, I could sense a strangely different feeling in the air and knew instinctively that something was about to happen. I watched Sister T. withdraw a letter from her pocket and waited with bated breath. I just *knew* that letter was about me. Taking her time, she slowly perused those meaningful pages before looking up and calling, 'Hope, come down here.' With great trepidation I obeyed. As I made my way past the other tables, I heard the muffled whispers: 'the white pigeon'. Without taking her eyes off the pages in her hand, she said, coldly, 'You are leaving today and returning to Hammersmith. Report to my office after breakfast. You will be given appropriate clothing and a pair of shoes for your journey. Now go and eat.'

But there was no way I could tackle those ugly doorsteps of bread and lard that were put in front of me, so I waited patiently for the usual dismissal and made my way along the stark, red-tiled corridor to Sister T.'s office. She handed me a pile of clothing: a jumper I had knitted myself and a dark grey skirt I had also made during needlework classes. There were several pairs of brown sandals, and I was asked to try them for size. There was also an old navy-blue coat which I practically drowned in, but who cared! It was part of my freedom regalia. Then she said, 'Is there anything else you want to ask me before the car comes for you?' I replied, 'Yes, Sister. Please may I have my silver ring?' My request evoked a look of utter disgust, which was voiced in the sarcastic retort, 'Proud to the end, the devil will get you, my girl, for sure.' Nevertheless, after rummaging in one of her drawers she produced the object in question. Even though it no longer fitted my finger, I treasured it for months after, as a trophy of victory, if nothing else.

I was then ushered to the main entrance at the front of the building and within minutes a small car arrived to take me to the main railway station in Manchester where I was to be put on the train for London. My instructions were to look out for a Sister Alberta when we reached the other end. The odour of engine smoke, plus the hissing of the tank's pressure build-up, which always preceded those old puffer-billies' take-offs was music to my ears. Here, at last, I was among ordinary, sane people, like my Nanny and her family. But for how long? And so my journey began.

Although there were still the green fields which I viewed with such joy through the limited space allowed by the sticky material that adhered to the windows as a precaution against blast, there was also the destruction. As we eventually steamed into King's Cross Station, I scanned the waiting crowds for a sight of a nun in the blue-edged navy garb of the Sisters of Nazareth. And sure enough, there she was, Sister Alberta, one of the nicest, most truly spiritual nuns I ever came to know during the whole period of my incarceration within the walls of that Order. She hailed a taxi and it was not long before I was once again passing through that barred door into the precincts of Nazareth House, Hammersmith, London W6.

What I did not know was that Nanny had applied for my release with the offer to provide me with a good home. But as I had been placed there by Court Order, and the Child Care Officer who handled the case was away in the war, the Convent authorities were reluctant to let me go to someone whom they saw as a stranger. It had to be my mother who collected me, no-one else. Nanny therefore wrote to her and asked if she would do the necessary. She replied that she would, but on condition that Nanny never bothered her about me again and accepted complete responsibility for me from then on. Also, she did not want her husband to know what was going on, so she would arrange to collect me and meet Nanny at Hammersmith Underground Station, at which point the handover would take place.

All this negotiating took a couple of weeks, during which time I was given various domestic chores to carry out. The weather was extremely cold and the water I was obliged to use for my scrubbing was barely lukewarm. As a result, my hands became sore and chapped. That dear Sister Alberta, noting my discomfort, came to my bed after lights out, armed with a tube of handcream which she rubbed into the open cracks. She begged me not to mention it to her seniors, as they considered such suffering to be good for the soul, whereas she did not quite see it that way. It was she who, albeit confidentially, comforted me with the knowledge that arrangements were taking place for my release.

And so, once again, I was given my marching orders and told to report to the main office after breakfast. My mother was there to meet me, looking somewhat embarrassed. However, she duly signed the necessary papers, and slowly that ominous, barred door was opened once again and I stepped out into the freedom of London. Not a word was spoken as I trotted along beside her towards Hammersmith Underground Station, but as we approached the entrance and I saw Nanny standing there, I rushed towards her outstretched arms. The gods had, at last, seen fit to restore me to those I truly loved.

As I held tightly onto Nanny's arm, my mother said, 'Now, Nurse Adams, I must insist that she is your responsibility from now on. In view of my own domestic situation I want no further contact. You do fully understand?' Nanny's answer left no doubt in any of our minds. 'I have always seen Jack as my child. I only wish you had let me have her in the first place and saved us all a lot of bother.' 'Quite, quite, Nurse. But that is all over now and I must get back to my family. Thank you. Goodbye'.

And so Nanny and I wended our happy way to Blackheath: not to 151 Westcombe Hill, since that was an almost empty shell but to 25 Collins Street, right near the station, and next door to Aunt Beck and her family, who lived at Number 26. Collins Street was adjacent to the railway marshalling yards, so it was a natural target for German bombers. There were therefore a lot of patched and broken windows, but none of that mattered to me. I was home once again, with Nanny and Uncle Alan. Aunt Beck, Uncle Bert and their son, Bert, all came out to welcome me. Nanny soon had the kettle on and I enjoyed the first 'cuppa', with milk and sugar, that I had tasted for several years.

But Nanny was growing old. She must have been well into her seventies by then, and several years of war, being bombed out and lack of sleep had taken their toll, so I was careful not to add to her stress. During those few weeks I stayed with her I offered to look for a job, but she felt I should try to put on some weight and to rest from the ardours of the past few years before embarking on any kind of career. There were days when we went to the pictures together, talked and read. But at night the skies wailed with the screech of sirens and the repetitive throb of German bombers, the deadly deposits of the latter serving to light up Blackheath and surrounding areas with the red-gold of a thousand fires. There was an air-raid shelter in the street outside but Nanny refused to enter it. She used to say, 'If it's my time to go, I'd rather do so in the comfort of my own home than in some cold bunker'. So we made ourselves cosy in the downstairs living room, where we kept a small fire going all night.

The bombing got worse and Nanny became worried for me. After exchanging some correspondence with Win and Charlie Beacon, it was decided that, in view of her age, and the ever-increasing danger, the best thing would be for me to stay with them in the safety of Sandridge. Ken's room had been empty since his death in 1936, and Win and Charlie had told Nanny they would be only too pleased to give me a permanent home, should the need arise. Nanny's family were very closely knit and it was the custom among such folk to look after their own. As far as Win and Charlie were concerned I was Nanny's daughter, so there was no more to be said. However, they too, were old age pensioners, so sooner or later I would be obliged to find a job, and to contribute in some small way to my keep. It was therefore agreed that I move to Sandridge, with the proviso that I could visit Nanny at weekends. It was on one such visit, in the Spring of 1944, that the following extraordinary event took place.

My weekend journeys involved catching a bus from Sandridge to St.Albans, and then what used to be called 'The Green Line' to Golders Green, from which point the Underground conveyed one to London Bridge. On the occasion in question there had been some delay due to an air raid, so I arrived at London Bridge Station slightly later than usual. There was a train already standing at the usual platform, and, somewhat out of breath, I asked a porter, 'Please, does this train go to Blackheath?' 'Yes, love' he answered, with the usual Cockney friendliness. 'On you get, or you'll miss it'. I hastily jumped into the nearest carriage as the shrill whistle heralded departure, but as the journey progressed, I realised that there was something wrong. Instead of the usual stations – Lewisham, St. Johns, etc. – the places at which we stopped were unfamiliar. I knew that I had boarded the wrong train. The next station we stopped at was Westcombe Park and I recalled there being a railway station at the bottom of Westcombe Hill, near which was a bus stop, number 48, I think, which we always caught when we were going to visit Aunt Beck. Hastily alighting, I made my way down the steps and across the road to where, I hoped, the bus stop still stood. Sure enough, there it was, just as I recalled. After a short wait, a somewhat war-worn 48 bus eventually lumbered into view under the old railway bridge.

In those days the windows of the London buses, like those of the trains, were covered in a strange, sticky material, which allowed only a small space through which one could peer to see where one was. So, as the vehicle trundled wearily up Westcombe Hill, I was able to catch a brief but sad glimpse of the old house at 151. After stopping at The Standard, where we picked up some more passengers, it was only a short run to Blackheath Station, behind which Nanny now lived. As we approached the relevant stop, I noticed a crowd of people gathered outside the station. There were also wardens, police, and several ambulances, and there was Nanny among them, her face furrowed with anxiety. I jumped off the bus and ran towards her, shouting, 'Nanny, Nanny'. She looked up, startled, and, as we embraced, she dissolved into tears of gratitude. The train I should have boarded had received a direct hit – most of the passengers were either dead or severely injured. I have often wondered which kindly spirit whispered into that porter's ear to direct me to the wrong train.

Following this frightening event, Nanny decided there would be no more weekend visits until the bombing eased off. From then on I would remain entirely in the care of Win and Charlie. I bade her goodbye for what was to prove the last time. Had I only been aware of this I would have made that final embrace last forever, but perhaps Nanny wouldn't have liked that, as she had been schooled never to display deep feelings in public. And so the next chapter of my life welcomed me with open arms, and 15, Spencer Place, Sandridge became my new home.

CHAPTER 8

15 Spencer Place

When I first arrived at Spencer Place, much was as I had remembered it from my last visit, which had taken place prior to my mother's intervention in my life. The house was on a small council estate, which comprised 20 three-bedroom dwellings, set high on a bank and arranged in horseshoe fashion around two small greens. Everyone knew everyone else. Doors were never locked. In fact, our front door was so seldom opened that, on the odd occasion when some stranger did ring the bell, it was extremely stiff to move! The back door was the way in and out for all. The large garden backed on to a bridle path, the other side of which were the estates of Lady Saltmarsh. During my 1930's visits, it had been the custom to take one's hand-churn across to her farm to collect milk fresh from her cows that morning. Due to war conditions, however, this was no longer the case.

Charlie and his son Eric, whom I judged to be in his mid-forties at the time, used to work in the garden. They kept chickens, so there were fresh eggs each morning, while the end section had been planted with vegetables of all kinds. Potatoes grown in the summer months were buried deep down in sacks, their placings appropriately marked, so that they could be dug up in the winter months when the necessity demanded. The front part of the garden which backed onto the house was, however, kept as just that, with a neat lawn, hedges, rose bushes and the usual garden shed. Eric used to charge accumulators (rechargeable devices for storing electrical energy in the form of chemical energy) in that shed, for a small fee, and the locals would deposit their 'empties' outside the back door for refill, accompanied by the few pence involved. Once recharged, Eric would leave these in the porch for collection at any time. Also in the shed were two bicycles and an old scooter that had belonged to the late Ken.

I had been allocated what had been Ken's room, which was the smallest in the house. Win and Charlie shared the large front bedroom, while Eric had the middle-sized room which, like mine, overlooked the back garden. Charlie had done little to change the room after Ken's death. The bookcase he had built for his son still contained all Ken's books. These were typical of the sort of reading enjoyed by male teenagers in those times: John Buchan, spooky tales, and adventure yarns of all sorts. I had a small bed, a mirror on the wall and a place to hang my clothes, but at that time, no other furniture. However, as I never liked girls' stuff anyway, Ken's books proved a source of inspiration to me.

For the first few weeks, when I was not visiting Nanny, I helped Win around the house, and Charlie and Eric in the garden. Our entertainment consisted of listening to the 'wireless'. Charlie liked ITMA for a laugh, and we all enjoyed those detective serials which dominated 'steam' radio in those days. Paul Temple was one favourite I recall and if anything was guaranteed to put Charlie in a bad mood, it was someone arriving at the back door just as the final episode of a 'whodunnit' was about to come over the air!

Discipline was rigid. No-one spoke during a meal. The Sunday ritual consisted of Win having a lie-in, while Charlie and Eric prepared the lunch. Before I had fully grasped the silence situation, I committed the heinous crime of offering an opening gambit just after everyone had seated themselves comfortably to eat. My words were greeted with a stony silence. Everyone put down their knives and forks, and I recall the look of sheer disdain on Eric's face. Then Charlie broke the silence with, 'We don't talk when we're eating, Jack. Mealtimes are for enjoying food, and you can't do that if you're nattering away about this or that.' I never made the same mistake again.

The other main discipline concerned my hours. Until I was sixteen, I had to be in by 9 p.m. in the summer months and 8 p.m. in the winter months. When I turned sixteen this would be extended to 10 p.m., and at eighteen I could stay out until midnight, on condition that I was escorted home by a responsible adult approved of by Charlie. As I have never been one for late nights, these arrangements were no problem for me.

Across the way at No.6 lived Charlie's father, old George Beacon, who was well into his nineties. A sprightly old boy, who still dressed smartly for his regular game of cribbage at the village pub, George lived with the memories of earlier times, when he plied his craft at the houses of the rich and titled. I would sometimes spend hours listening to his tales and learning therefrom. They reminded me of Nanny's stories of the many great houses where she had carried out her nursery/nursing duties in days past.

One Spring day, a few weeks after I had said my goodbyes to Nanny at Blackheath Station, a letter arrived. Win called me in to tell me that Nanny had passed over. She never explained the circumstances, but rather hinted that it had been a heart attack caused by the bombing. One day before I die, when I am feeling brave, I will consult the Records Office to find out what really happened; as Aunt Beck died at the same time, I rather suspect a direct hit. Perhaps I should let well alone.

All of us were distraught by the news. Nanny had, it seemed, been paying Win and Charlie to look after me, and now that money would cease. When they told me this, I announced that I would seek a job forthwith. I recall Charlie donning his best bib and tucker (he usually sported a striped shirt, minus collar, and a pair of braces) and carting me off to St. Albans to the Labour Exchange (what we now refer to as the Job Centre). The lady in charge was eager to help. There were lots of jobs available for a fourteen-and-a-half year old girl who wrote good English, knew her maths, and was willing to learn typing. I was sent for an interview at the Metropolitan College, a correspondence college in St. Albans. The office manager, a Mr. Cosslett, offered me a job right away. The hours were from 9 a.m. until 6 p.m., with one free Saturday morning in four, and I would be paid the princely sum of twenty-two shillings and sixpence a week. Fifteen shillings of this would go to Win and Charlie for my board and keep, while the rest I could keep for clothing and such bits and pieces as a teenager of the time would be likely to require. There was one problem, however. The bus fare from

Sandridge to St. Albans was threepence each way, which would leave me with almost nil! Charlie came to the rescue. He arranged, through a friend of his, to obtain a 'utility' bicycle; the word 'utility' in those days indicating something absolutely basic, single-geared and painted black. I could then repay him at two shillings a week, which was slightly better than the bus idea. That bike was destined to afford me much pleasure. In fact, it lasted right into my twenties. But then, in spite of the 'utility' tag, things were much better made in those days. In her will, Nanny had left me what little she had in her Post Office Savings Account, plus the wardrobe and dressing table that had graced my childhood bedroom at 151, Westcombe Hill, and were soon to perform a similar task at No.15.

But to return for one moment to the days prior to Nanny's demise. A letter, which had been sent from the convent to my mother, and had finally found its way to me via Nanny's address, came from two of my former tutors, who taught maths/science and anatomy and physiology respectively. These dear ladies had sent details and samples of my work to a doctor colleague who lectured at Trinity College, Dublin, and who was, it seems, equally impressed with it. In fact, it was unanimously agreed that I should, if possible, get back to school and take my Matric, as I was what they described as a 'natural' for a career in medicine. Realising that money was a problem, there being no grants in those days, they were trying every possible avenue to raise the necessary funds. Accommodation could be arranged with a family in Dublin, who would be happy to accept responsibility for me until I was ready to enter a hall of residence. Sadly, however, no money was ever forthcoming. Win and Charlie had nothing, and although all three academic ladies in question assured me they had bought tickets in the Irish Sweepstake specially for the purpose, Fate, on this occasion, was not to prove my friend. Would I have made a good doctor? A General Practitioner – no. But I know I would have made a good hospital clinician, as I have always had a nose for correct diagnoses.

The second letter which rocked the foundations of my security arrived shortly after Nanny's death. It was from my mother. She had, it seemed, received from some unmentioned source news of Nanny's passing. It was addressed to Charlie Beacon and he read it out to me. She wished Charlie and Win to know that she no longer accepted any responsibility for me, as she had made quite clear to Nanny; but, as Nanny was no longer with us, and I was now with the Beacons, if there were any problems whatsoever with me, such as insurbordination, teenage rebellion, or similar, they had her full permission to 'have me put away'! Charlie and Win were both upset, and, for a moment, it was suggested that the missive be put on the fire. However, Charlie thought it might work both ways, in that, should they wish to adopt me legally at some future date, there would be no impediment thereto. So it was placed among a pile of similarly meaningful documents on the mantlepiece, where it sat until I joined the WAAFS in 1948. For my own part, it made me extremely nervous, and I therefore went out of my way to do all those things that pleased my acquired 'family'. In fact, I was an exemplary teenager, although I did have one slip which, mercifully, Charlie never found out about. But more of that later.

Teenagers are expected to rebel. These days, such behaviour is blamed on their hormones. But, in truth, I was never a rebel. Rebellion took up valuable time and energy, so, as far as I was concerned, it was illogical. I have always hated upsets of any kind and have therefore gone out of my way to avoid them. In my early teens I made the occasional friend at work; one girl in particular featuring so much in my life that Charlie allowed me to stay the night at her home, with her parents, of course. There was also the usual crowd of village teenagers, some of whom were still at school. They used to hang around in a gang, standing for hours on the corner, doing nothing. On one occasion a girl from the house next door to old George Beacon invited me to join them, so I trundled down to where they were standing around as usual. I asked, 'Aren't we going to do something?' They all looked at me as if I had just uttered a blasphemous invocation to Old Nick. 'DO? – why do we always have to do something? We just stand around and talk. After all, what is there to do?' I promptly walked away, and went back to my room, where I could at least read and learn something. This, and similar encounters with the local teenagers, earned me such titles as 'weird' and 'daft'. However, they occasionally put up with me when we all went for cycle rides together, although if I am honest, I was never really accepted by them.

The summer of 1944 gave way to autumn and the inevitable chills of winter soon set in. I had settled comfortably into my job and had learned to type, albeit with two fingers only, which proved a distinct advantage. There were a few older men, tutors, working for the Metropolitan College, plus the Office Manager, but the Chief Accountant was a Scottish lady, a Miss Edith Adcock, who was very strict, and therefore not very popular with the youngsters. I stayed in the job until I joined the WAAFS in the Winter of 1948, slowly working myself up into a fairly good position. But more of that later.

Aside from reading Ken's old books, I also joined the local library but the books I borrowed were never fiction. It was during this period that I commenced my studies of palmistry, astrology, numerology and allied occult sciences. What I lacked, however, was the psychology of application; a lesson I was soon to learn the hard way. The girl friend I had acquired at work, let us call her 'Teresa', often used me as a kind stool-pigeon. Being slim, pretty and well dressed, she was able to attract any boy she wanted, whereas I was plain, plump and cheaply clad, as a result of which no-one ever gave me a second glance. This never worried me at all, because at the time I had no interest in boys. However, Teresa was always slightly suspicious of first dates, so she would arrange for me to stay the night at her home, take me with her when she met her various admirers and require that I follow them around, always keeping well out of sight. Should the occasion arise when one of these beaux went a little 'over the top', she would call to me for assistance and the two of us would chase him off! This arrangement worked well until she found 'the' one, at which point I was permanently dismissed.

But, to come to the palmistry bit: having decided that she wanted to tie the knot with said boy, she asked me to read her palm. I distinctly saw two marriages, and advised her accordingly, whereupon she immediately flew into a tantrum and stomped off, never to 'use' me again, nor even acknowledge me as a friend. It was not until years later, when

I was on leave from RAF Ruislip and I took Win to the pictures, that I saw Teresa in the box office. She recognised me immediately and asked a colleague to take over so that we could converse. In a flood of contrite tears, she told me that her former boyfriend had got her pregnant. She had been obliged to marry him, but he had turned out to be a no-good scoundrel and they had subsequently divorced. She was now courting 'George' and they were to be married quite soon. Upon recalling that, in my palm reading I had mentioned only two husbands, she felt safe in the knowledge that George was the right one for her.

Aside from my occult studies, the other interest that dominated my teenage years was music. Although I had been forced into the Catholic religion against my will, I had grown to love the liturgy, and its music in particular. So, while I had no intention of ever practising Catholicism again, I decided to see what the Catholic church in St. Albans had to offer in the musical field. I struck lucky. The conductor, I discovered, was a member of the BBC musical staff and his choir one of the best anywhere around. They sang the great motets by Schubert, Mozart, Bach, etc., also the earlier works of such musical giants as Palestrina. I presented myself as a 'Catholic', auditioned and was accepted immediately, since I read music and was already familiar with many of the works they performed. In fact, I never missed a Sunday although I often thought it strange that no-one ever questioned why I did not go to communion, or indulge in any of the more personal Catholic rituals. Perhaps they thought I partook of these on weekdays, thus leaving Sundays free for music only.

Both clergy and choir were a pretty jolly lot, especially

when it came to the regular parties which were held in the church hall (when it was not being used as a 'British Restaurant' – a sort of war time soup-kitchen for the homeless or those who had been bombed out). Catholic priests, I observed, were certainly partial to a drop of booze, or more than a drop on occasions. They also erred on the side of a flutter. News somehow spread that I had 'the gift', and on one occasion which I recall with much amusement, one young priest approached me, *during the Sermon being given by the parish priest,* in the following vein: 'I'm after hearing that you have contact with the *sidhe*, which tells me you've the gift.' 'So I'm told', I replied modestly. 'Then would you be after doing me a great favour and telling me which horse is going to win the 2.30 on Tuesday?' (He did mention the place and race in question, but these I cannot recall). I enquired of him as to the names of the horses running, and when he reached No.3 on the list I stopped him. 'I think that's the one'. He seemed well satisfied. The following week he was there again, this time with a colleague. 'I won half-a-crown on the horse you gave us last week – for the poor box, of course. Could you find it in your heart to ask the wee folks for their help once more?' Repeat performance, which again proved successful. However, I found it embarrassing that said cleric always made these requests during the period when the parish priest was giving his sermon of the week, which point I raised with him on the following Sunday. He dismissed my concern with the casual remark, 'Sure, we know that one by heart, we've heard it so many times before!'. I rather suspect that someone must have mentioned these goings-on to his superior, as the requests ceased somewhat suddenly, and not, or so I heard, because my forecasts had been incorrect. But in spite of all this I thoroughly enjoyed my singing, and learned a lot of material that was to prove of considerable help to me in later years, when I won a scholarship to the Royal College of Music.

The other highlight of my stay at 15 Spencer Place came later, when Charlie's sister, Elsie, and her husband Jack Playdon, together with their thirty-two year old daughter, Jean, came to live with and look after old George Beacon.

Before I embark on the tale of those happy days, I must confess my one teenage sin. A girl I worked with at the Metropolitan College had made friends with two sisters from a very wealthy family who lived in a large house in the suburbs of St. Albans. The parents were going away for the weekend, so the girls, who were around 18 years old, invited my friend and me to join them for the night. I was about seventeen at the time. The parents having dropped a note to Charlie to put things right for me, I took off that Saturday afternoon to meet up with my workmate, armed only with my pyjamas and toilet kit, ready for the night. However, when we arrived it seemed that the two resident girls had different plans. 'Now that we have the place to ourselves, we are all going up to the Palais in Hammersmith to dance away the night'. A wave of fear overwhelmed me. What if Charlie found out? I was assured that there was no way in which he could and that I would be quite safe. The girls' older sister gave us a lift to the station and we boarded the train for St. Pancras. Upon our arrival in the Metropolis, the Underground soon whisked us off to Hammersmith Broadway, the dance-hall in question being a mere stone's throw from there.

I recall the place being absolutely packed, mostly with

servicemen of all nationalities. If I remember correctly, the resident band was under the leadership of Joe Loss. What with the crowds and the loud music, the noise was deafening. Somehow I became separated from my friend and the two older girls, who had all acquired partners fairly early in the proceedings. Eventually an American sailor asked me to dance, but his whole attitude and body language worried me, so I hastily excused myself and headed for the toilets. By this time I was feeling sick and panicky, but, try as I could, I failed to locate the other three among the seething crowds. So I decided to do a runner and make my way back alone. I rushed out of that dreadful place, and over to the Underground Station as fast as my legs would carry me. Then on to St. Pancras, where I just managed to catch the last train to St. Albans (dear guardian angel!). From there I was obliged to walk the three and a half miles to Sandridge in the pitch dark. As my feet were already aching, I took off my shoes and made the journey barefoot. When I arrived 'home', all was quiet. Everyone had gone to bed and darkness reigned supreme over the sleeping inmates. Thankfully the back door was never locked at night, so I opened it cautiously and tiptoed silently up the stairs to my room. Any slight creak I may have made was drowned by the loud snores coming from Eric's room. I quickly undressed and fell into bed and a thankful sleep.

The next morning, as soon as I heard movement, I called to Win, telling her that I had decided to come home after all as I didn't like the older girls. I added that since I had arrived back just after they had all gone to bed at 10.30 p.m., not wishing to wake them I had crept in as quietly as possible. I hated telling them a lie, but I knew they would have been more than hurt had I told them the truth. That morning I caught the bus to St. Albans and sang in my choir as usual. Thank goodness we were not on the telephone, or there might have been a call enquiring as to what had happened to me. Explanations were proffered at work on Monday morning, when I told my friend I had been 'taken ill', which news she promptly conveyed to the other two miscreants. Never again!

CHAPTER 9

Horsing About

Win and Charlie had always kept cats, and, following the death of their old tabby shortly after I took up residence at No.15, they had taken in a stray who was about to give birth. 'Minnie' had four lovely kittens, two tabbies and two grey-and-whites. The latter two being the most favoured, it was agreed to keep them and they were named, appropriately, Pat and Spot, while suitable homes were found for the others. However, before they reached maturity, Minnie was discovered dead behind a neighbour's shed, the remains of what was obviously a very ill rat serving as a clue to what the vet established as death by poisoning. Pat and Spot, both males, were neutered, and soon settled in to become members of our closely-knit family. Every morning Pat, who was my favourite, used to wake me up by licking my eyelashes. Pat and I enjoyed a special kind of relationship so it was no surprise to me when, in later years, his little soul returned to me in a new body.

The only other animal to grace our home was Charlie's sister's dog, Jan, an elderly black cocker spaniel, whom we agreed to take charge of while Kit and her husband were moving house. Needless to say, I was the one left to walk the dog, which I did without reservation, and it was on one such walk that a very strange thing happened. I must have been about sixteen and a half at the time, and, apart from the anatomy and physiology classes I had attended at school, which had dealt mainly with the skeletal system and principle organs, I had no real knowledge of certain other bodily functions which could be seen as being more relevant to a teenager.

The lanes in those days were usually empty, so Jan and I would cross the fields and make our way back along those lanes without meeting a soul. However, upon this one occasion, a young man cycled past us at some speed, obviously oblivious to the angle of the approaching corner, which caused him to brake so sharply that the string holding the batch of books that was strapped to the back of his bicycle snapped, discharging the package right across the road. I ran to help him pick them up and noted that they were all medical books, including the classic Burke's Anatomy. The twine that had originally held them had shed a few inches in the process, so, try as he could, the poor man was unable to include them all within the remaining length. After hesitating for a moment he cast an apologetic glance in my direction, shrugged his shoulders and removed one of the books, which he handed to me with the words,'No offence, but you might find this of some use later in your life if not now, and I can always get another copy from the University library'. And with that he was gone.

I waited until he was well out of sight before opening the tome. It was a medical textbook which dealt with all the things

I had not learned at school, but which it was imperative that I should understand. As a consequence I was able to avoid those mistakes made by many of my peers. Once more, thank you, Guardian Angel.

It was around the summer of 1947 that the Playdons moved in with old grandfather Beacon. They had previously lived in Birmingham, where their daughter, Jean, who was thirty-two, had worked on a milk-round. Jean had two ponies already and her parents had promised her that when her father retired he would buy her a stable so that she could set up a riding school. They kept their promise and Jean started off with five horses, including her own two. The outdoor life suited her as she was asthmatic.

Jean was a strange woman, of the kind I had not previously come across. Today she would doubtless be dubbed 'gay', a fact which struck me at the time. She had a 'girl friend' back in Birmingham who would visit her occasionally, although I rather suspect that it was something of a one-sided affair, the 'friend' appearing straight, as far as I could judge. However, I could have been wrong, as in those days I possessed neither the experience nor the psychology to assess such matters. Jean had a strange but effective sense of humour. On one occasion, instead of riding our horses back to Sandridge we left them in the stables at the other side of town and came home on the bus, in our full riding gear, of course. As we took our seats, some clever-Dick remarked, 'What's the matter, ducks, wouldn't they let you take your 'oss on the bus?' To which my quick-thinking companion retorted, 'Actually, he prefers to ride his bike!' which had the desired effect – silence!

Running the stables all on her own did prove a bit much

for Jean at times, so she enlisted my aid, first of all as a dogsbody – mucking out, brushing the horses down and so forth. Finally she decided to teach me to ride.

Jean had been well schooled in horsemanship by an old cavalry officer, whose stringent disciplines she imposed upon me from the start. I was not allowed to hold a rein until I had mastered the art of 'kneeing', and she used to have me, along with her younger pupils, going round in circles, our arms folded neatly across out chests, heads erect and knees well in. In time I was allowed to use the snaffle, and eventually the double rein; and, when she felt I was ready, I was invited to accompany her when she took out a 'ride' . She positioned me at the rear while she led at the front, some six or seven children straggling along in between. Later, Jean and I rode together, and we were allowed access to the bridle paths and jumps on Lord Verulam's land. By the time I was eighteen, I had mastered sufficient of the preliminaries of horsemanship to merit her teaching me to tackle fairly high jumps.

I defy anyone who has ridden for some period to say they have never had a fall. I had several, in one of which I broke a couple of ribs and a collar-bone. The doctor who attended me was totally unsympathetic, and advised me to 'get mounted again as soon as possible – best thing for you, young lady!' Which was, of course, exactly what I did.

In 1948, the St. Albans City Fathers decided that the time was right to hold a special pageant in memory of a spectacular and historical skirmish between Roundheads and Cavaliers which had occurred on those very grounds just outside the city many years earlier. Since this 'skirmish' involved a cavalry charge, each and every horseperson available was roped in to take part, including Jean and the more suitable horses from her stable. The local gentry, who were quick to cast themselves as Cavaliers, hired appropriate costumes from professional agencies, whereas the rest of us, who were left to play Roundheads, were told to make papier mâché helmets as best we could and to wear trousers (our brother's, if we were girls), brown jackets and wellies, which, we were assured, 'would not notice from a distance', all eyes being, naturally, on the Cavaliers. A fair-sized orchestra was hired and the special guest was to be Her Majesty, Queen Elizabeth who is now the Queen Mother.

Jean and I, together with other youngsters from the many minor stables, were also required to work in the horse tent. Denham Film Studios stunt horse team, which was then under the direction of a Daphne Day, would be there for the real performance, so that the required 'stampede' could be effectively stage-managed. However, a local gentleman farmer, whose name I shall refrain from mentioning in case his descendants see fit to sue me, assumed an imperious position which, he seemed to think, gave him the right to treat the rest of us like something the cat had brought in that had gone slightly off. After taking a day or so of his abusive language and behaviour, we quietly planned our revenge.

A lady I worked with in my daily job just happened to be playing cello in the orchestra and her son, a professional musician, was on percussion. Now the Cavaliers and their horses were all assembled in front of the orchestra, with our arch-enemy positioned right in front of the percussionist. The idea was that he should raise his sword and shout 'Charge', whereupon the Cavaliers, in their wigs, feathered hats and velvet costumes, would have us poor Roundheads running for our lives. The theme music used was Walton's 'Crown Imperial', which, as anyone who is familiar with that piece will know, features one particular section where there is a *tremendous* clash of cymbals.

The pageant commenced and the point came at which Mr. Nasty was about to draw his sword and effect his dramatic announcement. But before he could unsheath it, our 'ally' in percussion leaned forward with his cymbals and brought them together in an almighty clash, right behind the rear of said gentleman's nag, which reared up, almost unseating him, and bolted. The whole Cavalier field bolted after it, with us in hot pursuit, waving our wooden swords and shouting for Cromwell! The Queen, and other dignitaries present, believing all to have been rehearsed, were generous with their praise, Her Majesty herself declaring it to be the most inspiring and exciting thing she had seen in a long time! Apparently, the 'bolt' was so effective that it took our Cavaliers some time to control the stampede, we 'oiks' having dropped behind, submissively, after the 'field' was out of sight of the audience.

That night Daphne Day and the film people held an all-night party in the horse tent, which I was obliged to attend, but hated. At break of dawn we were all expected to saddle up for a brisk gallop to brush away the cobwebs. I was allowed to ride one of her studio horses, a thoroughbred named Cooleen who was (I was assured) a direct descendant of a very famous race horse called The Tetrarch.

When I arrived home the following morning, I was so tired that I slept most of the day. Even in my teens I was never able to take late nights, the average dance, which in those days ended at midnight, serving to knock me out for several days. This lack of stamina has followed me all through my life, so I cannot, in truth, blame it on old age.

As the hazy days of that summer gave way to the lengthening shadows, I found myself feeling restless. Win and Charlie were starting to feel their age, and I had gone just as far as I could go in my job at the Metropolitan College. With the advent of my nineteenth birthday I decided it was decision time. I went to the Labour Exchange, stated my position, and asked the kindly lady for any sensible advice she might see fit to proffer. She suggested a spell in the Forces, where I could learn a trade. I sat and thought about it for a moment before asking which she thought would be best for me: ATS, WAAFS or WRENS? She suggested that I fill in the application forms for all three and let Fate decide: the first to reply would be the right one. I concurred, took the appropriate forms from her, and returned home, where I discussed the matter with Win and Charlie.

It seemed that they had both been thinking for some time that I needed to spread my wings. Before I could render what I felt might be an appropriate apology for leaving them, Charlie came out with, 'We're getting old now, Jack, and a young girl like you needs to get out and about in the world.' Although Win nodded in agreement, I could see the hint of a tear in her eye. I cannot honestly remember how many days I waited for the first reply. When it came, it was from the RAF. I filled in the form and sent it back, and it was not long before I received the appointment to attend Adastra House in London for an interview and appropriate medical. Strangely enough, the other two replies had come hurtling through the letterbox with that very same delivery.

I have to confess to having a lump in my throat as I caught the train to St. Pancras: I could sense the end of what had been a happy, uneventful, albeit instructive cycle.

Having passed my medical, plus the intelligence tests required for the Women's Auxiliary Air Force, I received my marching orders to report to the Training Centre at RAF Wilmslow (Cheshire) on 6th December, 1948. The winds of change had blown effectively, but were their tidings of good or ill?

CHAPTER 10

The Women's Auxiliary Air Force

By the time I enlisted in the WAAFS I was well and truly steeped in all things metaphysical. There was, however, much more to be learned, some of which involved a comprehension of the more practical facets of life and human psychology, which a spell in the Forces seemed guaranteed to provide. Upon my arrival at Wilmslow I met up with some thirty or more other girls who were also part of that intake. After we had all assembled and been checked in, we were taken to the Supplies Depot, where we were issued with our full quota of 'kit'. This included two standard uniforms (matching skirts and tunics), a 'greatcoat' (overcoat in civvie terms), two hats, gloves, stockings (heavy duty lisle – there were no nylons or tights in those days), and the most awful underwear imaginable. Regarding the latter, to my knowledge none of us ever wore it, especially the knee-length knickers which were dubbed 'passion-killers'. These were appropriately folded for the regular kit inspections and secreted away in our lockers meantime. Sometimes we were obliged to wear those heavy-duty stockings, route marches in particular demanding their use, especially in the winter months. But during most other times we preferred use the meagre allowance we were given at the weekly pay parade to purchase something more attractive and flattering.

The Training Squadrons were known by colours. Ours was Yellow Squadron and our arch-rival was Blue Squadron. Having collected our kit we were taken, in line, to the billets (Nissen Huts) that were to be our home during our training period. The corporal in charge simply allocated the first hut to the first batch, and so forth, indicating the appropriate bed-spaces to each of us in turn. Then followed my first lesson in the psychology of collectives: within the hour we had re-organised ourselves into three groups. The cockneys and their regional equivalents ended up at one end of the hut, the more educated among us at the other, and a middle group – the members of which seemed to disapprove of both ends – in the centre. Three of us formed a rather special trio which was destined to play a small but significant role in Yellow Squadron's activities in the weeks to come: Bobbie, an Australian girl whose father was a diplomat, Cristabel, an ex-public school girl who I later found out came from a titled family, and yours truly. We got on extremely well with the cockneys and their mates, but the middle group never really liked us.

Our first visit to the Mess was something of an initiation in itself. The 'boys', most of whom were National Servicemen in training, inevitably contrived to get ahead of us girls in the queue for food, and, while we were all waiting, they would chant every rude song they could think of, from the old Rugby specials to ditties appropriate to Air Force personnel. We were, of course, supposed to be utterly shocked. However, after a week or so, following the old axiom 'if you can't beat 'em, join 'em', we were singing along with them.

There were a few strange rules to be learned, especially in relation to property, be that our uniforms or our personal chattels. For example, on our usual morning visits to the NAAFI following an hour or so of square-bashing, we would hang our greatcoats on a series of hooks just inside the main doors. I think it was on my second visit that I dutifully hung my coat on a spare hook before savouring yet another of those delicious Eccles cakes in which the establishment specialised. Upon returning to collect my coat, I discovered, to my horror, that it had disappeared. Fortunately, the only article in the pocket had been a damp handkerchief. As I stood there wondering what to do, a corporal who was passing noted my dilemma and enquired as to my problem. I explained that my coat had been taken, whereupon she simply removed the coat from the next hook along and handed it to me. 'Take this one, it's about your size'. 'But it might belong to someone else', I protested. 'I doubt it', she replied. 'It probably belonged to the WAAF who took yours. That's the way it works, luv. Off you go, now.' Oddly enough, no one missed a coat, and the one I had acquired proved a much better fit, and far more comfortable, than the original. It also sported much shinier buttons!

In addition to the pre-breakfast morning parades and the daily square-bashing, the latter of which I thoroughly enjoyed, there were lectures and instructions regarding the role played by the WAAFS within the Royal Air Force. The all-round discipline presented me with a sense of security, and I was reminded of Nanny's 'Always know where you are, Jack'. Needless to say there were 'inappropriate' words for all the major marching tunes, the flag-up drum roll ditty being unrepeatable in this book. However, we were all around the eighteen to nineteen age group so it was a lot of fun.

When I had enrolled back at Adastra House in London, I had been asked to choose which branch of the Force I would like to work in. I opted for M.T. (Motor Transport – driving), simply because I had always wanted to drive and the likelihood of ever being able to afford a car in those days was about as real as the Angel Gabriel dropping in on the parade square. Ha ha, thought I, why not learn at the Government's expense? However, it seemed that some sixty per cent of male entrants had exactly the same idea in mind. Driving School Training (at RAF Wheaton, I seem to recall) involved handling not only Staff cars but also troop carriers and 'heavies' of all kinds. Therefore, when our period of training ended, there were no vacancies for WAAF trainee drivers at Wheaton, the menfolk, and National Servicemen in particular, having been given first choice.

The training period extended over Christmas and into the New Year. We were given Christmas leave, which I spent happily with Win and Charlie. I was also able to sing in the Midnight Mass at the old church. In fact, I spent all my later leave periods at home, the journey from the station to which I was eventually posted being negotiable by bus to St. Albans.

One of the highlights of this period was the weekly 'General Knowledge Challenge' between two squadrons, in our case, Yellow and Blue. This was where what became known as 'the brainy three' came into their own. The idea was that three members of one squadron took the platform and fired questions at all those present from the other squadron, each correct answer from the floor meriting a point. Yellow

Squadron always won hands down, but, in hindsight, perhaps a little unfairly, since our questions involved a degree of academic prowess and specialised knowledge, such as the habits of the Australian Aborigines, the third Roman Emperor in line after Domitian, the composers of various pieces of Baroque music and the speed of light. For that, if nothing else, the oft-times sneered at 'three', enjoyed a degree of appreciation.

Passing Out Parade was a grand affair, complete with band, and a salute taken by an Air Commodore, whose name I have conveniently forgotten. And so we each received our postings. Mine was to RAF Ruislip, where I was to stay 'on hold' until a suitable vacancy occurred at Wheaton. Not that one could sit about doing nothing, so I was seconded to the Signals Section where I was expected to learn to work a switchboard. The irksome thing was that the three girls from Yellow Squadron who had received the same posting were from the middle group in our billet, so, from the word 'go', I was odd man out and decidedly unpopular. The problem was further exacerbated by the fact that they were all GPO trained telephone operators, so, when I was obliged to 'go on the board', they made my life hell. But in time I effected my revenge, as my readers will shortly see.

RAF Ruislip being one of the official RAF Records Offices, in addition to the girls and boys in blue there was also a full staff of civil servants. It was a small, quiet station, with little activity outside the odd cup of tea at the local ABC cafe, punctuated by trips to London on the Underground when funds permitted. What the station did have, however, was a concert/drama group, the musical side of which was organised by Squadron Leader Marshall. Responsibility for the theatre itself fell upon the shoulders of a National Serviceman by the name of Tony Neate. One name among our group which I have often seen on television in recent years was Ken Parry, a character actor of talent. I appeared in several of the productions which took place in that theatre and sang in all the concerts that the good Squadron Leader saw fit to arrange from time to time.

In time I was to discover that Tony Neate had a great fascination for all things theatrical. He had already met several musicians from the world of jazz (can't recall their names, I'm afraid), while also enjoying the classical side. We became firm friends, and, as the months rolled by, what would be described today as an 'item'.

It was during my first few months in the WAAFS that I decided to seek out my natural sister, so I placed an advert in a popular Sunday paper and hoped for the best. It worked. Having no idea as to what to expect from this new arrival on her family scene, my sister's adoptive mother decided to pay a visit to 15, Spencer Place to check me out before allowing her daughter to meet me, not realising that she who had placed the 'ad' was now employed in H.M. Services. According to Win and Charlie, her attitude upon arrival was cavalier to say the least, since it provoked from Charlie the statement that 'our Jack has more breeding and common sense in the end of her little finger than you or yours are ever likely to see!' Once the atmosphere had calmed down, however, I was invited to meet Berrie at her home. She was twenty-one at the time and very beautiful, with Elizabeth Taylor-type looks and an enviable figure. I recall feeling rather dowdy beside her, in my woollen stockings and blue uniform. She had also been able to stay at school until she was eighteen, which rendered her an educational advantage over me. But in spite of sharing the same biological parents we found we had little, if anything, in common, and although we have remained in touch over the years, the relationship has been a cool one. So much for genes, but then how many people would want a changeling as a sister?

But to return to the Signals Section at RAF Ruislip. In spite of the rough ride I was given by the girls in the Telephone Exchange, I finally got the hang of the board, after which the sarcastic comments eased off. I found a good friend in one girl in particular, Sheila Morris, so we contrived to be on the same watches together. For those uninitiated in Services jargon, these watches had nothing whatsoever to do with timepieces, but referred to periods of duty, both day and night. I hated night duties. There were always two of us on at a time, one of whom was allowed to sleep on a put-u-up, while the other 'sat at the board'. There was a loud bell that could be switched on during a quiet night, so that both of us could get some sleep, but when it did ring, it was enough to wake the dead! Working in Signals did have its perks however. As the food in the main Mess was (for us WAAFS, anyway) inedible and eggs were on ration at the time, members of the cookhouse staff would trade them (and other tasties) for free night calls. As most of the cookhouse staff at the time were Irish, such calls involved the use of GPO lines rather than the RAF 'tie' lines. We were supposed to make tickets out for them, but – well – to every 'trade', its perks!

The months ticked by and there was still no news of my posting to M.T. In the end, I requested an interview with the

WAAF Officer in charge and stated my case. After making the relevant enquiries she informed me that, as a 'two-yearer', I had little chance of ever getting on the M.T. Course, unless I were to sign on for another five years. Not wishing to commit myself for such a lengthy period I took her advice and decided to settle into the Signals Section. By this time I had become a fairly proficient operator, although I was still only an ACW-2. Perhaps the time had come to think of moving up one?

There was another situation that was 'moving on', that being my relationship with Tony. We were both nineteen when we met, and, as we passed our twentieth birthdays, he asked if I would become engaged to him. In those days one always went through an engagement period of at least two years prior to marriage, which gave one time to work out the finer details while getting to know each other really well. When he was twenty, Tony's period of National Service ended, so he returned to civilian life and his job as an accounts clerk at Shell. However, we met regularly at weekends, or when my shifts permitted, and I was eventually introduced to his parents, who lived in Norbury.

As regards promotion of any kind, appropriate examinations, known as 'Boards', were held regularly for all Trades. These were posted on the Station Notice Board, and, if one was interested in bettering oneself within one's Trade, one applied to sit on the relevant Board. One day, while perusing the notice board, I observed that exams were being held at RAF Innsworth for Signals Personnel for promotion from ACW-2 (commonly referred to as ACW-plonk!) to ACW-1. I swatted up the paper-work and applied, but, in case I made an utter fool of myself, refrained from telling anyone. Since the

exams involved staying the night at RAF Innsworth, a useful
excuse was 'going on a thirty-six', meaning a period of 36
hours' absence, sanctioned by the WAAF Officer.

In those days, Innsworth was a ghastly place and
extremely difficult to get to, being in the middle of nowhere,
with little or no help from public transport. When a bus did
finally arrive, I met up with two other girls who were attending the same Board. Upon arrival at the Innsworth Guard
Room, the duty sergeant issued us with the warning to 'sleep
with your handbags under your pillows, and don't get
undressed. You'll be sharing a billet with some ACHGD's
(Aircraft Hands, General Duties – those incapable of doing
anything other than cleaning loos and the likes), with highly
suspect reputations', after which he enlightened us with a
catalogue of past thefts and other, less agreeable, goings-on.
We followed his advice, but the night was a sleepless one, so
none of us were all that spry when we presented ourselves
before the examiners the following day. However, I did pass
my 'One', and returned to the Exchange at RAF Ruislip with
the good tidings. After that, life among the telly-ops improved
considerably.

There were, however, certain incidents in which I was
involved which could be seen as unseemly, to say the least.
One Saturday, my friend Sheila and two other girls decided it
might be a good idea to hitch-hike to the West End, where
'Little Women', starring Elizabeth Taylor and June Allyson,
was showing at the Odeon Leicester Square. We made our
way to the main road and tried to hitch a lift. Sure enough, a
man stopped and asked us where we were heading, but he
could only take us as far as Shepherd's Bush, after which we

could get the Underground to Leicester Square. That man turned out to be film producer, David Lean, who in those days was married to actress Ann Todd.

We arrived at the cinema, paid for our seats and thoroughly enjoyed the film. What we did not know was that on that very day there had been a major football match between England and Scotland at Wembley, which Scotland had won, resulting in crowds of inebriated Celts taking over the West End. As we made our way out of the cinema, there they were, in their thousands. Seeing our uniforms a cry went out, 'WAAFI girls, hey, girls, gi'us a song', whereupon a group of them hoisted us on top of a Rolls Royce that was conveniently parked nearby. Realising that the best way to extract oneself from the situation was to go along with it until they became bored, I replied, 'Okay, boys, here's a little RAF ditty, and I hope you'll all join in.' After all, thought I, this might be the one and only chance in my life to perform before such a large audience. So, waving my arms in conductor mode, I started singing:

'They say that in the Air Force, the pay is mighty fine,

They give you thirty shillings, and take back twenty-nine,

Chorus:

I don't want no more of Air Force life,

Gee but I want to go,

But they won't let me go,

Gee but I want to go home!'

There were quite a few ex-service types among the 'audience' who were also familiar with both my own, and other, less reverent, versions of said ditty, so the chorus was well supported until ...

Suddenly, at the far side of the crowd, two white hats of the RAF Women's Police appeared. Trying to make their voices heard above the crowd, they were shouting, 'Airwomen, you are under arrest'. But the Scots would have none of it. While several of them surrounded us, hastily ushering us down the steps of the nearby Underground Station, others took hold of those poor policewomen, throwing their hats in the air and harassing them so that they were unable to pursue their line of duty. Once we were safely on the train, our Scots allies waved us goodbye and in due course we alighted at Ruislip Station. Being without the required late-night pass, we were obliged to use the secret way in, which some of the boys had set up at the back of the camp. And so we crept silently back to our billets, albeit a little the worse for wear (ripped stockings and a missing tie!).

On Parade the following morning, the Station Commander, Wing Commander Snelling, made one of his rare announcements. 'Notice has come to my attention from Central Police Headquarters that some WAAFS were seen behaving disgracefully in Leicester Square, while the Officers who were trying to pursue them in the line of duty suffered humiliation at the hands of a drunken mob. I have, of course, assured the Air Commodore that no such behaviour would have come from the girls on my camp, no late passes having being issued, and he tended to agree. Our culprits doubtless came from RAF Uxbridge, where, or so we have heard, there is a somewhat rougher element.' Although by then almost everybody on camp knew the truth, no-one said a word and the issue was never raised again.

The time had come for me to attend another Board, this

time to secure my 'props' – the propeller insignia worn on the sleeves of all LACW's, Leading Aircraft Women. This time it was a day job only, at RAF Chigwell. Apparently I passed with the highest marks known at that time, some 95 per cent, and the examining Officer advised me accordingly, while also sending a memo of recommendation to my Officer at Ruislip. I was now second-in-command in the Exchange, working under Corporal Law, who preferred to be called Angela but was known as 'Aggie' behind her back.

My newly acquired status was to prove of little use to me, however, as I was immediately moved from the Signals Section and placed on Ceremonial Duties, firstly with Air Chief Marshall Sir Basil Embry, and subsequently with the Duchess of Gloucester. These duties necessitated the wearing of white armbands and full dress uniform, much standing about, the usual protocol of opening car doors, handing messages to the appropriate Aide on a silver platter, and lots and lots of saluting. The scenario involved standing well back behind said dignitaries when they were attending official functions, the idea being to represent the rank and file of the Force. In return for the long stands in the cold, and their resultant leg- and back-aches, the perks included a good nosh-up in the servants' quarters after the bigwigs had partaken of their share of the luncheon or dinner.

As my two-year period was fast approaching its end, our WAAF Officer sent for me, in the hope of interesting me in signing on for another five years with the promise of a chance to take a Commission. It sounded good, but then there was Tony to consider. Besides, in all fairness, I had had enough of Service life and was looking forward to getting back into civvies once again. However, the issue was decided for me by a Higher Power. It all happened on the weekly Pay Parade. I remember feeling somewhat off-colour that morning, and by the time we were lined up to receive our weekly dues I was feeling decidedly ill. I think I must have passed out as I came round in Sick Quarters, from where I was transported by ambulance to the RAF Hospital at Halton in Buckinghamshire. The diagnosis? Severe pyelo-nephritis, a condition which was to haunt me for the rest of my life.

In due course, I was discharged from the hospital and had to return to RAF Ruislip to pick up my personal possessions and hand in my kit. The end was, in fact, rather traumatic. After a short stay with Win and Charlie, Tony's mother found some digs for me near to where the Neate family lived in Norbury, so that Tony and I could see a lot of each other and I could find appropriate employment in central London. Thanks to my Service record, I was able to obtain a splendid job, in which I was destined to receive my next lessons in human psychology.

What some of my readers may be wondering is whether my metaphysical interests featured at all during my two years in the service of His Majesty. The answer is, 'yes'. In addition to reading palms, consulting charts, and indulging my mates in all and any other avenues of occult knowledge, I also narrated those ghostly tales from my convent past, which served to give them the odd goose pimple, if nothing else. And as for Tony, of course we were both destined to walk the Path together for the next few decades, the child destined to be born from our spiritual partnership being the society known as 'The Atlanteans'.

CHAPTER 11

The Opening Door

During the last few chapters I have said little, if anything, regarding my feelings as an 'alien soul' in the more earthy type of environment such as that encountered in the RAF. As my life proceeded, the necessity to appear as normal as possible became imperative, any obvious aberration constituting a possible threat to my role as observer. But wherever I went, there were always those who sensed the difference and were consequently ill-at-ease in my company. One only needs to read current sci-fi to see how the hominid reaction to any intelligent life outside of its own collective is to treat it with hostility. Over the years, I have tried desperately hard to play the game of life by hominid rules, but, try as one may to say or do all the right things, one is inevitably 'sussed out' and ends up on the wrong side of them – well, most of them, anyway. On the other hand, it is difficult for me to pontificate on human ethics because although I wear a human body and am therefore controlled to a degree by human hormones, there is the inevitable, painful clash with the field/essence. Nowhere has this basic difference surfaced so much as in the area of the emotions.

The bond I enjoy with others of my kind, although a very close one, is not emotionally orientated. Emotionally based bonding is something I have never come to terms with, and probably never will. This has, of course, caused me to be misunderstood on many occasions. Also, as I explained in an earlier chapter, although we devas conform to the active/passive modes of universal existence, I have always found it extremely difficult to accept the role-playing, both practical and emotional, that accompanies accepted methods of hominid bonding. As a youngster I always got on better with boys than with girls. Cars, aeroplanes, mechanical things and the likes; boys' adventure books, even boys' clothing, all these appealed to me far more than things feminine. Although I am privileged to count several women (mostly married, or in partnership with a male) among my closest friends, I am certainly not gay. However, my best relationships with the opposite sex have always been with those men in my life who have treated me as 'one of the boys' rather than as a decorative or domestically useful female. As to my marriages, details of which I will bore my readers with in the ensuing chapters, I entered each of these with the best of intentions, only to find that, in spite of their protests to the contrary, my partners were seeking a normal woman rather than the freak they eventually found themselves tied to. As I have said to several of them, 'But you knew what you were getting, I made it quite clear before we tied the knot'. The reply was always the same: 'I thought you'd get over all that stuff, and settle down like a normal woman'. In other words, they hadn't listened to a word I had said.

Letting go has never been my problem. We devas never

'own' anything or anybody. Following my many 'dumpings', dear friends have often consoled me with the words: 'How terrible you must feel at the loss'. No way! In fact, with each relationship I have had, I have known well in advance how and why it would end. Such information is usually released to me in a dream, so I am psychologically prepared for the break as and when it comes. During the period in between, however, there is always plenty to be learned. As to my stance in the hominid male/female debate, logically there would appear to be matters better handled by a man than a woman, and vice-versa. Therefore, there are times when I am 'fluffy', in that there are tasks I would rather hand over to a man because I am not physically strong enough to cope with them. On the other hand, I will not submit to being in any way mentally inferior to a partner, or any man, for that matter, simply on the grounds of his gender!

Questioning people's beliefs or stances is inevitably a futile exercise. 'Horses for courses', the saying goes, and we can't all run at Epsom! On the rare occasions when I have had the guts to stand up and express views contrary to those of the 'collective', as I did in The Atlanteans, I have been ridden over roughshod, and given the 'Who do you think you are?' treatment. The fact that I am neither a social animal, nor politically correct, does not help either, my overview as an alien serving to highlight the folly of fundamentalism under any guise.

My dislikes/discomforts include noise of any kind, entertaining and being entertained (my closest friends proving the exception to this rule), and debate. The latter I tend to view as an excuse for verbal aggression among other, more psychologically-orientated, factors. My kind simply do not think that way. In our world things are as they are, and democracy, in the human understanding of the term, does not exist. However I do have my preferences when it comes to human political and humanitarian systems. For example, I am often asked why, as a non-hominid spirit, I am an unashamed patriot and Royalist. The answer is that, since I am a deva, I naturally know in which parts of this planet the elemental forces are the strongest, and where I am therefore the most at ease. If I had one wish, it would be to be remembered after my death as one of those great English eccentrics of my era, one who never conformed, but was always loyal. Loyalty is a prime virtue in both the Paschats and the Elemental Kingdoms: we look after our own – a sentence I cannot repeat enough times.

Although my hominid body assaulted me from time to time with a surfeit of hormonal activity when I was younger, I was somehow able to channel it into other avenues of expression. I have always had a very poor libido and what little I did have in my youth, which tended to be focussed on the reproductive aspects rather than pure physical pleasure, was mercifully put to rest overnight by the human menopause. However, since I was not programmed to produce progeny, this factor proved a cause of irritation – both ways – in my relationships and many were the times I recalled Nanny's preference for a 'cup of tea'!

But let us return to the narrative in hand. Following my demob from the WAAFS, I went for an interview for a job at The Officers' Association of the British Legion, the headquarters of which was at 28, Belgrave Square, in London.

There was only one woman already working there, a former WREN Officer. I got the job, and a very good one it proved to be. Although casework is not really my thing, it served to render me a deeper insight into the human psyche. Working under Squadron Leader Cox (all military titles there!), I soon learned how to assess the demands of those seeking assistance, write up their cases for our Committee's consideration, and effect appropriate recommendations. I thoroughly enjoyed working among the chaps, although they did tend to give me a rough ride at times. All in all it was something of a zany outfit, full of colourful characters with stories to tell. And what stories – psychic and more. I soon learned that military personnel from all three Forces were subjected to psychic experiences when under fire. It would take a whole book to cover them all, but here are two as a sampler.

Old Mr. Sanders – Sandy to us – had served in WW1. The area of land near the 'Front' that was patrolled by his unit was comparatively quiet, there having been no enemy activity for weeks, a situation which had tended to induce a state of false security. Guard duty was, however, still observed, those on Watch being required to walk to a pillbox located some three-quarters of a mile up the road, which afforded a good view of the enemy lines. One particular night when Sandy and his mate were out there on Watch, activity being nil, they settled down for a quiet doze. But hardly had they entered the realms of Morpheus when Sandy was awakened by one of the two men from the next Watch whose duty it was to relieve them at dawn. As an hour had barely passed since they had settled down for the night, this intrusion was hardly greeted with enthusiasm. 'What do you think you're doing, Reg, its only 2.30 a.m., three more hours to go, mate – b..... off'. Whereupon Sandy and his companion once again sought the comfort of their sleeping bags.

As dawn broke, the two men blinked in the smile of the rising orb and prepared for the trek back to camp. But no relief had arrived, and it was well past the time they were due. They noticed smoke rising from the direction in which they would be heading, and so, realising that something was wrong, they gathered up their weapons and headed for Camp. They had barely covered half the distance when they were met by by a small band of soldiers, including two sporting the armbands of the Medical Corps. 'You alright, mate?', their spokesman enquired. 'Yes, why, what's happened?' 'Last night a small Hun raiding party sneaked up our backsides. Six of the blighters there were. We managed to get four and wing another, but one sod fired the bloody place and escaped in the smoke. Old Reg bought it, and Bill's gone into dock.' Sandy was, needless to say, horrified. But a thought suddenly struck him and he asked, 'Hey mate, what time did all this happen?' 'Around two-thirty', was the reply. Reg's spirit had been ready to carry out its duty, even from the 'other side'!

The other tale involved a rear gunner, let us call him Dave, who was grounded by his M.O. (Medical Officer) on account of a strange experience he regularly underwent, which was judged medically to be caused by battle fatigue. He claimed he could hear voices calling him, friendly voices rather than those of the spooky variety, whenever his Lancaster flew over a certain point. This resulted in the rest of the crew logging the coordinates for 'a bit of fun'. After a week of sitting around doing nothing, Dave became bored. Aircraft came and went; others never returned. He longed to be back in his tailpiece, guns at the ready, protecting his mates. One evening when he was sitting in the Mess, an emergency occurred. The rear gunner from a Lancaster due to take off shortly had been rushed to hospital with appendicitis. A relief was required immediately, but would the M.O. okay Dave as a stand-in? After a hasty examination, he was pronounced fit for combat and made his way forthwith to the Lancaster. The aircraft was hit *at exactly the co-ordinates over which Dave had heard his voices.* The pilot managed to bring back what was left of it, but died later in hospital. His co-pilot, however, survived and was able to give the co-ordinates of 'Dave's Voices' as the exact spot at which the event occurred, when Dave finally answered the call of Spirit.

After I had worked at the O.A. for a while, I discovered that the mundane occult sciences such as palmistry, numerology and astrology were accepted by most of the men. However, it took a cunning ruse on my part to bring them all out into the open. When I was alone in the office they would often engage me in a metaphysical discussion, but when faced by their colleagues, such matters were treated with scepticism. One day, however, when we were all present, I obliged them all to face up to what they really believed, by bringing their private sessions into the open. After a few moments of protestation and huffing they all had a good laugh about it. From then on the taboos were lifted, all psychic and allied subjects became open to general discussion and, and believe it or not, agreement! But enough of the spooks. Suffice it to say that my years at the O.A served to enrich my knowledge of both psychology and metaphysics, thus opening the door to my next period of learning.

Tony and I were married on 2nd September, 1951. I was 22 on 17th September, and Tony had his 22nd birthday on 5th October of that year. We had found ourselves a flat in Streatham Hill which, believe it or not, also exhibited a worthy spook before we left there in 1958. As neither of us was ready to consider a family, on our wedding night we made a pact not to consummate our union until such time in the future when we felt both emotionally and materially equipped for such an event. In hindsight, I think I was subconsciously, if not consciously, aware that motherhood did not constitute part of my programme, the incompatibility between my basic essence and the hominid endocrine system rendering physical procreation impossible. But then my relationship with Tony was, from the word 'go', more that of two pals than of husband and wife.

In those days Tony was working in the City, so we both went about our respective jobs during the day, while busying ourselves with other activities during weekends and evenings. We were a highly creative partnership, counting among our successes The Norbury Revue Company, and SCOPE – Shows, Cabarets or Personal Entertainments, a small, local agency we set up to provide amateur or semi-professional services when and where needed. We had a variety of talent on our books, including sufficient musicians to put together a reasonable dance-band, an accomplished conjuror, several well-known singers, dancers/dancing troupes, etc. And as for the Norbury Revue Company, in addition to regular concerts, we put on such established favourites as 'Showboat', at the Civic Hall,

Croydon, with Tony producing and myself taking the soprano lead.

I had started taking singing lessons (as advised by Squadron Leader Marshall, who saw in my voice operatic potential), my teacher being Margaret Gordon (linguist and former tutor at the Paris Conservatoire). Miss Gordon's idea was that one should get as much audience experience as possible before tackling the profession, and the N.R.C. provided just such a platform.

Tony and I had a set routine, in that every Saturday would be spent with his mother and father. This involved the inevitable trip to Croydon, when old George would hide himself away in some electrical department while Tony, his mother and I would haunt the fashion areas. We would all meet up at a prescribed time and return to their house, where George's old mother, 'Nan', would have a tasty meal ready. When the time came for the two of us to return to our own home, we would often walk the whole distance from Norbury to Streatham Hill, the exercise and fresh air being good for office workers who are parked on their rears all week. It also provided us with the opportunity to discuss future plans, and to talk generally. Remember, there was no television in those days, so one was obliged to make one's own entertainment.

The other feature that lurked in the background of our relationship was matters occult/psychic. I had sensed for some time that Tony had psychic potential, but getting him to acknowledge this, let alone make use of it, was to prove something of a task. In fact, it was not until I went into Kismet in 1955, resulting in his being left alone every evening except Sunday, that I persuaded him to visit the MSA – Marylebone

Spiritualist Association – in Belgrave Square (which later became the Spiritualist Association of Great Britain, or SAGB), and he finally agreed to put his powers to the test.

After I had been studying with Margaret Gordon for some time, she felt that I should start auditioning to go professional. I had always wanted to be a classical singer, but experience had shown me that the only doorway into that side of the profession was via a music college, unless, of course, one had influence in the right places – which I did not. Miss Gordon advised me to turn up at every audition going, while also assuring me that I did not stand a snowflake's chance in hell of being accepted, due to my total lack of professional experience. 'It will get you used to standing up there and singing your piece. It doesn't matter whether you get the job, or if you even want it. Auditioning experience is valid training in itself, in that it helps you to overcome your nerves.' She was right, of course. I recall asking her what I should do if the job was some dreadful end-of-pier thing in some tatty place, and I didn't want it. 'All you do, my dear, is to pick up your handbag, pretend to look in your diary, and say, apologetically, "Oh dear, so sorry, I'm already booked for those two weeks", or whatever'.

A group of about seven of us used to trail round all the West End auditions, consoling ourselves with cups of coffee and pastries when we received the inevitable turn-down. In fact, in the end we became good friends. And then, one day, I was sent by my agent, Robert Layton, to an audition at the Stoll Theatre. The leading lady, Joan Deiner, had done a disappearing act and her understudy, who also played the part of a slave girl, was obliged to take over. Once it was understood that Ms. Deiner was not returning, auditions were held for the small role of the slave girl which was now vacant, her understudy, Sheila Bradley, having taken over from Joan on a permanent basis. This was my thirteenth audition!

Upon arriving at the Stoll Theatre, which in those days occupied a site in Kingsway, I discovered that I was one of about sixty girls who were after the part. An operatic-type voice was required, also dancing ability, so we all had to audition for both these skills. Eventually all were eliminated except for two: myself and a girl named Jennifer. Our fate, it seemed, lay in the hands of the wardrobe mistress, in that whichever of us the appropriate costumes fitted got the job. Sheila Bradley had a good, rounded figure with a generous bustline, and so did I, whereas Jennifer's lithe body was more suited to a catwalk than to a harem. Upon that point, and that only, I got the job. Such silent touches from the slender Hand of Fate!

But there was one more hurdle to cross. Equity representative Judith Shergold (wife of actor Barry Foster) asked me whether I was a member. I told her, 'no'. 'You have the job, therefore I can give you a card. But when you go up to the office, tell them you are a member, okay? Now what is your name?' 'Jacqueline Hope', I replied. 'Oh, dear, there is already an Equity member called Jacki Hope – a dancer. Think of something quickly – what's your middle name?' 'Murry', I replied, inadvertently neglecting to inform her as to the correct spelling. She wrote Jacqueline Murray on the appropriate card, and that name stayed with me throughout my theatrical career.

After watching the show for a few days, plus learning the

music, moves, etc., I made my début on the professional stage, in a show that was to run in the West End for two years. West End productions of this kind inevitably involve six days a week plus two matinées, so I was only able to see Tony on Sundays. He did, however, meet me at the bus stop in Tulse Hill every night and we would walk home together through the back doubles to Wavertree Road.

It was during these two years that Tony started his regular visits to the MSA. Through the various psychics he met there, he was invited to séances held in private houses by several of the well-known Spiritualist mediums of the day, who encouraged him to take a deeper interest, and to engage in preliminary excursions into the realms of the 'other side'. Prior to these times, my psychic experiences with Tony had been limited to the initial 'glass on the table' (which turned out to be amazingly accurate, as my readers will see in a future chapter), and psychometrising small, personal articles, including a sliver of wood from the stage floor of the Stoll Theatre, concealed in a plain envelope. The results were definitely promising.

It was also during this period that my cousin, Paul Thomelin, who had completed his National Service in the French Air Force, found himself footloose and fancy free. So he often took to accompanying Tony on his visits to Belgrave Square, where they would take part in one of Eric Stewart's famous discussion groups, about which my readers will be hearing later. Paul's father, Uncle Eugène, was a former French air ace in WW1, while his mother, Auntie Norah, was said to have been my mother's sister, although as I mentioned earlier, Paul and I later discovered that this was not quite the case.

Before Kismet's two-year run at the Stoll ended, a combination of dancing barefoot in the cold in flimsy garments, and the fact that it was a very hard show workwise, brought back my old kidney trouble. On hospital orders, I was obliged to leave the cast a few weeks before it was scheduled to go out on tour. So once again Tony and I were able to spend some time together, and, along with Paul, we inevitably haunted the hallowed premises of the MSA. It was there that we met Edwin Naylor, who was destined to feature strongly in the future of The Atlanteans. Tony's psychic powers had been developing rapidly, to the extent that I was able to take him further. We experimented with psychometry, messages from loved ones, automatic writing, and so forth. Always I was the protector and logician who insisted on every point being checked and double-checked to avoid landing up with a load of imaginative subconscious eyewash. Our experiments included Tony using one method to tune in and myself another, to see if the results agreed. And they did. We were soon joined by Edwin Naylor and Mary Prestage, a soprano friend of mine, both of whom shared our interest in all things metaphysical. The stage being finally set for the next production, the curtain was now due to rise. A comedy or a tragedy? A goodly proportion of both, as it happened.

CHAPTER 12

The Atlanteans

Following the Kismet episode, I suffered severe renal problems which kept me out of work for a few months. During this time, Tony, Edwin, Paul and I would regularly attend the aforementioned discussion groups, which were held weekly at the MSA. Tony, Paul and I were still in our twenties, and Edwin was thirty-something, which made us the youngest members in the group. But what a gathering of amazingly colourful characters! I suppose I should have mentioned earlier how Tony, on his first visit to the MSA, was approached in the canteen by no fewer than four 'Jesus Christs', each claiming that the others were false gods. So we were all well primed regarding the mentally ill, and those inadequates who had chosen to assume some psychic persona in order to compensate for their inferiority complexes. During my days as an exorcist I came across many such people; sad human beings who could find no other way to attract attention.

But to return to said discussion group. Eric Stewart was, at that time, President of the MSA, while his predecessor, W. Howard Lievens, a scholar of some distinction, with

Polynesian leanings, was usually in attendance. At each session a subject was chosen for debate the following week, but regardless of the selected title, Lievens would inevitably bring it round to 'Well, now, the Polynesians had an answer for this ...', during which lengthy explanation we all went to sleep. Well, not quite, but nearly! There were two mediums present: Olive Field, a mystical lady with decidedly Christian leanings, and Sylvia Grey, whose approach scanned a wider metaphysical field. It was to the latter than I came to owe much of my later learning. Other colourful characters included Daniel Allinson, a raw-boned Scot who seemed to be undergoing a permanent libido/kundalini conflict and a burly Yorkshireman who showed his displeasure at comments with which he did not agree by rolling his sleeves up and asking the offending speaker to see him outside. I recall in particular one session when the subject set for discussion was 'What proof have you had for life after death?'. Said Northerner's contribution went something like this: 'I woke up in the middle of the night. My wife was sleeping soundly beside me, but there was a bright light in the room and standing in this light was my mother, only she looked like she used to as a lass in the photo my dad had on the old piano. She reached out to me and as I made to touch her, the bedclothes shot back like a roller-blind!' Noting the looks of either scepticism or amusement on the faces of certain members present, he promptly arose, took off his jacket, rolled up his sleeves and stated firmly, 'And if anyone here says that was not my mother, then I'll see him outside, and right now!' Needless to say, there were no takers.

The artist Anita Purser was also a prominent member of

this group, her approach veering towards the scientific. So whenever Olive Field closed her eyes and waxed poetic on one of her usual 'spiritual' journeys, Anita would shake her head in disgust and murmur, 'A lot of sanctimonious slush. It's little wonder that great scientists like Sir William Crookes and Sir Oliver Lodge despaired of all this holier-than-thou-type mediumship!' Tony and I were later invited to Olive's home, where she gave us both a fairly accurate forecast for our future. Tony, she said, was destined to become a fine trance medium, but when it came to me she seemed mystified. 'There is something about you I can't understand. My guides are also perplexed. You are not a medium as such, nor even a psychic in the accepted sense of the word. You are from "somewhere else", but I am out of my depth here.' I later approached Sylvia Grey on the matter and sought her opinion. She passed the question back to me: 'What do you want to be?' 'A proficient occultist', I found myself replying. 'I am already familiar with the mundane occult sciences'. 'Then go away and study the mythology and religions of all the earlier civilisations; psychology, both Jungian and Freudian; the magical beliefs and systems of other cultures, extant and otherwise; the Devic Kingdoms; anthropology and the history and prehistory of the planet; and the sciences generally. For without an in-depth knowledge of these subjects, you will have no criteria against which to evaluate the accuracy or otherwise of your inspiration and will simply teeter at the edge of reason, always lacking the terminology to express what little you do discover.' A tall order, perhaps, but then I was acquainted with much of it already. And so I took her advice, and to this day I thank that dear lady for a superb put-down, which served to spur me on to open my mind to my own destiny in the service of those I am here to represent.

It was during this time that Edwin, Mary and I met regularly at our flat in Streatham Hill. We knew there was something special to be done, some important message, perhaps, for us to discover and make public. But what was it? By this time Tony had several spirit contacts who used to come through to speak to us. These included a French lawyer by the name of René Talliard, the famous singer Dame Nellie Melba, and Tony's personal guide, a young girl whose name escapes me but who was destined to introduce us to the new Force in our lives, Helio-Arcanophus, former High Priest of Atlantis.

One evening when we were all sitting quietly, the atmosphere seemed to change significantly and we all became aware of the presence of an exalted entity. Speaking through Tony, if somewhat hesitatingly at first, the name he gave us was, he explained, simply a title which, in translation, meant 'Chief High Priest of the Sun'. He also made it quite clear that he had never been any supposed celebrity from the past, religious or otherwise, hence his reluctance to provide us with a 'name'. He had reigned in the Old Country during the Zodiacal Age of Virgo, well before the fabled 'fall', when Atlantis was at the height of its spiritual power. And the more he told us, the more I 'remembered.' Strangely enough, I had become obsessed with Atlantis well before this event took place. In fact, I could not read a book about it without bursting into tears. Memories came flooding back of a beloved land wherein all was fair and just; of belonging to a closely-knit family, a brother, especially, who seemed to be reaching out to me from across space-time. And I knew that this great Being was one and the same as he who had spoken to me in the bathroom in Wells Street, and later appeared in the cathedral in Liverpool and the church at St. Albans. There was no mistake – I had come home.

As time passed, others also came to hear H.A. speak. And they grew to love him as much as we did. And then, one day, he made a suggestion. 'Since you all seem to feel so strongly about the Old Country, why do you not start a society and call it The Atlanteans?' It seemed a good idea at the time, so we all went for it. However, forming a group of this nature required the knowledge of someone skilled in corporate management, who could advise us how to draw up the correct documents of Association and so forth. And just such a person appeared at – yes – the MSA Discussion Group, in the person of Major Leith-Hay-Clark.

This all happened at a time when Tony, Edwin, Paul and I were beginning to feel somewhat isolated among the older folk who attended the group. We were looked down on as being young and inexperienced, and therefore hardly capable of pontificating on matters spiritual. The problem was inevitably brought to a head when Eric Stewart chose as the subject for the next discussion group 'The Spiritualist attitude towards sex'. Needless to say, none of the older folk present wanted to know, and neither Tony nor Edwin felt inclined to volunteer. So – in desperation, perhaps – Eric Stewart put it to me: 'What about you, young lady?'. After a bit of prompting from the others, and from Major Leith-Hay-Clark, I reluctantly agreed and set about writing my piece in the light of both my studies of psychology, and of the experiences I had undergone at the Officers' Association.

The following week I duly presented it and, to my amazement, it went down quite well. However, when the next issue of 'Two Worlds' emerged, Maurice Barbanell, who had apparently been listening to my talk through the open door of an adjoining room, returned a scathing comment, the words of which I can remember to this day. 'What sort of a state has Spiritualism come to that we have to rely on some silly young actress to pontificate on our attitude towards sex? Are there no sensible adults who could have taken the Chair and given us the real facts? Since I find this difficult to understand, one can only assume the obvious – who is befriending her?'

On top of all this, we were constantly told we were too young to know anything, which the dear Major Leith-Hay-Clark countered by saying, 'Rubbish. Take my word for it as an older man. When it comes to wisdom, or the recognition of that gift in others, you will always find yourselves labelled 'too young', right up until you reach old age, after which you will be told you are past it.' Whereupon he took us to one side, advised us to set up The Atlanteans forthwith, and said he would help us with all the necessary registration and documentation, which he did. And so, in the presence of Edwin, Mary, Tony and me, The Atlanteans was finally born on 11th April, 1957.

Shortly after these events took place, our landlady, Mrs. Rawkins died, and her son, Sydney, wishing to sell the property, gave Tony and me three months' notice. Oddly enough, Sydney himself died shortly after and both Tony and I saw his ghost, looking over the bannisters from the upstairs landing. After consulting with Edwin and Mary, we decided to look for somewhere more central, and, through the Chesterton

Agency in Kensington, found Flat 5, Mulwarrie House, 150 Lexham Gardens, London W8. The accommodation, which was at the top of the building, comprised a long corridor, four bedrooms, a living room, kitchen, bathroom and separate loo. It was, in fact, ideal for a few people, each needing their own privacy, but being happy to share in the commitment of general living. Let me hasten to assure the suspicious-minded among my readers that over the five years that Mulwarrie was occupied by Atlantean members, everything was strictly above board, and minus Nanny's 'hanky-panky'. Those members who had boy- or girl-friends were obliged to carry on their courting outside the premises. Only Tony and I, having tied the knot, shared a room.

The flat being somewhat run down, we set about putting it into reasonable decorative order. My dear Win, in fact, supplied us with two sets of curtains, among other, smaller items of furniture. If this all sounds like spiritual bliss, dear reader, step down from your rainbow – the worst, as well as the best, is yet to come.

Like Topsy, The Atlanteans grew and grew, and very soon the small rooms at Mulwarrie no longer accommodated the growing crowds. More suitable accommodation for our regular meetings was eventually found in the area, notably the vegetarian restaurant in the Earls Court Road, and the Headquarters of the Vegetarian Society, opposite St. Mary Abbots Hospital. In addition to trance addresses by Helio-Arcanophus and our other mediums, I would give talks on subjects metaphysical and we also engaged guest speakers, so that our audiences could hear alternative views.

From the foregoing my readers will by now have gathered

that Tony was not the only medium in our society. We were also privileged to have the services of Muriel Graves, Edwin Naylor, John Crutchley and Michael Thorburn, the latter being responsible for channelling several of the lectures which later appeared in The Atlanteans' printed booklets. Some of these stayed on in the society, while others left to set up their own groups. Helio-Arcanophus (whose name, by then, had become shortened to 'H.A') always insisted that we never take the word of any one medium as gospel, but that we check and double-check with other psychic or occult sources. He also advised us to broaden our knowledge of all allied subjects, thus allowing each 'sensitive' adequate terms of reference via which to express those teachings given from other dimensions of existence.

I will refrain from boring my readers with the more personal travails that I underwent during those early days, but suffice it to say that conditions were chaotic. The group seemed to attract different sorts of people, experience inevitably teaching us how to distinguish the genuine seekers from the ego trippers and psychic butterflies. Which brings me to what I feel to be one of the most wonderful H.A. stories from those early times.

Among the small group of us who gathered together one evening awaiting a session with H.A, there was a young woman of about 20 who obviously believed herself to be a spiritual cut above the others. After offering us a few moments of enlightenment, H.A. enquired as to whether there were any questions he could answer for us. The aforementioned female was quick off the mark. 'Sir, could you tell us who, among those gathered in this room, is the most spiritually highly evolved?' I recall cringing with embarrassment, but I need not have worried. 'Yes, my dear, I would be delighted', H.A. answered. He then turned his medium's head and pointed to his right. 'Over there, on the back of that chair, there sleeps a little black and white cat, which is, without doubt, the most spiritually evolved soul in this room.' Silence! I cannot recall this instance without shedding a tear. Needless to say, the enquirer's membership of the group was short-lived.

During this period I had signed on with a new agent, Myrette Morven from Fraser and Dunlop, so there was quite a variety of work coming my way, including my first pantomime, Cinderella, with the Bromley Repertory Company. My Principal Boy was none other than Sheila Hancock for whom I was able to forecast a brilliant future in television.

My next job was 'The Beggar's Opera' with the Windsor Repertory Company and it was during this run that I experienced another of my spectacular escapes. It happened during a period when I had moved temporarily out of Mulwarrie, and taken a bedsit at the house of an older member who lived in Bayswater, the lady in question having felt that it would be better for me to distance myself from the closely-knit arrangements at Mulwarrie while I was working such difficult hours. It so happened that another member of the cast lived in a house just across the road, so we would accompany each other to the theatre and back at night. 'Pru' was also interested in my 'other' activities, and H.A. in particular. Although we usually took the train back to London, on this occasion a senior member of the cast offered us a lift, which we naturally accepted.

During the homeward journey we witnessed a nasty accident. A young man on a motorbike in front of us skidded and hit a gravel container. His leg was literally hanging off and I gave him healing while the others knocked at a nearby door for help to call an ambulance. It was sometime, however, before the poor man was safely on his way to hospital, which naturally made our driver, who had also arranged to pick up her husband, late for her appointment. So, when we arrived at the top of the Harrow Road, she regretfully informed us that we would have to leg it for the rest of the way.

Anyone who is familiar with that area will be aware of its insalubrious nature, so Pru and I made our way, uncomfortably to say the least, towards Bayswater, ever alert to the type of persons believed to haunt those streets at such an hour. Before we were even half way home we became aware that we were being 'paced' by a large black car. Hasty backward glances warned us that the passengers, three men and a woman, were definitely of the unsavoury variety and we noticed the woman pointing to us and making some comment to the men, whereupon the car stopped, and two men got out and began following us. As we started to run, so did they, and, in a fit of panic, Pru begged me, 'Please ask your H.A. gentleman to help us.' I answered, breathlessly, 'You ask him, too. Let's call for help together'. And we both shouted – 'Helio-Arcanophus'. Suddenly a double-decker bus appeared from a road to the right of us. It was empty and obviously on its way back to the depot. The driver had noted our plight and decided on a quick course of action. Pulling the huge, red vehicle up beside us, he shouted, 'Quick girls, hop on'. We were saved! The conductor then asked us where we lived.

'Durham Terrace, Bayswater', we told him. After a quick consultation with the driver, he returned to where we were seated near the door. 'Don't worry, girls, we'll take you all the way home!' And so one large, red bus trundled into the darkened silence of Durham Terrace, depositing Pru outside her front door and me outside mine. Of course we thanked the two men profusely, but the driver, who was the older of the two, simply said, 'I've got two girls of my own about your age. Need I say more?'

It was also at 22 Durham Terrace that I first experienced the onslaught of the type of alien phenomena that was to teach me the art of psychic/occult self-defence, for without first-hand experience, how can one possibly evaluate this, and learn from it? My room was on the first floor and the house faced a church, the clock of which chimed on the hour. It was during the second week of my stay at No.22 that I experienced a terrifying dream, in which I was being attacked by negative forces. I awoke in the middle of the night to find my bed suspended some three feet in the air – and precisely at the moment of my awakening, the church clock struck three. I immediately changed the energy frequency in the room to inhibit further manifestations of phenomena and the offending furniture descended slowly to the floor. I then effected a 'clearing', turned on the light and had a drink of water. From that moment onwards, every 'initiation' I underwent which involved out-of-the body battles with negative forces, always occurred at exactly three a.m. My career as an occultist had well and truly commenced.

Upon learning of my experience, Edwin hired a car and came over to collect me and my meagre possessions. 'You are not staying in that awful place another night', he told me, 'There is someone living there who does not wish you well'. And this turned out to be true; the woman who had masqueraded as my friend came out into the open forthwith, and showed her true colours.

Shortly after, I auditioned for a new West End Production, 'The Crooked Mile', which starred Millicent Martin, Jack McGowran and Elisabeth Welch. I was lucky. The show made its début in Liverpool in the summer of 1959, also playing Manchester for two weeks before opening at the Cambridge Theatre in London. It was a happy show and I made several friends among the cast, one of whom I have stayed in touch with to this very day.

It was during the London run of this show that something happened that would, once again, change my life and point me in the direction I had wanted for some time. One evening Sheila Chester, an attractive young member of the cast, who had an excellent voice herself, commented to me, 'You have a true, classical voice; you should be in opera and oratorio, not this sort of stuff'. I explained to her how I had always wanted to work in that field but lacked the training which only a music college could give. 'I trained at the Royal College of Music', she replied. 'I'll tell you what, I still have contacts there. I'll see what I can do for you'. I remember thinking to myself, hot air, heard it all before. But I was destined to eat my words. Two days later, upon arriving for the evening show, Sheila said to me, quite casually, 'Oh, incidentally, I have arranged an audition for you at the Royal College of Music at 10 a.m. on Thursday. So don't let me down'. At first I thought she was having me on, but after she insisted on the truth of her

story I felt obliged to give it a try. On the following day I
arrived early at the Cambridge Theatre and had a good sing
through several arias which I thought might be the sort of
thing my auditioners might require.

The day in question, one of those chilly early December
mornings, duly arrived, and, as instructed by Sheila, I
presented myself at the theatre of the Opera School where I
was met by a group of examiners including Richard Austin,
who was then Principal of the College Opera School, producer
Douglas Craig, two professors of singing, and Pauline Elliott,
the Opera School secretary.

There was the usual darkened stage, lit only by a small,
bare bulb, plus the illumination provided for the accompanist.
I sang *'Ebben endro lontana'* from *La Wally*, which was followed
by a few moments of silence while the experts conferred. Then
I was asked, 'Have you anything else you could sing for us?'
'Una voce poco fa', I replied, which seemed to meet with their
approval. Having achieved my high 'C's and 'D's without
much effort, I once again waited patiently for the Committee's
decision, hoping for the best but expecting the worst. After
what seemed to be an eternity I was called down to confront
them, only to be told, to my amazement, that they had decided
to award me the Richard Austin Opera Scholarship. They
enquired as to when I could start and if I had any means of
maintenance. I explained to them that I was working in a
show that was due to finish at the end of the following
January, so it was agreed that I could start full-time on 1st
February, but attend some voice lessons during matinee-free
days meantime. As for maintenance, having gained the
Scholarship I would be entitled to a Major County Award, so

an audition for this facility would be arranged for me with the London County Council at County Hall.

In time all was settled and I commenced my course in the first week of February, 1960.

CHAPTER 13

Will The *Real* H.A. Please Stand Up?

It was during the first few years in the Society's life that H.A. (through Tony) suggested that I write a book about his life and my own in those far-off days in Atlantis. Never having written anything before, other than poetry and the odd article, I was somewhat daunted. Also, my facility for detailed recall had not yet fully developed, so I was obliged to rely on information given through Tony. Although I was subconsciously aware at the time that these accounts were not entirely accurate – H.A., via Tony, being the *ex cathedra* of the Society – I was reluctant to proffer alternatives which would have proved useless. The end product, *Daughter of Atlantis,* which was duly published, was little more than a poor pastiche of the reality that was the Old Country (fortunately, I was later afforded the opportunity to correct it). Consequently, I never mention the earlier book to anyone these days, not feeling it to be 'my' work as such.

As I have grown older, my memories of Atlantis have become much clearer and the fact that I have been obliged to do my own inner and outer seeking, rather than relying constantly on material fed to me via a medium, has assisted that development considerably. Names now flow easily into my mind – minor episodes of life there which I could not recall in earlier years; scents and sounds of an age and culture still viewed as pure myth by many academics. But like Troy, it will some day emerge from the mists of time, shed its mythological shroud and rise triumphantly from its watery bed to assume its rightful place in the annals of world history.

When I eventually left The Atlanteans in May 1975, I felt free to explore my Atlantean roots. And when asked by HarperCollins to write a book which was to be latterly entitled *The Ancient Wisdom of Atlantis*, I was able to bring through a few of the real truths behind the Atlantis of H.A.'s time, and its accompanying ethos. I would therefore like to clear up, once and for all, some of the speculations as to the origin, nature and one-and-only former life on this planet of the entity known as Helio-Arcanophus, including his real name in those times, and those of his closest family.

When one entered the Atlantean priesthood, once one had 'qualified', the last portion of the name of the deity in whose service one was to be employed was added to the latter part of one's name. The Being we now know as H.A. was born Yeris, son of Saras-aeia (a scientist Priest of the Goddess Philaeia) and Kulata-Sîn (priestess of the Goddess Khiet-Sîn). In time, when Yeris was received into the priesthood of the Sun Deity Helio, the 'io' was added to his name, which became Yeris-io until such times as he became firstly High Priest, and then Chief High Priest, of the Sun – Arcanophus – and sole ruler of the Island Continent.

Yeris was still quite young when he married his first wife, Kalis-ona, a Priestess of Heliona, the Sun Goddess. The couple had four children:

Filon-aeia (priest of Philaeia)
Lyel-aeia (priestess of Philaeia)
Pera-nuih (priest of Danuih)
Felis-ona (priestess of Heliona)

Later, following the death of Kalis, he remarried Ylani-ona, priestess of Heliona, by whom he had one son, Alei-tuih (Priest of Akhantuih). How do I know all this? Because I was Felis-ona, and now, having finally made contact with that devic aspect of myself which was created to be a representative, and eventual manipulator, of the energy known as Time, I am able to project my consciousness in comfort to those times, hear the sound of the names in question and translate them to their nearest possible equivalents in modern-day parlance.

During my eighteen years' service with The Atlanteans, however, there were things I could never tell a soul, knowledge I was unable to share with anyone. Some members guessed at my origins, some did not. But then one cannot carry out the old ways in today's world, in which they would be totally alien. However, during the whole of that period, H.A. never denied the fact that I had been his youngest daughter. The Atlantis of 'our' day, meaning my father's and mine, was a theocracy and NOT a democracy. There were therefore no votes and people were allotted their place in the community according to their soul-age, or field band-width. So when, at the age of three, each child was presented at the local temple, the highly trained priests, using a section of their brain that latterly became atrophied – that same part which could calculate maths to the nth degree without the need to write an equation – defined the best rôle in life for the child in question. Although the progeny of a farm-worker could also be an advanced soul, many destined for the priesthood were born to priests and priestesses, simply because like attracts like. What a wonderful system of government, where no-one was chosen for their T.V. image, financial backing or double-dealing, and which sported a free welfare state, the like of which has never since been matched.

So much for the H.A. of the past. But what of the present and the future? Since he is so much an integral part of my whole beingness, the next problems that need to be dealt with before I can proceed with my narrative are: who or what is this Being? Who really does channel him? And at which levels? Although I may be judged by some to be in no position to effect any rulings in this matter, I was, after all, born with certain knowledge, albeit ignorant of its idioms. What I have picked up along the route are the semantics, or some of them, essential to an understanding of what is broadly termed the 'psychic faculty'. I studied its mundane applications during my teens and from then on dedicated my life to learning about, and trying to comprehend, its various levels of application – a period scanning some 69 years. I therefore feel that experience alone, if nothing else, entitles me to offer some criteria against which those who are seeking the cold logic of truth, rather than the deceptive warmth of self-delusion, may effect their own judgement.

Let us look at it rationally. Adherence to the following may help to facilitate identification of the level from which any entity is communicating:

(a) The breadth of its knowledge/messages/instructions,

especially if relating to Cosmic cognition.

(b) Its ability to keep one step ahead of modern-day scientific discoveries, logic demanding that such information, if latterly proven to be accurate, must obviously have emanated from a higher mind/intelligence, which has access to other, more elevated dimensions.

(c) Its comprehension of the psychology, stage of spiritual development/understanding, and therefore the needs, of the listeners/enquirers.

In this debate there is one fact that needs to be fairly and squarely faced, that being even the most honest and spiritually inclined sensitive is going to prove a stumbling-block for those beings who wish to convey any really advanced information if he/she does not possess the appropriate cerebral software. This says much in favour of channellers, and psychics generally, consulting more erudite works in order to familiarise themselves with the terms of reference more appropriate to the message or scenario of the communicator. Software/hardware – these are, of course, purely metaphors of the age, ones which will doubtless be discarded in years to come in favour of some new terminology more relevant to the prevailing *zeitgeist*. And, while we are on the subject of the kind of psychic discipline that is encouraging of good mediumship/channelling, it goes without saying that either the use of mind-bending chemical substances/drugs, or over-indulgence in alcohol, can have an adverse effect on the brain, thus limiting the level of contact and impairing considerably the quality of reception.

In Chapter 1, I offered some brief definitions of the better-known practices that shelter under the somewhat dubious umbrella of psychism. However, the best explanations of what actually takes place during *genuine* paranormal practices and their accompanying phenomena, are to be found in the semantics of science and I would therefore define what is commonly referred to as 'magic' or 'occultism' thus:

A body of knowledge concerned with natural cosmic laws which, due to an over-emphasis on the worlds of physical matter, has become severed from the scientific mainstream. So called 'occult mysteries' are therefore nothing more nor less than ancient scientific facts that became encoded into terms of reference easily understood by the unlettered, and many of which, over the centuries, degenerated into superstition, their true meaning having been long since forgotten.

Magic or occult energy works at three main levels:

1. The manipulation of particle aggregates (matter) via the agency of mind.

2. The conscious negotiation of particle/wave packets in non-locality (subtle energies on the inner planes in popular esoteric parlance).

3. Imitating certain basic universal principles or patterns which can have the effect of setting corresponding events into motion at the physical level – a process referred to as 'sympathetic magic'. Of course we can always simplify the above by replacing the terminology of modern physics with appropriate elemental or angelic nomenclatures! (see Chapter 21).

In due deference to the views and researches of brighter minds than my own, perhaps I should also add to the above, Rex Stanford's PMIR (Psi-mediated Instrumental Response), in which he suggests that many of us are unconsciously using magical powers to manipulate events to our advantage, hence there is no such thing as 'coincidence'. But now we are entering the world of parapsychology, which demands that I cease this line of enquiry forthwith.

While on the subject of psychology, one cannot help wondering how many of those misguided people whose idea of 'occultism' is prancing around in fancy-dress, or the apparel of earlier cultures, really understand the nature of the energies they are playing with and the oft-times disastrous effects their undisciplined actions can have on both their own psyches and somas and those of other, less strong-minded individuals who might fall under their influence. Having dealt with many such 'casualties', I am only too aware of the pitfalls involved in what I would irreverently describe as 'metaphysical entertainment', the primary aim of which is to experience some kind of paranormal 'high'.

But I digress: let us return to the question of mediumship and in particular those cases involving communication with H.A. There have, I gather, been quite a few people who have claimed to receive messages from, or be controlled by, H.A., but at which frequency? Let us use my computer as an analogy to highlight some of the problems facing accurate reception from 'higher sources'. Due to power fluctuations caused by the fact that the village I live in is supplied by a sub-station, I am obliged to connect a small adaptor/gadget to said machine which monitors the electrical input and keeps the flow on an even keel, thus avoiding loss of material/information, etc. Likewise, good psychic training can help the brain to accommodate fluctuations in communication frequencies which are/can be induced by energies emitted by those present at the time of reception, or the mood-swings (chemical changes in the brain) of the medium him/herself.

Because of the highly radioactive natures of their fields, powerful beings from the faster time-frequencies (other universes) are often obliged to use intermediaries in order to make contact with us lesser mortals. So, no matter how accurate the transmission, if the receiver is faulty, the real facts may become obscured by interference of one kind or another, thus creating yet further impediments in our quest for truth. But surely each person views truth from his/her own personal standpoint or current conviction, which means that changes in our attitude towards it inevitably alter in the light of new perspectives? It can also, at times, prove to be both kind on the one hand, and devastatingly cruel on the other.

Although there may be times when a medium/ channeller's facility for the absorption of higher energies is effective, there are other occasions when he/she is, perhaps, not actually receiving anything. However, his/her cerebral data-banks having retained the memory of earlier communications, the tendency is to fall back on these, and, should the 'void' continue, to repeat those same messages over and over again until they degenerate into a series of homespun philosophies which are purely the product of his/her subconscious mind. As long as there are people willing to accept such meanderings the supply will, sadly, continue. In all matters relating to the metaphysical, care should always be taken to avoid falling into those two extremes of New Age psychedelia on the one hand, and rigid adherence to specific fundamentalist dogmas on the other, mental inflexibility of any kind being conducive to cramping the kind of logical thinking required to effect a fair assessment of any material purporting to emanate from extrasensory sources.

There is, however, another side to this 'accuracy' debate which is seldom taken into account, that being the ability of the listeners/pupils fully to understand what they are being taught. To illustrate my point, I could not do better than heed the Gnostic views regarding who accepts what, and at what level. These wise people saw humankind as being divided into three categories: Hyle, Psyche and Pneuma. I quote from the Victorian scholar, G.R.S.Mead:

'Thus it was a custom for them to divide mankind into three classes: (a) the lowest, or "hylics", were those who were so entirely dead to spiritual things that they were as the hyle or unreceptive matter of the world; (b) the intermediate class were called "psychics", for though believers in things spiritual, they were believers simply, and required miracles and signs to strengthen their faith; whereas the "pneumatics" or spiritual, the highest class, were those capable of knowledge of spiritual matters; those who could receive the Gnosis. It is somewhat the custom in our days, in extreme circles, to claim that all men are "equal". The modern theologian wisely qualifies this claim by the adverb "morally". Thus stated, the idea is by no means a peculiarly Christian view – for the doctrine is common to all the great religions, seeing that it simply asserts the great principle of justice as one of the manifestations of the

Deity. The Gnostic view, however, is far clearer, and more in accord with the facts of evolution: it admits the "morally equal", but it further asserts difference of degree, not only in body and soul, but also in spirit, in order to make the morality proportional, and so to carry out the inner meaning of the parable of the talents.' *Fragments of a Faith Forgotten, (1900) pp. 139-140.*

Oh, had I the courage to write thus!

But to return to H.A. All said and done, being the advanced intelligence that he is, H.A. is not exclusive to any one medium. It is well worth remembering that when it comes to connecting with such an Entity of Light, what any of us receives from H.A. constitutes less than a droplet from that reservoir of Eternity that is fed from the Ocean of Time. So who, and what, is he? I have already commented on this in some detail in my book *Cosmic Connections,* but for those unfamiliar with this work, and because this also applies to my own story, allow me to explain.

In a dimension of time far beyond the comprehension of most hominids, there exist certain powerful 'fields'- Essences, Spirits, Angels in our parlance, perhaps – who are responsible for the manipulation of the energy known as Time. The existence of such Beings having been known to the Ancients from time immemorial. These are to be found among what are referred to in Christianity as 'The Angelic Choirs', in the Bible – the 'Elohim' or 'Nephilim; in Ancient Egypt – 'The Neters', and so forth. (According to Dr.Heinrich Brugsch, the word 'Neter' actually translates as 'the operative power which created and produced things by periodical recurrence, and gave them new life and restored them to the freshness of youth'). These great Time Entities are the Creators of Universes, in that Time has to be slowed down in order for matter/mass to manifest at a given frequency, while subsequent energy recyclings also demand time changes, each 'episode' presenting a different form of experience/ knowledge. As I mentioned in the Introduction, five different energies are engaged in this process. These are known in metaphysics as the Elements of Fire, Air, Water, Earth and Time, and in science as corresponding to the Strong Nuclear Force, the Weak Nuclear Force, Electromagnetism and Gravity. (The concept of Time as a source of energy is not, as yet, generally accepted in mainstream physics.)

In the dimension from which such Beings emanate, all Time exists simultaneously, in that everything that has ever occurred in this and other multifarious universes is contained in the data-banks of that moment, to be accessed according to the evolutionary requirements of each species. Many scientists, and mathematicians in particular, have now reached this conclusion. When I first wrote about H.A. in this context, my communicator, Danuih (Gaia, Planetary Genius of Earth) referred to him as a Time Lord, adding that she had little regard for any sexist objections. The planetary Genius of Vulcan subsequently offered a more acceptable (politically correct?) term – The Timeless Ones. Well, H.A. is just such a Being.

While on the subject of Time, I have often been asked what would happen if a psychic inadvertently tuned in to information for which the world was not ready. Fear not, for the Strands of Time are surreptitiously woven so as to prevent premature access. This 'law' is known in metaphysics as a 'ring-pass-not', and in science, 'The Principle of Conservation of Order'.

So where do I, as H.A.'s daughter in Atlantis, fit in? In the Summary of *Cosmic Connections* there is, commencing on page 194, a section under the heading 'THE OBSERVATIONS AND CONFESSIONS OF A TIME ESSENCE'. In this I have made it quite clear that I am neither Master, Adept, nor any such exalted personality. Such icons have no reality outside of the hominid collective, which unconsciously created them as criteria against which to measure individual stages of development. My 'field', essence, or spirit, if you prefer, is a single aspect of a five-fold Time Entity which experiences alternating periods of separation from the matrix (chaos) and unification therewith (order). I and the other four Essences which form our group were first brought to this planet by our 'Father'. May I hasten to add that this is a purely arbitrary term, the Being in question being totally androgynous – (H.A. – the fulcrum around which we orbit). In the long, long prehistoric past, our separation, or fivefold individuation from the matrix (which was essential for the negotiation of hominid bodies), represented a period of chaos that was to last for thousands of Earth years. In future times, when humanity has learned to appreciate the true nature of Time, people will come to understand more about our kind, and the nature of our commitment.

Since our first exposure to Earth conditions, *each of us has incarnated only once*, for a specific purpose or mission. Thus the five of us, Filon, Lyel, Pera, Felis and Alei, were born the children of Yeris, who became Arcanophus – Chief High Priest of Atlantis. Incidentally, as far as Earth (and certain other planets which were designed to house life at a similar frequency to our own) is concerned, one of the rôles undertaken by senior Time Essences (I am, as yet, very much a junior!) is the introduction of a new gene, which, once it has spread worldwide, will effect physical mutations designed to alter the pattern of human consciousness in preparation for the next great era in the history of the body of Danuih (Gaia). The full effect of this will not be observed, however, until certain major upheavals, destined to take place on this planet in the future, have effected the necessary 'culling'.

Knowing the hominid predisposition towards 'identity discs', if I am to be labelled, perhaps The Fool in the Tarot would be appropriate. Like him I am the Eternal Time Traveller, who, accompanied by my faithful companion (feline in my case), is ever ready to rush headlong into the uncharted territories of the unknown.

Time Essences do not conform to the hominid gender pattern. As members of the devic kingdoms, they are able to function via either positive/active or negative/passive modes, as the situation dictates. However, when entering a species which states this requirement, they are obviously obliged to conform, although, once that choice is effected, they are programmed against deviation. During their sojourn with any species alien to their own kind they are accorded no special privileges which means they are not exempted from the frailties and sufferings to which all hominids are exposed. In fact, experiencing these adds considerably to their data-banks, but they do receive a degree of protection, which is governed by the specific rôle they have come to play in the drama of life at the level in question. The hominid experience is particularly painful for them for several reasons, the main two being that due to their basic nature on the one hand and a feeling of isolation from the 'family group' (which is conducive to melancholia) on the other, they inevitably experience difficulty in conforming to the required norm. Also, being precluded from using their knowledge for any form of material gain or advantage, they may appear ineffectual at the everyday level, and therefore reliant to an extent on minimal assistance from either 'external sources', or kindly hominids who have become spiritually (subconsciously) alerted to their needs. So now you have the full story of my former existence, and of my unbreakable bond with my Father, the entity known generally as 'H.A.'

It is interesting to note that not all the psychics I have met seem able to recognise either H.A's devic (alien) origins or my own, whereas several psychologists have! Dr. John Evans, for example, identified it from my earlier writings and Dr. Rick Mansell, who attended one of the Atlantean meetings at the Vegetarian Society, rumbled me straight away, and confronted me accordingly. What did he say? That, I am afraid, I cannot tell you.

CHAPTER 14

The Reluctant Exorcist

During the latter part of 1959 I sensed that my relationship with Tony was somehow slipping. Perhaps my career, with its unsociable working hours, was the culprit, or maybe our relationship had simply outworn its purpose. My fears were confirmed when I overheard a conversation between Tony and another male member of the society, in which he stated quite clearly that he wished our marriage would end, so that he could make a different kind of life for himself. Mind you, it wasn't put quite as kindly as that, but one has to take into account that when men discuss such matters among themselves, the old bravado inevitably rears its inflated head. As I explained earlier, we devas do not 'own' anyone, nor does anyone 'own' us. Nevertheless, nine years of marriage to Tony, plus the three years we were together prior to that, had served to create a bond between us. The matter came to a head shortly after, when H.A. asked to speak with me in private. The marriage, he said, having served its purpose, could now be dissolved amicably and arrangements to that end put into motion. Since neither of us had, to my knowledge, committed any errors in the conjugal area, a 'situation' had to be set up, that being the custom in those days. A female acquaintance of mine had been asked to co-operate (for a fee), so all we had to do was to wait for the case to come to court. I do, however, recall the feeling of loneliness and loss which accompanied the outcome.

Joining my class at college in February 1960 raised my spirits somewhat, and it was then that I met, and befriended, fellow student Sally Dowdall (later to become the internationally known soprano, Sally Le Sage), sister of the then professional singer Ann Dowdall. Sally showed an immediate interest in The Atlanteans and hastened to tell her sister all about it. Although a staunch supporter of Moral Rearmament, Ann agreed to attend one of our meetings, where Sally and I introduced her to Tony. They seemed to take to each other immediately, and the following summer, after Tony's and my divorce had gone through, they were married, and a new era commenced in The Atlanteans which was ultimately to result in my leaving the group forever.

In those days, The Atlanteans had several branches – Bromley, Bristol, Cheltenham, Croydon and Brighton spring to mind, and it was the custom for those among us who were lecturers or mediums to visit these branches fairly regularly. Now that I had my evenings free, it was easier for me to pull my weight, whereas when I had been in the theatre, the bulk of the work fell upon the shoulders of the others. We had a very strong healing group, under the direction of Gillian Kings, whom I also introduced to the occult. I had met Gillian at an audition (she, too, was a singer), and a few months later she joined me at College. From the very beginning I knew that there was one gift my devic origins afforded me, that of

exorcist, and it was with Gillian as a partner that I carried out
most exorcisms during my time with The Atlanteans. I later
realised that I could do them on my own, but the method I
taught the others was much safer for hominids. Nor did I need
to be present when effecting the removal of unfriendly, or
'lost' energies; in fact, some of my best exorcisms were done at
a distance. I recall one in particular, where a room in
Cheltenham was exhibiting positive signs of a haunting.
While projecting my consciousness to the place in question,
although I had never been inside that house, I was able to
describe the room in detail including objects, photos, etc., on
the mantlepiece. In this particular case the lost entity was easy
to help, although there were sometimes instances where one
met with opposition.

   At this point I have a confession to make which, I hope,
those dear friends of mine who used to work with Gillian and
myself in this field will forgive me. The method I used,
especially when working alone, simply involved *changing the
frequency to one which obliged the entity to vacate its haunt, by
proving uncomfortable for it.* But don't get me wrong. I was
always careful to see that such a soul was given healing and
handed over to its helpers, or to those in the appropriate
dimension who had its best interests at heart. When one did
come up against the 'nasties', it was always amusing to note
their perplexity when subjected to a totally alien – devic or
Paschat – energy field, (into which modes I would sometimes
shape-shift!), wherein they had no power, and from which
they were therefore only too pleased to escape. I have tried to
teach several people to use this frequency-changing system,
but with minimal success: the type of energy I employ, which

works via higher frequencies on the electromagnetic scale (in much the same way that a magnetic tape is 'cleaned' to allow for its re-use), appears to be something exclusive to my own kind. When effecting a clearing of this, or any kind, one should always remember the old scientific adage that nature abhors a vacuum, and fill the vacated space with an energy more appropriate to the needs of those who have sought one's help in this capacity. Remember the Biblical statement: 'If you close not the door, shall not seven more enter'? Interestingly enough, back in the early seventies there was a T.V. play, by writer Nigel Neale called *The Stone Tapes*, in which a heavily haunted mill was finally exorcised by the use of high-frequency electrical emissions.

As my readers will no doubt appreciate, having indulged in this practice for so many years it would be impossible to feature all the work I have carried out in this field, both with Gillian and on my own. Also, a degree of confidentiality being involved, one or two of the people I have helped have asked specifically that I do not mention them by name. This is especially the case with a particular family who sought help outside the religion to which they normally belonged and so I have decided to tell a little tale which will, I hope, throw some light on to the stance held by one of the major world religions.

Having been raised in a Roman Catholic environment, I was always taught that the Jesuits were *el supremo* when it came to dislodging unwelcome entities, and those in the employ of Old Nick in particular. A male member of our group, who had been educated at a major Catholic Public School, held a degree in geology, and had also served as a commissioned officer in the Army, agreed to come with me to

Farm Street, the H.Q. of the Jesuits in London, to see what we could find out about the Jesuit *modus operandi*. Passing ourselves off as medical students hoping to specialise in psychiatry, the practice of which might possibly bring us face-to-face with cases of possession, we sought a private interview with an exorcist priest and were duly invited to see a certain Father Barratt.

Upon arrival we were shown into a darkened room in which there was a somewhat spooky high-backed chair, which looked as if it had seen better days in some ancient ecclesiastical establishment. Enter Father Barratt, a small, white-haired old man of benign appearance, who greeted us cordially before taking his seat in said piece of furniture. After hearing our 'side', he commenced with an admonishment to 'Steer well clear of the devil, as he can assume many forms', and then, realising that he had a captive audience, he milked every moment of the next two hours.

Alas, I do not have the space to repeat all his colourful tales, but here is one in particular, which I feel serves to highlight the Catholic Church's approach to the problem of unwelcome visits from the region of Hades. The story goes thus: During a period when Father Barratt was attached to a small mission in the outbacks of India, a distraught father approached him (accompanied by some twenty or more relatives) to seek his help in disposing of a demon which had attached itself to his teenage daughter. Armed with his bell, book and candle, our worthy Jesuit set forth to carry out the required exorcism, but hardly had he set up his pieces for the necessary ritual when the demon in question addressed him thus through the girl: 'You are wasting your time. Go ahead and play your little games if you wish, but you do not have the power to dislodge me!' However, Father Barratt was not put off by his initial failure, as he had been taught that it sometimes took the power of more than one priest to send Old Nick on his way. He therefore sought the help of two priests from neighbouring missions and the three of them together went about the required procedures. But before the first line of the initial invocation had passed their lips, the demon once again pre-empted them, speaking through the girl: 'Oh, dear, I see we have more company here today. Very amusing, I am sure. But please, gentlemen, do not waste your time, as I have no intention of moving out, no matter how hard you pray to your God!'

Becoming somewhat perplexed (and more than a little frustrated) by then, Father Barratt approached his Bishop, a wily old man who, being obviously better versed in the ways of such phenomena than his juniors, promptly declined to have anything to do with it. And so, for the time being, the poor young girl was left with her demon, much to the frustration of her family. Attendance at the Jesuit mission dropped off, the locals having lost faith in the ability of its God to sort out their problem. However, it came to pass that a holy man, accompanied by his chela (student/disciple), happened that way, whereupon the distraught father and his family immediately turned to the newcomer for help with his daughter's malady. Surrounded this time by a very large crowd, the Guru bent down and took a few pinches of earth, to which he added his own spittle. As he was about to reach out to anoint the forehead of the girl, the demon spoke out with alacrity, 'All right, all right, I know that you are more powerful than I, so I am therefore obliged to leave this host forthwith. But I must say I've had a good time while it lasted!' Whereupon the girl collapsed in a heap, and, when she came round, all traces of the intruder were gone forever.

The grateful villagers lost no time in presenting themselves at the Jesuit mission, eager to render full details of the miraculous event, while also demanding to know why all the power of their Church could not dislodge the entity, whereas the holy man was able to do so without a struggle. Needless to say, Father Barratt and his friends, being somewhat narked, decided to seek the guru with the idea of prizing out his secret. When the worthy cleric finally caught up with him, his approach was forthright: 'How is it that the power of The Holy Church of Rome, acting in the name of its Founder, Jesus Christ Himself, was insufficient to dislodge the Devil from that girl, and yet you, a lone mortal lacking the support of a Church or established faith, were able to put it to flight?' A broad smile spread across the old guru's weather-beaten face as his eyes met those of Father Barratt. 'Ah, my son, it is like this: about God you think you are knowing much, but about the Devil you are knowing nothing!', whereupon his roughened, brown feet once again trod the soil of his native land, and his lilting laugh haunted Father Barratt for many a year to come. As we used to say in the theatre,'What an act to follow!'. My own humble efforts pale in the light of such wisdom.

Germane to the above is a short conversation that I had with an Irish Catholic priest some years ago, when he told me (in a moment of confidence) that during his training, women were often described as lesser mortals who fell into one of three categories: harlots, incubators and nuns. He was careful to add, 'the exception being, of course, those who are of the *sidhe*, rare though they be, for even the Holy Saints have no power over the likes of *them*.' So, for what it is worth, here are a few meagre examples of how the *sidhe* function in the exorcist mode, from this member of said faery fraternity.

The first of these took place on a large estate in the north, where part of the grounds were let out as stables. The lady in charge thereof used to take out groups of people for long rides which all went very well until they reached a given point in the route, when the horses would show signs of distress resulting in several topples. Anxious to find out what was 'spooking' this particular spot, the lady sought help from Gillian and me. My first action was to project back through time to the period at which the haunting commenced, and there, sure enough, lay the root of the problem. I found myself in the Border Wars period. A small *posse* of soldiers were seated around as though waiting for something or someone. I asked them why they were waiting here. The corporal answered me: 'Our captain has gone on ahead to recce, and our orders are to wait here until he gives us the all-clear. But he hasn't come back, and we dare not disobey an order.' My next move was to make contact, through Time, with the captain. This actually proved quite easy, as his spirit had already been trying hard to let me know that he himself had been killed, and his small troop ambushed and slaughtered to a man. Using a particular type of 'time-linking' energy, and with Gillian's help, I managed to get the two factions together. Upon seeing their officer the men were delighted, and naturally asked him how the war was going. 'It is all over now, men. We have won. You may return to your homes in peace.' Whereupon they immediately vanished and the hauntings ceased forthwith, thus allowing the horses to pass peacefully on their daily ride.

The next tale involves another stately home, in which the major staircase was haunted by a woman in a heavy silk dress, whose footsteps and the rustle of her gown against the stairs, could be heard regularly by everyone. This time there were several of us present, all seated at various stages down the massive staircase, waiting patiently for the arrival of the stately spectre. In accordance with The Law of Summons, I sent out my silent command: 'Will whoever is haunting this property make her presence felt before me this instant'. As we all sat there, tensely, the upper stairs commenced to emit the dreaded squeak accompanied by the rustle of a long, heavy garment. And there before Gillian and me stood the spectre of a noblewoman of considerable rank and distinction, to which fact she was quick to alert me. 'I am not accustomed to being summoned by a commoner, so who are you and what do you want with me?' I asked why she had come. 'As you well know, I have no choice, having been informed that there are laws other than those imposed by the State, which I am obliged to observe.' I informed her that I represented the residents of the house who wished to know why she was haunting their staircase. She replied, haughtily. 'Because I gave my word on my deathbed that as long as they kept my portrait I would watch over them and protect them. Now may I go?' I dismissed her with a 'thank you', and, once again, the ghostly footsteps were heard, this time ascending the winding flight.

When this was all over, our hosts asked Gillian and me to

describe what we had seen. This we did, whereupon we were taken to an attic room in which there stood an enormous painting of the apparition! It was then explained to us that there was a family legend concerning the portrait and the promise made by the lady concerned. I was obliged to give my word to the family in question that I would not disclose the identity of the woman, nor their own, for that matter, as certain senior, fundamentalist-Christian family members would be horrified were they to learn that the services of 'pagan-exorcists' had been sought.

Case No.3 involved a lady and her young child, who were renting a flat in Hampstead. During the night they became aware of strange, agitated voices carrying on a conversation in their living room, while the whimpering of a child was also highly audible. But when they opened the door and put on the lights, there was no-one to be seen. Having a friend who was an electronics engineer, the lady in question decided to arrange for him to record these sounds, just to prove that they were not all in her imagination. And so the appropriate machinery was set into motion, and, sure enough, the sounds came out quite clearly in the recording.

Someone had apparently told her about my work, and so, wishing to rid herself of the phenomena, she asked me to clear the place for her. This time, however, I was on my own. Listening to the tapes took me right into the past situation – an argument between and man and a woman, and the cries of a mentally abnormal child whom they had kept locked up, the age in question being one in which such afflictions were not viewed as kindly as they are today. The man eventually walked out, and, when she could take no more, the woman took her own life and that of her little girl. What I needed to do was to get all three spirits to face up to the situation they had failed to address correctly when alive. This I achieved through a kind of inter-time healing, which resulted in their feeling drawn to return to earth bodies together in what for them constituted 'the future', to make reparation for their past misdeeds. The present resident was, in fact, that very mother, her child the one she had borne in the past, and her technically gifted boy-friend, the former father. What goes around comes around, as the saying goes! After clearing the vicinity, I filled it with the Isis Ray and the voices ceased forthwith. I later heard that the man had set up a successful business. They had bought their own house, his (now) wife was very happy and the child, a little boy this time, had turned out to be highly gifted. I have been asked to explain how it is possible to link spirits together from different periods of time: as a Time Essence I am blessed with the facility to effect such linkings via a point in space-time at which time as we know it on Earth has no relevance.

Here is an amusing episode, which will, I hope, cause a laugh if nothing else. A certain 'lovers' lane' was manifesting signs of an unwelcome resident which delighted in frightening away those Romeos and Juliets who saw fit to carry out their courting activities within its vicinity. Another occultist I knew at the time was called in and he conducted a special rite which was guaranteed to send the 'bogey' on its way. And so it did, much to the delight of the local courting couples. However, the question was far from resolved. The next field along belonged to a local farmer, whose cows had always grazed happily in those mellow pastures. These poor creatures became the next target of our unfriendly spook, to such an extent that the farmer thought they had contracted some dreadful disease which could only lead to the slaughter-house.

When I heard the tale I knew immediately what had happened. The entity in question had simply been moved on to the next field, rather than away from the vicinity of Earth all together. I remember him being a pretty nasty sort of character when I tackled him, which obliged me to take the frequency up fairly quickly in order to inhibit any phenomena. But it was all sorted out amicably in the end, much to the delight of both the farmer and his meadow-ladies!

My last two tales carry more psychological undertones. The first involved the case of a highly respectable, well-educated lady in her thirties who had suddenly taken to being 'possessed of a devil', which, during those periods when it was in control, would hurl abuse and foul language at the rest of her family. In despair they sought my help, and, on this occasion, I asked to be left alone with my 'patient'. The first thing I always did before entering exorcism mode was to check that there was actually an intrusive entity around, and that the manifestations were not simply an attention-seeking ploy, a figment of an overactive imagination or a sick mind.

In this case there was no invading entity to be seen, which told me I was dealing with a psychological factor. During my days as a case worker, my senior officer advised that, in the event of there being any doubt as to the authenticity of a story, the procedure was to effect a confrontation, with the idea of inducing an abreaction. And so I put the question to her straight:'Why are you making all this up? Whom are you trying to impress? Because there is nothing there, no devil, no evil spirit, just your mind endeavouring to manipulate its environment; but to what purpose?'. After initially employing her demoniac invective in protestation, she finally abreacted into a convulsion of tears. Her family, it seemed, were very rich, and, although she had been given a first-class education, she was told there was no need for her to work. As the years went by and her family had refused to listen to her pleas, she had become more and more frustrated. In the end she had thought to herself that if they wouldn't take any notice of her, perhaps they would listen to the Devil. And so the charade had begun. I asked what sort of career she had in mind. 'I've always wanted to run my own business', she told me. 'Right', I said. 'We'll settle this one once and for all'. And this is what I did.

I called the whole family into the room and spelled it all out to them. At first my words were greeted with horror and disapproval, but slowly, as my 'patient' confirmed it all, several of them also dissolved into tears. There was much hugging and TLC, and when I eventually left, my 'halo' was, well, not quite so lopsided! I later heard that she had entered a successful business partnership with a man whom she had eventually married. So much for Old Nick!

A word of advice to aspiring exorcists: beware the psychological trap, and, when there is a serious mental illness involved, hand over to those trained and equipped to deal with it. It is also worth bearing in mind that inspiration and delusion are less than a hair's breadth apart, and likewise with ecstasy and frenzy. On one occasion, when I was lecturing in the West Country, I was interrupted by a man from the audience who informed all present that he was possessed of an evil spirit and had been to all the top occultists in this country (he gave a list of names), none of whom had proved as powerful as either himself or his entity. He said that he had been told that I was supposed to be something of an exorcist and asked if I would like to add my name to his list of failures. Rather than embarrass those present, I pretended to look him over, tut-tutted, and said, 'Oh dear, you do seem to have a problem, but, as you say, you are far more powerful than I, so what I suggest is that you deal with the entity yourself, then I will sit in this chair, and you can do me the honour of removing *my* three resident spooks!' Although my humour evoked a few titters from the audience, it failed to impress the organiser, who accused me of refusing to help, and of making fun of a poor, suffering man. Help he definitely needed, but from a qualified psychiatrist, not an exorcist.

Now I rather think that that is enough of yours truly and her exorcist activities. After all, as I said earlier, one could go on *ad infinitum* which, in the final analysis, proves nothing. Whereupon I rest my case.

CHAPTER 15

The Laurels Will Be Placed On The Corpse

A strange title for a chapter, perhaps, but if I explain who said it, and why, it might make some sense in the light what follows.

During the period prior to playing in *The Crooked Mile*, a series of small but significant events occurred in my life, events which have somehow become out of sequence as far as this narrative is concerned. One such occurrence happened when I was invited to a gathering somewhere north of London, at the end of one of those extended Underground lines which serve the Metropolitan suburbs and south Hertfordshire. Philip Friend, a reporter at the time with 'Two Worlds' (in addition to other, more popular publications), had instigated my invitation, so it was no surprise to find, on my arrival, a gathering of many of the top names from the psychic world, notably Maurice Barbanell. For some reason best known to himself, Barbie had taken a dislike to me from the word 'go'(perhaps my energies upset him). So it was little wonder that when we came face to face he greeted me with, 'And how's your little racket going these days?', meaning The Atlanteans, of course. Although I am not always so quick off the mark, on this occasion the Muse of Humour did not let me down, and I replied, 'Well, actually it needs restringing, so I shan't be playing Wimbledon this year'. Silence. He simply moved on to annoy someone else.

It was not the party as such which proved the highlight of the evening but what happened when, upon observing the lateness of the hour, I made my excuses and dashed back to the Underground Station just in time to catch the last train, which just happened to be one of those which passed through all the smaller stations between there and the Metropolis without stopping. After getting my breath back and finding an appropriate seat, I scanned my surroundings and noted, to my horror, that apart from myself and a man, the carriage was empty. But the worst was still to come. No sooner had the train commenced its journey than the man rose from his seat and came towards me, obviously very much the worse for drink. I tried looking the other way, pretending I hadn't noticed him. But after mouthing some pretty filthy suggestive obscenities, he lunged at me.

At this point I should explain that my occult initiations to that date had earned me the service of four young, single elementals: Djinn (fire), Sappho, (air), Minna (water), and Peter (earth). Each of whom would be willing to come to my aid should the need arise. In that moment of panic, protection became my prime concern, so I called on my faithful Salamander, 'Get him, Djinn, get him!' The response was instantaneous. The man leapt to his feet and started tearing open his collar. His face turned crimson, and he screamed that he was 'on fire'. By the time the train eventually stopped he was writhing on the floor by the door. Two of the embarking passengers, believing him to have had some sort of seizure, called for help, and, as the doors closed once again, I noted that he was receiving appropriate attention. Suddenly realising I had forgotten to call off Djinn, I did so immediately, and he returned to my field-space. I then sent the poor man some healing.

H.A. later admonished me with the words, 'My dear, you do not need to use a sledge-hammer to crack a nut'. It then dawned on me that a little assistance of a distracting nature supplied by Sappho (Sapphy, affectionately) would have been much more suited to the occasion, and certainly less painful. However, when one is subjected to an attack on one's person, one does not always have time to work out an apposite occult strategy, although latterly I did learn the art of using energies that were more conducive to minimising both initial discomfort and any later side-effects.

It was during this period that Tony and I were invited to the home of a Mrs. Bessent, (not to be confused with Annie Besant), a Theosophist and astrologer of some repute, who had spent many years in the East. During tea she asked both Tony and me for our dates and times of birth, saying that she would send her analyses to us later. This she did, and although the document itself has long since perished, I can recall to this day most of the contents of my own chart. They were uncomfortably accurate. Remember, at that time I was hell-bent on a singing career, and there seemed little to stop me. But she was adamant in her insistence that I would end up as a writer. Some of her words I memorised, and can repeat to this day: 'Never expect fame and fortune, and, should these ever appear in your path, you will be moved from that direction by circumstances beyond your control. You will not fully understand what you have really come to do until you are long gone, when *the laurels will be placed on the corpse'*. This advice has been of considerable use to me, in that I have never expected anything from the material world, and never will.

During these early days in the history of The Atlanteans, and possibly because of my own theatrical connections, the society attracted quite a few celebrities. These included film star Chili Bouchier, several other well-known actors and actresses, and Rosemary Knight, one of the casting directors from the J.Arthur Rank organisation (for which I did a few bits of filming before I went into 'The Crooked Mile'). Rosemary's husband, Castleton Knight, or CK, as he was known, had produced the film of the coronation, for which he had been offered a knighthood – which he refused. (Rosemary and I subsequently struck up a friendship which was to endure until her death from cancer in the late seventies).

The Atlanteans was, by then, growing apace. On one occasion we were approached by George King, whose 'Aetherius Society' was also in its growth stage. He had, it appeared, a proposal to make to us. Mary having left to live in the USA, our main Council at the time consisted of Colin Bennett, Edwin Naylor, Tony and myself, each of us anxious to hear what Mr. King had in mind. What he proposed was an amalgamation of the two groups, according to *his* agenda, which was: no women in positions of authority; he would be senior medium with Tony as second; the other two men could help with the administration; and the ladies (only yours truly at the time!) would be allotted the secretarial duties. Keeping a straight face was, of course, very difficult, but we somehow managed to put up a reasonably good show and sent him on his way with a promise to consider his kind offer, and to notify him of our response within the next few days. Although several appropriate expletives sprang to our minds at the time, the letter of refusal that we sent him, which we all signed, was politeness itself. It was never acknowledged.

Another incident which took place around this time, and which might interest my readers, demonstrates how the devic energy deviates from the psychological 'norm'. It concerned the eminent psychiatrist, Dr. William Sargent. During his researches, Dr. Sargent had become convinced that certain rhythmic drumbeats could alter consciousness to the degree that all ethical considerations became blurred, resulting in a temporary return to the primitive state. A television producer with whom I had become slightly acquainted at the time asked if I would be willing to take part in an experiment with Dr. Sargent, in order to prove his point. We met at a flat somewhere in central London, where the psychiatrist had the appropriate recordings all set up. I was asked to sit back comfortably in the chair, let myself go with the beat, and see what happened. However, suspecting a bit of hocus-pocus, I devised a way of sidestepping the energies which were obviously emitted by these ritual drumbeats. For this purpose, prior to Dr. Sargent's throwing his switch, I selected a song by Henry Purcell of which I was particularly fond, which I programmed into my brain. So powerful was the Purcell that it completely drowned out the drums, to the extent that when the dear shrink switched off his recording I burst into song with the last few stanzas of the piece in question.

He was thoroughly perplexed. 'You are the first and only

person who has ever reacted in this way to these drumbeats. They are designed to induce a state of frenzy which by-passes normal disciplines and reasoning powers, and renders the subject open to suggestion. You must tell me what you did.' I replied that I had simply inserted a pre-programme at a slightly faster frequency than that of the drums, which served to block out their sound. Although the physics angle seemed logical, he could not understand how such energies could be manipulated *from the brain*. What we are dealing with, of course, is a field/essence reaction, although at that time my data-banks did not have the programme which would have enabled me to address the problem in terms appropriate to both medicine and physics, so the worthy shrink was left floating in a sea of doubt. Strangely enough, while taking a break from editing this morning to glance at my daily paper, what should I come across but the following report:

YOUR MIND CAN MOVE MATTER, SAY SCIENTISTS
'Mind over matter is more than just a theory, according to some scientists. They claim that it is possible to influence inanimate objects without touching them by concentrating hard enough. A team at Princeton University in New Jersey tested 100 volunteers, and say they were able to control a random number machine which displayed figures as a series of ones and zeros. Their success rate in getting the counter to come up with numbers they were concentrating on was better than could be expected by chance, and better than the one-in-a-billion probability that psychokinesis does work, the scientists say. 'We believe that we now have pretty incontrovertible evidence for this phenomenon',

said Princeton Professor Robert Jahn, who has been working to prove the theory for 12 years. He stressed that the skill of psychokinesis was not limited to a few unusual people. 'It seems to be a common ability', he added. His team believe humans tap into only a fraction of the brain's true potential.' (*Daily Mail, 16/11/97*)

I have been preaching this for the past forty years: there is obviously a right time for everything. But allow me to pick up my tale at the point at which I was at college, and busy helping to run The Atlanteans in my spare time.

Although residents came and went during the five-year Lexham Garden period, after Tony left to marry Ann, the four regulars were Eddie, Colin, Sally and yours truly. There were also a number of members, mostly single men, who lived in bedsits round and about the area, who would invariably gather at Mulwarrie for a chat or an evening out. Sometimes we would all go to the 'flicks', while at others we would simply meet up at some small bistro for an omelette or a baked potato, meat consumption of any kind being out – orders of H.A. After our regular Sunday meeting, twelve or more of us would often pile into cars and head for the 'Stockpot' in Knightsbridge, which was usually filled with characters equally as colourful as ourselves, and sometimes more so. These were very happy days, those 'good times' about which Sally and I still reminisce, when The Atlanteans represented a sort of family situation for many of us. But then groups, societies, cults, call them what you will, are, as any psychologist worth his or her salt will tell you, emotional minefields. The tendency is for some members to regard them as family, myself being no exception, so that when others break away to resume normal lives, while still retaining their membership, rifts inevitably occur which tend to affect some people more than others, depending on their psychological make-up.

It was during the period following the marriage of Tony and Ann that I was invited out by Brinsley Le Poer Trench (later Lord Clancarty), a UFO buff who edited a magazine on the subject entitled 'Flying Saucer Review'. Brinsley was considerably older than me, but he was what I would describe as a dear, woolly sort of soul, whose only ambition was to write books about UFO's, which he eventually did, *The Sky People* being the first. Sorry to disappoint those readers who might be hoping for a drop of Nanny's 'hanky-panky', but we were simply friends. Mind you, the fact that I had a reputation for NOT slipping easily between the sheets did seem to perplex some people. So much so that, in order to get them off my back and appear 'normal', when asked, 'What was it like with ...?' (whoever), I would tease them by replying with oohs's and aah's, wows, and fabs, which they could interpret in whatever way they wished. (The usual assumption being that these referred to bedroom frolics.) In this way I could get away without losing face (on the purely human side, of course) while not necessarily telling the truth. In fact my relationships with the three boy-friends I had during that period, Brinsley, Michael C., and Donald S., never got farther than a kiss and a cuddle. Sorry, folks!

But to return to my personal career. Aside from a sudden and severe illness which hit me around the time that Tony and Ann were married in 1961, my first two years at the Royal College passed successfully. I won a coveted prize for singing

– above all things – Wagner lieder! (Can't think why, but since it also involved a sum of cash I could hardly complain.) There was also some good concert work available for advanced students, details of which were usually posted outside the Registrar's office for those interested. And when Hammer Films were making 'Phantom of the Opera', it was to our College that the producers came for the voice-overs. In fact, I was also included among the minor members of the cast, which involved several days' filming. All good stuff for the bank balance! But my real sense of triumph occurred when our Principal, Keith Faulkner, auditioned every voice in the College for the solo parts in the St. John Passion at Chichester Cathedral, and Sally and I were chosen.

At the commencement of my third and final year, my Professor, Ruth Packer, suggested that it might be expedient for me to start thinking about what work I would do when I left. And, strangely enough, it was at about the same time that I was alerted to the fact that a soprano was needed immediately at Sadlers Wells Opera (later to become the English National Opera, when the Company moved from the old Sadlers Wells Theatre to the Coliseum). Richard Austin, then Principal of The Opera School, suggested I attend the audition for the vacancy (with Miss Packer's consent), although the latter was careful to caution me that it was too early in my career to harbour any bright expectations.

It was a chilly day in early March when I attended that audition. The number of applicants seated around, anxiously waiting to be called in, was enough to put one off to start with. I took my place among them and sat dry-throated, and fully resigned to Miss Packer's forecast, to the extent that when my name was called I entered the audition room with little hope of success. I recall thinking, 'Well, I suppose it's all good experience'. There was the usual long table, with some five people seated behind it who peered alternately at their notes and the shaking figure standing before them. I was asked what I had brought to sing for them: it was *Signore Ascolla*, from 'Turandot', which they requested in English (Oh, I entreat thee, Sire), whereupon the accompanist was gestured to proceed. I think I sang it reasonably well, but one can never tell. There I stood, anticipating a polite dismissal, while the auditioners conferred amongst themselves, a sense of resignation having served to calm my nerves, if nothing else. Tom Hammond, who happened to be head man there in those days, then addressed me. 'Have you anything else with you?' Somewhat taken aback, and thinking 'in for a penny, in for a pound' I answered, *'Merce dilette amiche'* from 'The Sicilian Vespers'. (Miss Packer, herself a great Verdi singer in her time, would have had a pink fit had she known of my audacity.) 'I think we would like to hear that', he replied, once again motioning the accompanist to proceed with the spirited Verdi introduction. Maybe it was because both Miss Packer and Keith Faulkner had insisted that I was essentially a Bach/Baroque singer, who should not be allowed within miles of Verdi, that I sang in a couldn't-care-less mode. My examiners sat bolt upright in their seats, and, when I had finished, after a short consultation I was called before them to be told that the job was mine and asked when I would start. I explained that I was still at College, but was advised that Mr. Austin would be contacted, and the situation explained to him. My grant would also need to be refunded.

When I arrived back at college, the general advice rendered was to accept the job, even though it was initially in the chorus, as my potential as a performer had also been noted with considerable interest. I had only two weeks in which to make my arrangements and find some 'digs' before the Company set off on the road, although I was obliged to present myself for rehearsals forthwith. For a person who hates travelling, or going anywhere for that matter, the touring prospect was daunting, to say the least. But it went with the territory, and I knew that without professional operatic experience, I hadn't a snowflake's chance in hell of ever having a career in classical music.

And so I signed on, leaving the management and running of The Atlanteans to the remaining members of the Main Council, and Tony's wife, Ann, who had, by then, assumed a position of prominence in the society's affairs. Had I known then what I learned later, however, I would never have accepted the opera contract. The preceding events having taken place while Keith Faulkner was in hospital, upon his returning to college and hearing what had happened, he was shocked at my decision and asked to see me when I returned to London with the Company four weeks later. He had, apparently, planned a career for me in oratorio and concert work, into which he had intended to launch me at the end of my third year – contacts, an appropriate agent, the lot. He commented that singing in an operatic chorus, even if I did manage to get some small parts, would spoil that straight line in my voice which was so essential for early music. He was, of course, quite correct. Joining ENO was a decision I have regretted to this day, although, no doubt, the experience must have proved valuable somewhere along the line.

At this point I must remind my readers of a remark made in an earlier chapter, when I mentioned how, in the early days of our psychic investigations, Tony and I had, on one occasion, experimented with a glass on a table. Well, the message we received at that time, when I was only twenty-two years of age and had never engaged in a single singing lesson in my life, was that I would eventually become an opera singer, and that the first opera I would sing in would be 'The Magic Flute'. Upon my arrival at Sadlers Wells Theatre, prior to the commencement of our first tour, the opera in rehearsal was – 'The Magic Flute'. And it was during a subsequent tour, when the girl playing the part of Papagena sustained a fall prior to opening with that opera in Oxford (I was the understudy, or 'cover' as they preferred to call it), that I made my début as a soloist and continued in the rôle for the rest of that year. Among that audience were Atlantean members Stephen Taylor (editor of the local newspaper) and his wife, Olive, who ultimately became my dear friends. Both have now departed this Earth, but theirs was a friendship that I cherished for many years. Of course, anyone who has any knowledge of the Inner Mysteries of Hermetic Masonry will be familiar with the metaphysical/initiatory implications of Mozart's brilliant work.

While I was away on one of the Company's extended tours, the five-year lease on our flat at Mulwarrie ran out, so we were all obliged to seek alternative accommodation. Rosemary Knight owned a flat in Kensington, which she offered to rent to me on the understanding that whenever she was in town she could use the spare room; so, I was able to move in there. But it was on the second floor, and on a busy road, so I had no option but to leave my beloved cat, Woodwee, he of the 'old soul' story related earlier in this narrative, with Tony and Ann, who had bought a large house in Ealing. Mercifully he died shortly after. Although we both missed each other dreadfully while I was away on tour, knowing he was well looked after by Sally and the boys did help a little. That same spirit, which is now in another furry little body, is seated beside me as I write.

My period with ENO was anything but easy, although it did have its moments as the next chapter will serve to highlight, and, thanks to Mrs. Bessent's forecast, I was somehow resigned to whatever problems I was faced with (although punctuated by the occasional good time, these were legion).

CHAPTER 16

The Winds of Change

Touring with an opera company can be fun on the one hand and exhausting on the other. And we toured – all over U.K. and Europe to start with, destinations further afield appearing as our reputation as a Company spread. Within any group of people who are thrown together for long periods, there are the inevitable personality clashes. I was fortunate in that I made two good friends in my 'mates', Jill Ashby and Jane Whitehead. We used to arrange to 'dig' together when possible and one amusing incident resulting from this springs to mind. Jill and I were sharing a bedroom at a hotel in the Midlands somewhere. Her bed was positioned in the corner opposite mine, and it was her custom to read for a while before settling down to sleep while I edited the voluminous notes sent to me by the Atlantean Secretary, Betty Wood, who used to take down H.A's talks in shorthand. On one particular night there was no editing to cope with, so I pulled the bedclothes over my head and went straight off to sleep. It seems that after about half an hour, I suddenly sat bolt upright in bed, still fast asleep, and announced in strident tones, 'I have discovered the secrets of the Universe!' Anxious to share such a revelation, Jill grabbed a pen and paper from her handbag and asked me to tell her what I had found out. Apparently I turned my head in her direction, eyes still tightly closed, and snapped, 'You mind your own business!' whereupon I promptly returned to the horizontal in true pratt fall style (straight down like a stiffened board). The next day I was inundated by members of the Company asking me to tell them the secrets of the Universe. The joke lasted for several days.

Not all my workmates were as friendly as Jill and Jane, and one girl in particular set out to make life difficult for me. As the old Chinese saying goes, 'Destined enemies always meet in narrow passages', and although I cannot, in this case anyway, view this lady in the 'destined enemy' mode, my vibes certainly appeared to irritate her, to the extent that I was obliged to seek help from the management to get her off my back. Luckily she left soon after, but rejoined the Company at a later date, when I had gone. I have always found that whenever I am involved in a group of people of any sort, there is inevitably one in particular who targets me. Having discussed this with many people over the years, it would appear that it is, perhaps, my elemental energies which serve to aggravate them in some way. But then, it has ever been the way with hominids to attack either that which they either cannot understand, or over which they feel they have no control.

Just prior to, and during this period, I had two boy-friends, Michael C. (as opposed to the Michael I eventually married), and Donald. Both dumped me. The former did so with dignity, but the latter led me a merry dance. In fact, it was not until Henley Thomas, himself an actor and one of our Atlantean members, noticed pictures of his wedding in the national press that I finally got the message. But what really got my goat about the whole affair was the fact that, during the on-off periods of our relationship, he constantly chided me for having soft toys on my bed (a stuffed owl and a cat in this instance), suggesting such things to be a sign of childish immaturity. But when his wedding photo appeared in the press, his bride was seen to be carrying an outsize teddy bear! He also told me that he would never be able to introduce me to his parents, as not only would they disapprove of me on sight, but would doubtless consider me to be two storeys short of a penthouse!

But was I *really* upset? This is where the advantage of being an alien comes into its own. When commiserating with me, my friend Sally, knowing my love of real jewellery, suggested that we both go to Richmond, where there were some excellent antique jewellers, the purchase of some coveted trinket possibly serving to assuage my sorrow. Sure enough, in a small shop off the main thoroughfare, I espied a beautiful pair of gold and peridot drop earrings which I hastened to purchase. In fact I insisted on wearing them and as we left the shop I said to Sally, 'You know, Sal, if I am absolutely honest I prefer these earrings to Donald'. The switch from the element of water (the emotions) to that of earth (possessions) served me well; I never gave that man another thought. Should the situation demand it, I can also switch to air (detachment) or fire (creativity). Useful, no?

During most of the time I was with the Company, and while we were playing in U.K., Betty Wood would send me the material she had taken down while Tony was being controlled by H.A.; the idea being that these lectures could eventually be put together in booklet form. However, when I came to read some of those typescripts, the contents of which bordered on matters touching science, psychology, or the deeply metaphysical, I was obliged to effect some re-writing, or risk the Society being ridiculed. Most times, and with Betty's help, I got away with this, but occasionally I would find my corrections altered back, particularly if something I had said appeared to go against the cherished theories of certain members. So, where was H.A. in all this? Watch this space.

It was during these long periods of absence that a degree of resentment was beginning to ferment among certain senior members of The Atlanteans, although, perhaps, not without good cause. In addition to my not pulling my weight, there was also a feeling that perhaps my theatrical work was a form of ego-tripping or showing off. This attitude was made abundantly clear to me when the Company returned for a London season, and I was able to sort out the problem in a private session with H.A. Although H.A.'s usual practice was to direct the question back to the questioner, he somehow managed to make known his personal judgement, albeit cloaked in solicitudes which, in my own case, left me with little choice – ego or karma! In hindsight, and bearing in mind that I was, as Mrs. Bessent insisted, destined for a career in writing, perhaps I did the right thing at the time, although the motives of the instigators bear questioning.

It was circumstances that proved to be the deciding factors in this instance: a combination of health problems, aggravated by long spells of touring and nights of editing after the show, eventually took their toll. All this, plus the aforementioned challenge – Was I really an ego-tripper? Should I not be concentrating entirely on my spiritual life? – served to accelerate the process and my old renal trouble reared its ugly head. I ended up in St. Paul's Hospital in London with suspected T.B. of the kidneys, which, although it turned out to be a false alarm, finally obliged me to leave the Company. However, I am convinced to this day that, had I not been so deeply involved with The Atlanteans, and had I enjoyed the support of a sympathetic partner or a loving family to return to for warmth and TLC after long, arduous tours, I could have made good in the operatic profession. As it was, after my final farewells I closed my make-up box for the last time, forced by circumstances to seek elsewhere for a means of making a living.

Rosemary having finally sold the flat, I found myself some suitable 'digs' near Earls Court Station and promptly set about finding work. These were my 'bedsit' days, when I was taken care of at night by several spirit cats. These dear souls would sleep on my bed, their presences becoming almost physical at times. I would wake up and feel them as my toes explored the weight of their little 'bodies'. Then, slowly, they would edge their way towards the region of my head, their sensual purrs gently assaulting my aural senses. When I turned on the light there was nothing, but when the darkness again pervaded my wee room, there they were again, ready to purr me to sleep! It gives me great pleasure to inform my readers that three of those very spirits are now with me, in furry bodies, having never really left me.

There was, at the time, quite a bit of session work to be had, and my agent managed to find me the odd television show and some bit parts in films. These were often spaced out, so, in between, I made good use of the training I had received while in the Signals Section of RAF Ruislip and signed on at a Temp. Agency, switchboard work seeming to be quite plentiful. In fact I found I needed to go no further than a large advertising agency in Knightsbridge, where I was destined to meet a lady who was to become one of my dearest and closest friends to this very day. Her name – Val Leitch. Val was the supervisor of a large switchboard which served those high-powered executives who inevitably haunt the world of advertising. Val and I got on so well that I was asked to return there time and time again. Eventually she joined the Atlanteans, and, like many others among the earlier members, relinquished her membership when I left.

Aside from the session work and temping, there was also quite a lot of singing with smaller, less well-known opera companies and groups such as Opera Italiana, where I found myself a soloist alongside some very eminent names from the operatic world. I used to keep my old posters, but time has wearied me of such trophies so I cannot recall all their names. There were also recitals, and, along with the Coutts family, I formed The Helios Ensemble, which specialised in those baroque works which I loved so much, and for which I knew I had exactly the right voice.

I also tried to make up for my periods of absence from The Atlanteans by putting in a lot of time in their office, so, all in all, I was kept fairly busy while also managing to sustain a reasonable standard of living. It was while I was working in

The Atlantean office that I was to form another of those strange friendships – karmic, no doubt – which were destined to play a significant role in my future years. We received regular letters from an elderly gentleman who lived in Scotland. As he was obviously a scholar of considerable learning, I embarked on an exchange of correspondence with him, which eventually led to his inviting me up to Scotland for a few days, all expenses paid. Normally I would have eschewed such an offer, but he was careful to specify that his cousin Mary, and her husband, Robert, would act as chaperones – in case I was a little apprehensive at meeting a stranger for the first time. Robert and Mary had three young children, so the picture I mistakenly built was of a cosy family home, with 'grandad' living next door.

After discussing it with the others, the unanimous opinion was that I should at least give it a try. After all, I never took any holidays, and a break from the old bedsit would do me the world of good. The gentleman in question, a Mr. Bernard, who signed himself by his nickname of 'Boyne', sent me a first class train ticket to Berwick-on-Tweed, where he would meet me and drive me to his home at Makerstoun. It was a morning in early December when I caught that express, savouring the luxury of the first class compartment until we rumbled into the deserted platform at Berwick. Upon disembarking I scanned the platform for my host. And there he was, a frail 77-year-old in a deerstalker and plus-fours. He greeted me warmly, and together we took off on our journey to 'cousin Mary's place'.

By then it was dark, so I couldn't really see where I was going, although I was aware that we were crossing what seemed to be acres and acres of countryside. 'Ah, here we are', Boyne announced, but all I could see were two huge, gilded gates, which were duly opened by a lodge keeper. Beyond them lay a long, wide and splendid drive, which eventually led us to a typical British Stately Home – the Mary and Robert in question being Lord and Lady Biddulph. We were greeted on our arrival by 'Nanny', who explained that her employers had been detained in Europe due to inclement weather in the Channel, and would not be home for a day or so. They offered their apologies, and trusted that 'Nanny' would take good care of me meanwhile. The following morning Boyne arranged for me to be accommodated at Ednam House, an hotel of some repute in Kelso, much favoured by the aristocracy.

That first night at Makerstoun was rather scary. Nanny showed me to my room, which turned out to be a route-march away from the opposite wing, where she herself was resident. I sat down on the massive bed and surveyed my surroundings. Everything there was enormous – the wardrobe, the dressing table, even the door handles. The bathroom, which was *en suite*, was equally daunting. Needing to freshen up before retiring, I turned on one of the massive taps. Nothing happened. And then, quite suddenly, there was a Hadean rumble followed by a gush of hot water that would do credit to a geyser and the huge bath started to fill so quickly that I was obliged to turn off the water with alacrity. After enjoying a good soak and donning my pyjamas, I sat on the bed to remove my slippers and suddenly became aware that I was being watched. Several pairs of spirit eyes were well and truly focussed on me. Were they viewing me as an intruder or a friend? Not wishing my slumbers to be punctuated by rattling chains or the likes, I stood up, 'drew' a circle of Light around my bed and promptly announced to my viewers, 'I am very tired and I need to sleep, so you may not enter inside this circle of Light which I have drawn. This your home, and I respect that, so will you kindly also respect my presence as a guest in your house, and grant me the privilege of a phenomena-free night?' Although, in due deference to my request, they all stood back, I knew they were still around, so I turned off the lights and promptly fell into a rewarding slumber. The following morning, when Nanny brought me a cup of tea I was already awake, washed, and ready to meet Boyne on his arrival, when we would wend our merry way to Ednam House.

During the next few days I learned a lot about my host. A man of considerable scholarship, he had forsaken a life in science (Honours Degree in Chemistry) to work in the Far East, where he had mastered five dialects of Chinese, plus Japanese (in addition to his several European languages). He used to sign his letters to me with the Chinese ideogram – *Shinyu* – meaning 'beloved friend and guardian', and taught me to do likewise, a small folly which endured between us until his death at the age of 97. In a later chapter, when I tell about the Crystal People, the relationship between Boyne and myself will become only too obvious. Although he had never married, he did once propose to me, but realising that although we were spiritually linked, our present paths in life contained too many incompatibilities to bridge, I was obliged to decline his generous offer. However, we remained close for the rest of his life. For a while he lived in a small cottage on the

Makerstoun Estate, followed by a period of residence at Thirlestane Castle in Lauder after the death of his cousin, Ivy, Dowager Countess of Lauderdale. When younger members of the family took over the ancestral home, he moved into one of the fishermen's cottages on the Thirlestane Estate. A humble man, whom I grew to love dearly.

Realising that I might feel uncomfortable alone with him, he invited my friend Gillian to visit with me. These visits became a bi-annual affair, and both of us would return armed with presents and goodies of all kinds. He really knew how to spoil a woman! But aside from the accepted peck on the cheeks, the subject of a closer relationship was never mentioned, nor even hinted at, again.

Over the ensuing years I learned much about Boyne's deep wisdom; allow me to illustrate with one small example. One day, when driving through a nearby village, he happened upon a Meet, complete with huntsmen in their resplendent pink, their hounds and outriders about them. Also in attendance was the local vicar, who had been asked to bless the hunt before it took off. Although it was not within his jurisdiction to interfere with this 'sport', the action of the vicar struck Boyne as being somewhat unfair. He therefore stepped out of his car and addressed his concern to the cleric, suggesting that since the fox was also one of God's creatures, it, too, was deserving of His blessing! The residents of that area, being unwilling to fall out with the local gentry, thought it best to go along with the whims of an eccentric old man, so, following a few nods of approval, the vicar shrugged his shoulders and proceeded to bless the fox. On that occasion the dear creature eluded the hunt!

Although it was Rosemary Knight who actually taught me to drive, it was Boyne who bought me my first car. When Gillian and I paid him our regular visits – all expenses paid – he would ask me to take him for long drives around the Border countryside, which I eventually came to know quite well. There was also the occasional trip to Edinburgh for a round of the shops, when he would delight in treating both Gillian and me to something special to wear or to keep.

To round this story off, I have to come up to date. In November 1996, a dear friend of mine brought a visitor to see me: the well-known medium, Jim Chivers. After sitting quietly facing me for a few moments, he suddenly said, 'I have a gentleman here, an elderly, refined gentleman, an aristocrat. He lived somewhere up north – I am being shown a great house with huge grounds. He asks me to tell you that all the time he knew you he wanted so much to hold you in his arms and tell you how much he loved you, but propriety forbade such an unseemly advance on the one hand, while he was anxious not to frighten you away on the other.' Recognising Boyne straight away, and therefore being greatly moved, I answered, 'Please tell him that I, too, loved him dearly, and still do. In fact I often dream that I am wandering around Thirlestane Castle looking for him. I know our link goes beyond this world, to another planet in another solar system, where the inhabitants could love in a pure way, free of the shackles of convention and earthly carnality.' What a richness of spirit that old man brought into my life. It is to him that I owe much of the scholarship that has enabled me to write several of my books – over the years, he passed on to me priceless volumes, which I shall cherish until I die. He always felt that writing was my métier, and frequently encouraged me to enter that field. Sadly, it was not until after his death that my first book was published.

Around this period, the Atlanteans sported a surfeit of eligible young men, three of whom actually proposed to me. News of this came to the notice of Tony and Ann, and I was promptly requested to attend a session with H.A., he having made it known that he wished to address me on the subject. The problem seemed to be that certain members who were established in secure relationships felt that my 'running around like an emotionally loose cannon, followed by a posse of young men', did little to enhance the society's image of serious stability. It was therefore suggested that I effect a choice from among the eager applicants, and thus settle the matter once and for all. I said that in truth I did not fancy any of them, whereupon it was put to me that physical attraction should not be the only criterion involved in selecting a partner, mental compatibility and a joint interest in, and dedication to, The Atlanteans being more important.

It was not until a month or so later, around the Christmas of 1964, that I started seeing more of Michael Thorburn, although I was not completely sold on a serious relationship. He was fourteen years my junior, although he assured me that this meant nothing to him (oh, had I but known). Eventually he asked to speak with H.A. about it, and, in spite of any misgivings I might have had, there appeared to be no opposition to a possible union between us. Michael was a man of few words, a deep, brooding sort of character, but as far as I was concerned he gave the impression that he would defend me with his life. In fact it was God help anyone who spoke rudely to me, or who was, in his eyes, taking advantage of me in any way. This whole scenario engendered in me a feeling of security, and at this point I'm afraid I have a confession to make: aside from Tony, each of my subsequent marriages have been strictly for security, for 'knowing where I am'. I always hated being a spare wheel, rolling about without direction or stability, although I really did try hard to show some affection.

As my relationship with Michael started to become serious, dear old Eddie tried, as diplomatically as possible, to talk me out of it, although he was unable to give me any real reasons why. Shortly after, he was taken seriously ill and rushed into St. Mary Abbott's Hospital, where cancer of the liver was diagnosed immediately. Ten days later he was dead. In hindsight, he was my *real* protector, although there was never even the slightest hint of a personal interest between us: we were just 'brother and sister', nothing more. Later in life, when I undertook an in-depth study of psychology, I came across the warning, 'Never marry or partner with a knight in shining armour, because when the supply of dragons runs out, you are next on the list'. As far as Michael was concerned, I have never seen a truer word written, nor heard it spoken.

Michael and I were married the following Spring, but within a few weeks of our union I discovered to my horror that he was epileptic. Then I knew what Eddie was trying to warn me about – he had apparently had a *grand mal* in Eddie's bed-sit one evening, but obliged Eddie to swear secrecy. I was informed that, legally, I could have obtained an immediate divorce, but it seemed somehow wrong to take someone on and then dump them because they were ill. I saw him through the four and a half years of his illness (which was eventually stabilised), and for The Atlanteans' sake, if nothing else, stayed with him until we both eventually left the Society in 1975.

My Mother in her mid–30's.

Beresford Hope as a young man (with
soldier friend in uniform).

Murry – with Grandfather 'ELF".

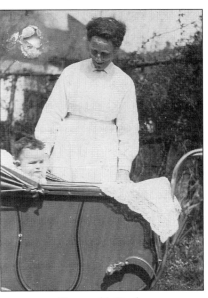

Nanny with Berrie.

"BLUE' Granny – 1920's.

Nanny and Murry.

Berrie and me at Nanny's before we were separated.

My French cousin, Paul Thomelin, taken during his national service in the French Air Force.

My sister Berrie – in her 20's.

2809014 – LACW Hope RAF Ruislip, 1950.

My first portrait, aged 16 – for Win and Charlie Beacon.

Win & Charlie Beacon in the garden at 15 Spencer Place, 1947.

With my first husband, Tony Neate, circa 1952.

Top left: Gillian Kings, who was in charge of healing in the Atlanteans, and with whom I carried out many exorcisms.

Top right: My second husband, Michael Thorburn, taken on our wedding day in May 1965.

Centre left: A group of old Atlantean members outside the Atlantean HQ in the Earls Court Road, London.

Below: Singing 'Eurydice' to Gwyneth Jones' 'Orfeo' in 1962.

Above: "Boyne' (Edward Bernard) as a young man (Boyne died aged 97 in 1983).

Left: I wrote the 'Occult Question Time' column for PREDICTION magazine from 1974-1978.

Thirlestane Castle, Lauder, Scotland, where Boyne and I spent many happy hours in the company of Boyne's cousin, Ivy, Dowager Countess of Lauderdale.

Left: With Siamese, Isis, on the publication of my first book, *Practical Techniques of Psychic Self-Defence* (Harper Collins 1984).

Bottom left: With American husband, Jed Collard, at our home in Cheltenham 1984.

Below: The wild ocelot male who responded to the Paschats (California 1980's).

On my 60th birthday.

Outside my present home with Val Leitch, my oldest and dearest friend, 1997.

My Grandfather, Grand Duke Alexei Alexandrovitch.
(Photograph reproduced by kind permission of Leppi Publications.)

CHAPTER 17

The Final Curtain

During the first few years of our married life, Michael and I shared a flat in Ealing with three Siamese cats, two of which had been wedding presents from a lady who used to run the Occult Question Time column in PREDICTION magazine. Michael shared my love of felines, although he was sometimes less tolerant of their foibles. After his particular form of epilepsy had been diagnosed at a leading London neurological hospital, he was obliged to use the drug Epanutin, which prevented him having further fits. This treatment, which lasted for over four years, precluded him from learning to drive, while also imposing certain physical limits which tended to curtail our activities at many levels. I had a small sports car at the time, but, funds being low, I was obliged to sell it, together with most of the jewellery collection I had acquired during my touring days. Although to all intent and purpose he appeared reasonably normal, there was always the possibility of a recurrence of the *grands mals*, and I was therefore compelled to forego any musical jobs that might involve periods of absence and find temp work locally. Fortunately, Michael also managed to find a job which did not overtax his health.

However I did keep up my singing, and even managed to squeeze in some lessons with the celebrated oratorio singer Margaret Ritchie. There was also quite a bit of local work available, such the Bach 'Passions' at Easter, and Messiahs at Christmas. My first temp job was in the Children's Department of the London Borough of Ealing. As I mentioned in an earlier chapter, it was while I was working there that I was able to access the files that contained details of my own case! When the Education Department moved into its new offices, I was offered a transfer to the Schools Lettings department, where I was destined to meet up with Winnie White (now Mrs. Nicholas), who has remained my friend to this very day. Our department head was something of a Jack-the-lad, so my time spent in that environment was both pleasant and rewarding. It was while I was working there that Tony and Ann offered to loan Michael and me the deposit necessary for the purchase of our own home. After having a good look round, we chose a small, terraced house in Denison Road, the generous garden of which backed onto a secluded green, to which only the local dustcart was allowed access. Nice and safe for our cats.

The other interesting thing about this house was that the vacating tenants were the well-known and highly respected astrologer and writer, Janet Augustin, and her then husband, Michael. The sale went through easily, and Michael and I set about doing the place up to our taste. Working for the Council proved valuable in this instance, colleagues from the Works Department just happening to come across a few 'rejects' – kitchen sink, bathroom fittings and the like – which they were willing not only to let us have, but also to install for us. It was around this time that the Council offered me a permanent position, which, bearing in mind our new mortgage and Michael's dodgy health, I saw fit to accept.

The two problems I had with Michael almost from the word 'go' were his embarrassment over our age difference and his violent temper. When among The Atlanteans the former did not seem to bother him, my being President possibly helping. But when he was among those of his own age group, it was a different matter altogether. I recall one instance in particular when, our offices being close to each other, I decided to meet him as he left work. Upon seeing me standing there, he crossed the road and literally ran away from me. When I arrived home he was furious: 'Don't ever do that again. Seeing me with an old bag like you means I will be the laughing stock in the office tomorrow. The chaps I work with all have wives of their own age, and young children'.

In hindsight I must have been nuts to have put up with this sort of behaviour, but my need for security inevitably getting the upper hand, I eventually submitted, to keep the peace if nothing else. However, this and similar actions did prompt me to consider a return to my real profession, so I wrote to Covent Garden requesting an audition for the chorus, which was all I could expect at that age, and without the necessary solo experience. I sang *Ernani, involami*, and it actually went well. Although there was no vacancy for a top soprano at the time, I was informed that my name would be kept at the ready in the event of one arising in the near future. And that offer did eventually come, but not until after we had moved west. Had I known this prior to our decision to move, things might have turned out differently.

It was around this time that H.A. via Tony announced that we should all think about vacating the metropolis and moving to the Cheltenham area. We had a thriving branch there and certain of its members would be only too happy to help us to find jobs and settle in. Tony and Ann were the first to move, Tony taking a partnership in a company owned by the father of one of our Cheltenham members, along with the lady's husband. These two dear people, Patsy and Roy Claridge, were also destined to play a significant role in my future, as the ensuing pages will tell.

On H.A's advice, and with the help of Roy Claridge, Michael and I found a nice little bungalow in Charlton Kings, a suburb of Cheltenham. We put our house on the market and found a buyer immediately. Our property having increased in value, we were also able to repay Tony and Ann in full, thus relieving us of that particular liability. Roy also helped Michael to find a job in the area, while I was able to arrange a transfer to the Education Department of the County Council in Gloucester. Several other Atlanteans also sold their homes and moved west with us, while a buyer had also been found for the property which the society owned in the Earls Court Road. The money from the sale being insufficient to cover the purchase of a suitable headquarters in Cheltenham, those members who were in a position to so do, assisted with appropriate loans. It was around this time that Michael was able to come off Epanutin, his consultant neurologist having given him the all-clear, which meant he could at last consider driving lessons.

Although to all event and purpose the society appeared to

be thriving, there were certain undercurrents brewing within its ranks which were to contribute to the eventual breaking up of the group as I knew and understood it. Over the years preceding the move westwards, although I had always been, and at that time still was, President and Senior Occultist, I had constantly experienced a sense of not really being in control as far as the society was concerned. Nor had this been all in my imagination, as one particular instance, which took place at a main Council meeting, will serve to illustrate. Being run 'committee' style, our custom was to meet at regular intervals to discuss the way the society was going, consider any changes or whatever; but although I was President, I had little say in all this, and unless fellow Committee member Eddie was also present, it did not pay me to speak out too loudly for fear of being put down. Tony's father, George, had been Treasurer at the time, and what George wanted, George inevitably got – one way or another. On the occasion in question, a certain matter had arisen which concerned fund-raising. Realising that the suggested line of action was totally unethical, I had finally plucked up courage to voice my opposition. At first it had been greeted with a stony silence. Then a certain senior Committee member – no names, no pack-drill – had stood up and given me the slow hand-clap, chanting, 'You're not on the stage now, so stop showing off.' Not another member among those present had moved a muscle, let alone spoken up for me. I recall feeling a sudden sense of isolation, and a tear must have appeared in my eyes, as the next comment had been, 'Oh, dear, she's going to turn on the tap...' However, I had hastily recovered my composure, determined not to give them the benefit of that one. The person in question had later apologised in a jokey sort of way, saying that he and George hadn't really had any intention of carrying out the plan discussed, so why the fuss? Needless to say, when Eddie had returned the following day there was all hell let loose. But then, had he been present, he would never have tolerated such behaviour in the first place.

As for Committees, I later resolved never to come within light years of one for the rest of my life. Winston Churchill once said, 'If Moses had been a Committee, the Israelites would still be in Egypt'. True words, indeed! But then, I am hardly the stuff of which leaders are made, my motto being, 'Never a follower nor a leader be', which is well illustrated in my birth chart – the rational-minded discipline of Virgo, the farsightedness of Aquarius, and the compassion (I call it weakness!) of Pisces. But then, leaders are usually known for the way they manipulate the minds of those who are not sufficiently enlightened to effect their own decisions, swings of opinion easily defining the latter!

But I digress. The property market having changed rapidly, Michael and I decided to sell our bungalow and seek a humbler abode, the price difference allowing us to buy a decent car. Michael had by then passed his driving test and his enthusiasm for his new toy afforded me a welcome break from the wheel. We found ourselves a tiny cottage that had previously served as a cobbler's shop, and which, after a complete refurbishment, turned out to be an ideal home for the two of us plus three cats. It was in that very living room that a small group of us would gather to hear Michael channel H.A., for, in spite of all his faults, he was an excellent medium, and several of the teachings we were given in this way later found their way into the Society's printed booklets.

Around that time I was also invited to contribute to a book about divination – my first venture into serious writing since the disastrous *Daughter of Atlantis*. At that time Philip Pond, who was editor of PREDICTION, having been informed of my knowledge of matters metaphysical, offered me the 'Occult Question Time' column on the magazine, which I accepted. Later, when we returned eastwards, I worked for him in the capacity of roving reporter, which rôle served to open my eyes to the myriad approaches to the real metaphysical world, thus broadening my horizons considerably.

As time progressed, I became more and more uncomfortable with my position in the Society. Sometimes I felt as though I was kept in a cupboard and conveniently brought out to open bazaars, answer awkward questions, or deal with those metaphysical problems with which others would rather not become involved. If I ever did have the temerity to express an opinion that was 'anti' that of the dominant clique, I was either subjected to the 'stop showing off, you're not on the stage now', syndrome, or it was hinted that because I was barren, I was only half a woman and therefore lacking in certain essential areas of human experience. Not that the latter comment was ever made to my face, but it was repeated in the presence of several other single female members, who were so offended by it that they turned up on my doorstep in floods of tears.

The months flew by, and I became increasingly stifled by the level of mental/spiritual programming generally encountered among the Atlantean hierarchy. I felt suffocated, unable to explore and express other, more advanced avenues of metaphysical thought. After talking this over with several leading members, it was eventually agreed that a broader stance was called for, and that instead of simply relying on Tony's mediumship to supply us with ideas and further studies, we should explore the wisdom, knowledge, systems and disciplines of other, earlier cultures, notably that of Ancient Egypt. I therefore introduced the Four Festivals, which were based on the Atlantean originals, while also encouraging dialogue with those Ancient Egyptian archetypes which had emanated from the Old Country in the first place. At the time this approach proved highly successful, as it gave those attending these Festivals an opportunity actually to participate in the proceedings, instead of simply listening to endless channellings. As part and parcel of this new image, the Committee also decided to do away with both the Presidential and Secretarial titles, (mine and Tony's respectively), replacing them with 'Chief Occultist' and 'Chief Administrator'.

It was during this period that H.A. suggested the 'community' idea. Although I was not completely convinced that this was what he really had in mind, certain senior members devised the idea of selling their homes and buying a large complex, to be run along Findhorn lines. However, admission to this somewhat exclusive habitat would be limited to couples with children, which naturally placed them in a quandary as to what to do about Michael and me. The pot stewed awhile, during which nothing was said – not openly, at least. The matter came to a head in a somewhat accidental way (as magical matters are wont to do!). Several of us had planned a get-together to discuss the matter one evening. But when the time came, Michael and I were informed that as something else had come up, perhaps a 'rain-check' could be taken at a later date. So, the evening being free, we decided to treat ourselves to a meal at our favourite vegetarian restaurant. One of the features that attracted us to this restaurant in particular was that instead of being open plan, it sported small, cosy little niches, into which one could tuck oneself and enjoy a quiet meal, well away from the chatter of the other patrons. On the evening in question, Michael and I, having settled ourselves in one such corner, were about to start our meal when we heard familiar voices issuing from a nearby corner, from which the occupants were not afforded a view of us, nor we of them. The subject being discussed was how to set up the proposed commune for couples with children and exclude Michael and me, plus one or two other families who did have two children, but who were, it seems, deemed unworthy, on social grounds, of such inclusion. Fortunately, the members in question finished their repast before we did, and left without becoming aware of our presence. But for Michael and me it was 'curtains'. I had finally made the decision that I should have effected years earlier – to leave the Society for good. Maybe it was I who was guilty of holding up *their* progress, and I who should face up to the fact that I had let them down. Who knows? Perhaps it was simply time for me to move on, anyway. And yet, in my heart of hearts, I could not help feeling that the *real* H.A. would not have approved of such covert plottings and plannings.

In hindsight, and after discussing the whole episode and its preceding events with impartial observers, including a friendly psychologist, I found myself wondering why I had stayed around as long as I did, my submissive mode no doubt resulting from a natural feeling of being 'different', and therefore having to bend over backwards to gain acceptance. Salamander loyalty also comes into it, I suppose, but loyalty to H.A. rather than to those who found me difficult to understand, and therefore to 'handle'. Not that I bear any ill feelings or resentment against them: 'horses for courses' as I've said before, and we can't all run on the same circuits, or at the same speed. Besides, my devic energies would be totally incompatible with the hominid 'family' group situation. Therefore, to this day, I harbour no rancour or resentment. After all, they were probably right. I am far too much of an individualist to fit into the sort of set-up that they had in mind. So, all facts taken into account, I am prepared to give them the benefit of the doubt, and let Ma'at be the judge of any rights or wrongs on either side.

And so Michael and I put our cottage on the market, with a view to moving eastwards. At first it was Brighton we had in mind, but when the deal on a property for which we had made a bid fell through *after we had exchanged contracts*, it was Atlantean Main Council member and close friend Joyce Mitchell (later to become best-selling author and dream expert, Nerys Dee, who died in 1995) who came to our rescue by allowing us to take up temporary residence in the ground floor of a large property she owned on Clapham Common. Conditions there were, as she explained, primitive in the extreme, but as she was about to sell the place she had no intention of spending any money on it. Fortunately for us, that summer of 1975 turned out to be a scorcher, so the lack of heating proved no problem. Michael found a job in Croydon, and, while driving around that area, we were both taken with the small village of South Nutfield, in which, to our delight, there just happened to be a property for sale. By September we were cosily ensconced therein.

After I left The Atlanteans, the changes effected by the remaining members of the hierarchy were radical (how frustrated they must have been by my presence among them, poor things). In my day all services were free – healing, psychic advice, etc. Many was the time when Gillian and I travelled some distance, at our own expense, to administer to either an ailing member or his/her family or friends. The only charge ever made in my day was £2 per annum for membership, which entitled one to the monthly magazine *The Atlantean* and the newsletter, *Atlanteanews*. All such practices were subsequently dropped and Mammon commenced to raise his ugly head at every corner. The 'message' also changed radically, from one of the old Atlantean idea of cosmic universality and the future role of this planet, to what I choose to term, albeit irreverently, 'Californian psychobabble', and the New Age preoccupation with the Self. Sadly, there are far too many so-termed 'seekers' who still believe that the only road to enlightenment is the 'searching within' when, for many of us, anyway, it is only by looking 'without' that one can fully comprehend one's true place in the Cosmic scheme of things, comparison always proving an adept tutor.

There was still one bitter knock awaiting me around the corner. When I left the Society quite a few members left with me, some of these remaining my friends to this day, although many have now passed over. Michael was insistent that I should carry on our 'work', so we set up a small group which would meet once a month at our home in Nutfield. Oh, had I heeded those warning bells! This group was to consist of the two of us, plus Patsy and Roy Claridge, Millicent Rosslair (former Cheltenham Branch members), and, on Michael's insistence, two younger people (he was obsessed about being so much younger than the rest of us), a male and a female – no names, no pack-drill. From the onset, and sensing certain metaphysical incompatibilities between these two and the rest of us, I was unhappy, to say the least. But when I approached Michael on the subject he accused me of being jealous of their youth, especially the girl, so I was forced to forego my initial judgement and see how things went. If I recall, we had only two sessions before the trouble arose. Around the time when the third session was due, I was told, through a third party, that the two younger members had decided to pull out due to problems that had arisen in their lives, which they were convinced were caused by me. But it didn't simply stop there. They also had a sitting with a medium who assured them that I had gone onto the 'dark path', and they were therefore advised to avoid me at all costs. To crown it all, they also consulted those who were now running The Atlanteans, who, although they have since protested to the contrary, certainly rendered an impression which served to confirm the fears of their enquirers at that time. Why does logic always fly out of the window when fear rears its ugly head? And to think that these people had worked closely with me for all those years – surely they knew me well enough to know that the last thing I would ever do would be to engage in any practice that was not of the Light? Had I not spent years teaching them this very thing? As I said, this was all denied at a later date, but at that time it really hurt.

I resolved that I would never again, for the rest of my life, and in any circumstances, ever work with a group of any kind. As I explained earlier, elemental energies can upset many people, especially those who are not ready for them. Also, it was interesting to note that neither Patsy, Roy nor Millie experienced any ill effects. In fact, quite the opposite, since they benefitted considerably from our work together. Patsy and Roy are among my dearest and closest friends to this day. (Millie, bless her, passed over in the course of old age a year or so ago). However, just in case my ego had got the better of me on this occasion, I did check with two eminent metaphysicists, and a well-known and highly respected medium of the time, all of whom were beyond reproach, who were more than happy to give me a clean bill of spiritual health. And during a subsequent conversation with the celebrated writer and occultist William Gray, he was quick to point out the amusing side to all this, wryly commenting, 'My dear, you haven't passed the first stage in your initiation until you have been labelled 'black'. Take it as a compliment, as it is, after all, simply a way of telling you that the protesters and their allies fall so far below your energy level as to find its elevated status uncomfortable!'

CHAPTER 18

All Change At This Station

Due partly to my work on PREDICTION, I started to find myself in demand for lectures all over London and it was also during this period that I experienced my initial encounter with the media. My first T.V. appearance, which was on the Derek Nimmo Show, was enough to put me off, although from an 'evidence' point of view I scored top marks. Among the viewers was Dr. Carl Sargent, a Cambridge parapsychologist who, under the auspices of the BBC, had devised a series of tests which were designed to either prove or disprove the psychic faculty. One of the things I was required to do was to describe the person depicted in a series of photographs concealed in blank envelopes which he handed to me one at a time, recording my comments on a specially prepared document. When the task was completed he told me he could not allow me full marks, as I had slipped up with one particular envelope, having 'seen' the head of a horse when what I should have seen was the figure of a young girl. Upon opening the envelope, however, there, sure enough, was the girl, but she had her arm around the neck of her much loved pony! My energies obviously responded more strongly to those of the pony than those of the girl. But, science being the exact study that it is, as a human figure was requested I had obviously failed. By the way, the other comment Dr. Sargent made was that although I was accurate as far as the other envelopes were concerned, I appeared to pick up their content before he actually handed them to me, to which phenomenon he ascribed the term 'precognitive telepathy'. But then, what do you expect from a Time deva?

While on the subject of Time, I was also featured in the BBC Programme 'Arrows of Time', along with Dr. Lyall Watson, among others, and therein lies another strange tale. Some weeks prior to the actual transmission, when being interviewed by Leslie Smith, I referred to a T.V. programme which featured Dr. Watson, in which he had made a certain statement. Unknown to me, the producers contacted Dr. Watson, only to discover that the programme I had described, which included the given statement, was not scheduled to be shown for several weeks. At no other time, and in no other programme, had Dr. Watson made any such statement. Smith asked him how he could account for my precognition (which I, in all honesty, had not given with prophecy in mind. I really believed I had seen the programme in question, but could not remember how or when. Perhaps I had dreamt it). Watson replied that if one is in this space-time, one can *remember* the future.

Interestingly enough, at the purely material level my preoccupation with Time has been an ongoing thing since childhood, as may be evidenced by the fact that I have been obsessed with the subject for as long as I can remember. In my early 20's, for example, I wrote several short stories with Time themes – 'The Time Camera', 'Out of Time', and 'And the Future Happened', some of which were subsequently published in the Atlantean magazine.

Following these episodes, work in this direction, both in and out of the media, came thick and fast: and the more I became involved in it, the more I realised just how much I hated it. I was required to produce 'evidence' for numerous scientists, some of whom, as a result, accepted the authenticity of the paranormal, while others simply found convenient excuses to dismiss it as superstitious nonsense. Even if one scientist was convinced, his methods were immediately questioned and one was required to perform the whole thing all over again for another set of 'experts'. But it was not only the scientists that one was up against, as we shall see.

To digress for one moment: one beautiful metaphysical experience I did have during my sojourn in South Nutfield was to hear the voice of the fabled *baen sidhe*. It was a bright moonlight night when I was suddenly awakened by the sound of a strange, unearthly singing. I crept from my bed to the back of the house, a window there affording me full sight of both our own garden and old Bill's next door, from which the sound was coming. I did not see her, but my heart sang with her, and I knew she had come to collect one of her own kind within the next three days, for such is the legend. Old Bill was a much-loved member of the village community, well known for his acts of kindness to all. A natural pagan, he used to make corn-dollies, into which he would infuse the energies of the corn essences. Three days later, he died.

Back to the mundane. Michael lived in constant fear that the young men he worked with might find out that this strange 'psychic' who appeared on their TV screens was his wife, and make life difficult for him as a result. And this was not the only problem that was destined to separate us once and for all. Those old Atlantean comments about babies had taken a strong hold of his consciousness, and he was constantly rubbing in the fact that the men he worked with all had slim young wives who gave them children, not barren old hags like me. (At the time of our marriage, he had stated categorically that he did not want children, under any conditions, and could not, in fact, stand them! But people change). Moreover, although his epilepsy had never returned, he was beginning to show signs of another, more worrying, health problem. In fact I was about to approach my G.P. on the subject when the matter was brought to a head by Michael himself claiming he had 'flu and a high temperature'. The doctor was summoned and what took place between the two men is best left unsaid, although the older man obviously discussed it with me later, thus affording me the opportunity to voice my own fears, which were based purely on day-to-day observation. However, as is usually the case, Fate once again took a hand in the proceedings, thus turning the page of the next chapter in my life.

As a result of my T.V. appearances I became inundated with requests for help of all kinds, while also finding myself a convenient 'Aunt Sally' for shies from a wide selection of deranged people. Although most of the letters I received were fairly straightforward, there were also the threats, some of which were illogical in the extreme. At Michael's insistence, I had taken on the PREDICTION column under the name of Athene Williams, Williams being a family name, and Athene, the Goddess of Wisdom. Our telephone number was ex-Directory, but unfortunately there was also a 'Miss Williams' living in the same street, who obviously felt no need for such a precaution. On one occasion a certain woman who was anxious to make contact with me rang her number. Without realising what she had done, Miss Williams inadvertently gave her ours. Disaster! I received a highly abusive telephone call from this stranger, accusing me of having stolen her husband, and telling me that her three burly sons would be coming round to sort me out, after which my face would be unrecognisable. Not having a clue as to what she was talking about, I assured her I had never met her husband, whoever he might be, whereupon she yelled down her receiver, 'He hasn't made love to me since he saw you on T.V., so this has got to be stopped once and for all.' Needless to say, I alerted the Police, but this was only one of many threats I received, not all of them from irate wives.

The next most popular 'abuse' came from Christian Fundamentalists, who accused me of witchcraft, and delighted in quoting the passage in the Bible which states 'thou shalt not suffer a witch to live'. They assured me they would catch me one dark night and 'carry out the Lord's Commands.' It got worse and worse, and I became more and more desperate. Where could I hide; to where could I escape from it all?

And then came the final straw. It was the summer of 1978, and I was engaged by Jo Logan, Editor of PREDICTION, to work on their stand at the Festival of Mind, Body and Spirit at Olympia. It so happened that Michael also had to go on a course that week (or so he said), so it appeared to work out conveniently for both of us. However, an unfortunate series of events took place, which, since I have assured my publishers that there would be no sleaze in this book, would be best omitted. Those among you who have travelled along this road will, no doubt, have recognised the sign-posts without my pointing them out. To cut a long story short, by the end of that week Michael and I had agreed a divorce, he having found a considerably younger and (by his standards) more presentable woman.

In one sense I was relieved. Michael was a very violent man, who had at times exercised his strength most painfully on my frame. In one instance I had to go to hospital to have the top of the middle finger of my left hand sewn on after he deliberately slammed my hand in a door. He also blacked both eyes, and, when the doctor in attendance asked what had happened, he told him I had fallen over the cat. My G.P. subsequently checked this out with the hospital in question, and noted that it had been recorded as an incidence of domestic violence. There were other instances, too. Remember the 'knight in shining armour' I referred to in an earlier chapter? Now meet yours truly, the convenient dragon! To be fair, even those among The Atlanteans who were not all that keen on me were sympathetic when it came to the subject of Michael. He seemed to have a lot of anger deep down in his psyche, which had to be vented on someone.

The only problem left facing me was to find somewhere to live where I could have my three adored cats, Horus, Isis and Nephthys. Although there were rentals available round and about the Redhill/Nutfield area, none of these would allow me to have my cats, so, as the divorce neared its vital stage, I became more and more anxious about where to go and what to do. It so happened that I had for some time been receiving correspondence from an older man in Canada, who, upon hearing of my predicament, offered me a good home over there if I would marry him. Never having met him, I was not in a position to make such a commitment, and so, as he lived in Victoria B.C., we arranged to meet half-way, in New York. Joyce, who lived not far from South Nutfield, talked me into going, and even drove me to the airport on that occasion. And so I met 'Robert' in New York.

He was a deal older than myself, and had been married before, but was long since divorced. He seemed kind and caring, and adopted a fatherly attitude towards me, which was just what I needed at that time. But once again I failed to apply my knowledge of psychology and to realise that a man who behaved thus would never permit his partner to have a mind, or even a thought, of her own. After we had spent some time travelling round together, he returned to U.K. with me for a few days only, at the end of which time I somehow found myself agreeing to marry him after my divorce had gone through, and to make my home in Canada.

However, the divorce situation took a sudden turn which required that I leave my home immediately if it was to be heard at the date arranged by our solicitors. Fortunately, my dear friends Patsy and Roy Claridge came to my aid yet again, offering to have me and the cats to stay with them until such time as I left for Canada. I was therefore obliged to pack my bags immediately and to dispose of what few possessions I had left that would not be needed in my new home. Only my precious books were left behind with Joyce – was that a premonition, or simply a coincidence? (No such thing as the latter). For those astrologers among my readers, on that very day an eclipse fell in exact opposition to my Sun. I stayed with the Claridges for a few weeks until all the paper-work had been completed, and they kindly agreed to look after my cats until I was settled in Canada, after which I would send for them.

On the 5th November 1978, I bade a fond farewell to a large crowd of my friends, several of whom were highly tearful. Only Roy seemed unperturbed by the situation and I later learned that he had assured those present, 'She'll be back, and sooner than you think!' How right he was.

I left Heathrow for Vancouver, where I changed flights for Victoria. For the first few weeks Robert was kind and caring. Although he lived in a scruffy little apartment, he had money in the bank, and had assured me that we would buy a house together, after which I could arrange with Patsy to have the cats sent over. But somehow all this never happened, and, as the weeks rolled by, the realisation suddenly dawned on me that it never would. Also, I had started to notice that Robert was showing certain recognisable symptoms, but lack of professional qualification in the relevant area prevented me from voicing my fears. By the end of January I was desperate. What the hell had I let myself in for? How could I have been so stupid, and, above all, how could I extract myself without either of us losing face? Once again, my own kind came to my help.

I received a 'phone call from Joyce – my darling Isis (Issy) was seriously ill – dying, in fact, and I was needed to be with her immediately. One good thing about Robert was his love of animals, his old dog, Sheba, being resident with us at the time. Upon hearing of Issy's distress he suggested that I go to her immediately. Having left almost everything to Michael, all my remaining worldly possessions (with the exception of my highly valued books) I had packed into two large and one medium-size suitcases. These, I told Robert, I would need to take with me because it would be extremely cold in the U.K. I booked the first available flight and he saw me off at the airport. As I waved goodbye, I knew I would never return. The date? February 5th 1979. Astrologers, please note.

Issy had indeed been very ill, but Joyce had (conveniently, perhaps?) somewhat exaggerated the seriousness of her malaise, and she was, happily, on the mend. I was met at Heathrow by Patsy's father, Ted Crabtree, Roy being away on business at the time. The moment my flight landed, the three cats all made for the front gate, where they waited patiently for Ted's Mercedes to pull up outside. Needless to say, they were overjoyed to see me, as were Patsy and her family. A few weeks later Robert came over to visit and it was then that Roy raised with him the subject of buying a property over here, since he was reluctant to commit himself to one in Canada. Now Roy is a consummate salesman, and in this instance he wasted no time in pointing out to Robert the advantages of owning property abroad, well out of sight of the Canadian tax man. A tour of the properties available proved a small, one-bedroomed flat in central Cheltenham to be an ideal choice. The previous owner having passed away, the executors, possibly anxious to close the case as soon as possible, were offering it for a mere £8,000. Robert immediately came up with the necessary, while I used the money I had received from my half of the property that I had jointly owned with Michael to furnish and completely refurbish the place.

Robert, however, did not take to England at all. In fact he hated it and could not wait to get back to Canada, although he did visit me from time to time. On some of these occasions he was quite pleasant, but as time went by I came to realise more and more that all was not right. In fact, following one particular disturbance which took place around 3 a.m., I became so frightened that I turned to my doctor for help, and, upon hearing my description of the symptoms, she became concerned for my safety. By this time Robert had started to show another side of his character. Once he realised I was slipping from his grasp, he started bombarding me with insulting missives full of untruths. The whole situation became so distressful that Roy arranged for me to consult a friend of his, a local solicitor, who, after hearing what my doctor had to say and taking all the facts into consideration, suggested that divorce proceedings be put into motion immediately. Strangely enough it was not until later that Robert's first wife, a dear soul who is now in her late seventies, was able to put us in the picture and enlighten us as to the facts. My doctor's advice had certainly been correct: there were lots more disquieting details, which, taking into account the fact that he is now a very old man, are best left unreported. He fought the divorce tooth and nail, but the nature of his letters, which by that time were quite wild, obviously had little effect on the British judiciary. The divorce went through, and once again I was free, among friends, and with a roof over my own head and those of my three darling cats.

The flat was eventually to prove a problem, in that Robert,

being unfamiliar with British law, had insisted that it be put in his name only. Of course, when he tried to enforce his sole right to the property, his appeal was thrown out of Court. The Judge decreed that in the event of the property being sold I was fully entitled to half of the proceeds, but since I was resident in this country, and had no other home, I could stay there for as long as necessity demanded. This naturally produced a tirade of abuse against British law, and endless insulting letters to me. The problem was eventually resolved when I met the man who was destined to become my next husband, but meantime quite a few events were taking place in my personal life which were serving to shepherd me along an entirely new path. However, in spite of all his failings, I do feel I owe Robert a debt of gratitude for providing me with a roof over my head, if nothing else, at a time when I badly needed one.

During the first year Robert and I were separated but still married, I took on a temp. job at Cavendish House until such time as I could find employment (which thankfully turned up) appropriate to my own qualifications. Ann Neate, who had been teaching singing at the Cheltenham Music Centre, was about to move out of the area, so, as the job was no longer a viable proposition for her, she recommended me to the Principal as a replacement, and, in the January of 1980, I started teaching there. In time my list of pupils grew, and I was fortunate in finding the services of an excellent accompanist, Mary McGregor, which facilitated my method of instruction considerably. I also took on a drama class of 7 to 10 year olds – with considerable success – pending the absence of their regular tutor due to a long period of hospitalisation. It was during this time that I first met Jed Collard, who was also attending the Centre, but we did no more than pass the time of day.

Although I had still not regained sufficient confidence to resume my career as a soloist, I had, on a recent occasion, given some professional help to the Cheltenham Opera Company, which resulted in my being engaged by them to produce their presentation of Mozart's *'Cosi fan Tutte'*. During the initial stages of this production I was destined to become re-acquainted with Jed Collard. At the time he was in the throes of a divorce, so I was careful to keep well out of the way. But, having done a lot of singing in the States, he was greatly interested in *'Cosi'*, and offered to work back-stage during the production, which ran for almost a week to packed houses.

Jed turned out to be quite an interesting character. After getting his Degree at The University of Maryland, he had joined the U.S. Foreign Service, in which he had served for some years in the capacity of Vice Consul in several countries. He later switched to the Civil Service, and, prior to coming to the U.K. to marry a woman he had met some time previously and who was by that time divorced, he had also embarked on a musical career. Jed had an excellent voice, of the big, loud variety, which, had he started a career in opera some years earlier, might have taken him a long way. A Sun Gemini with a Leo Moon, he was highly gregarious, and he and Roy seemed to hit it off, initially, anyway; in fact, they even started a business together. But the astute Roy, who was then Sales Director of an established Marine Engineering Company, fortunately discovered a clause in his contract which precluded him from taking on other directorships, so he was obliged to extricate himself posthaste, and, it so happened, in the nick of time.

Once Jed's divorce had gone through I started seeing him, at first on a friendly basis and then more personally. Together with Patsy and Roy we often made up a foursome, even going on holiday together. He was certainly an affable sort of chap, and could be good company. Although he had never really studied metaphysical matters, he did not reject them out of hand and his interest therein developed slowly as time went by. Prior to my forming a relationship with Jed, I had discovered The Lion People, but, as I feel these dear souls are deserving of a chapter to themselves, I shall skip that period and return to it in chapter 19.

By now my friend Joyce had taken over the 'Dreams' Column in PREDICTION, and had already produced a book on the subject that had really taken off. One day the publishers in question asked her if she knew anyone well-versed in the subject of Psychic Self-Defence and sufficiently erudite to write a book about it. As I had originally taught her this very subject, she had no hesitation in recommending me; and so I wrote my first professional book, which was quickly followed by a commission for a publication on the subject of Ancient Egyptian Magic. I had just completed this second book when Jed and I decided to become an 'item'. After my flat was finally sold, Jed and I bought a house together, and we were married shortly after.

Prior to my leaving for Canada I had done a lot of work with The Runes. In fact the American writer, Ralph Blum, had approached me for tuition in the subject and I had handed all my researches and papers over to him before crossing the 'pond' to marry Robert. As a result he had produced a book about Runes which became an all-time bestseller. Jed had come across this book, and, having learned of how I had resurrected the Runes from years of obscurity, suggested that I top Blum's book with my own in-depth knowledge of the subject. Anxious to avoid jumping on to someone else's bandwagon, I made an even better suggestion; 'Jed, why don't I design a divinatory system based on ancient Egyptian archetypes and their relevant energies?' He went for it. I produced the necessary data, Martin Jones tackled the art work, and together we managed to get printed and published the first decks of what came to be known as '*Cartouche*'. Anastasia Angelini, a friend of mine in the States, then suggested that I write to St. Martin's Press in New York (who had published 'The Book of Runes' for Blum), to see if they might also be interested in Cartouche. Being more familiar with U.S. business methods than me, Jed insisted on writing what he felt to be an appropriate letter to St. Martins Press, enclosing a sample deck. They loved it and decided to take over the whole project forthwith. In time their end-product, which consisted of a large deck of cards accompanied by a hard-back book (which I had hurriedly written for them), neatly packed in an appropriate box, was duly published, and Jed and I were invited to New York for the launching. That was in 1985. Since then, copies sold worldwide have topped the eight hundred thousand mark. Unfortunately I have not been the recipient of the royalties since 1991, having signed them over to Jed when he and I were divorced. Yet another example of my 'peace at any price' stance. But from the point of view of this narrative we are getting way ahead of our time, a lot having taken place in the years Jed and I were together. I shall pick up the threads of the tale after I have included one of my most important personal 'rediscoveries'; that of The Lion People, or Paschats, as they later became known.

CHAPTER 19

Enter The Lion People

The events which I am about to describe took place shortly after my brief sojourn in Canada, and when I had become settled in my small Cheltenham flat with my darling cats. I was in my early fifties at the time and had temporarily abandoned my singing career. I had not, as yet, discovered my somewhat dubious talent for writing and felt that I was in a sort of no-man's land. The old Atlantean bogey about a woman being useless if she was childless seemed to be haunting me and I was anxious to confront the problem. It happened that a friend of Patsy's had heard about a really good lady hypnotherapist. Perhaps if I could access either my own subconscious, or my devic self, I could check out whether I was still on my correct devic track. Besides, there was another reason for showing an interest in hypnotherapy. All my life I had been haunted by a strange memory of being among intelligent, lion-like creatures. At times when I was at my lowest ebb, I would suddenly find myself in the presence of such a being, and, as I imbibed its energies, a sense of calmness, peace and control would pervade my whole being. But who were they? That was a good question to put to our hypnotherapist.

During the sessions that I underwent I never once lost consciousness, although my awareness did shift to another level, at which the floodgates of memory were slowly and surely opened to me. The results tended to bewilder my therapist, the following being one example. As is usual in regression, after getting me to relax in her large, comfortable chair, she instructed me to go back, right back as far as I could go. She no doubt expected that I would end up either in the womb or in Nanny's arms following my mother's rejection. But nothing of the kind.

Before I proceed, I feel I should point out that the following is only a brief (recollected) résumé of the original, which, although it was taped and typed out at the time, was lost during a flood, when the box containing it was completely waterlogged and the contents ruined. The first question she put to me was, 'Where are you now?'. 'On a distant Sun', I replied. Somewhat perplexed, she asked me what I was doing there. 'Fusing hydrogen atoms to make helium', I replied. She asked me why. 'Because I am working with the fire elementals, and that's what we do', I replied. Rather than stay with that line of enquiry, which she obviously found disconcerting, she decided to bring me further forward in time. 'And where are you now?' 'In the ship, but we are in trouble. The time mechanisms have failed and we can't get back to our own planet.' 'You say, 'we': how many of you are there?' 'There are eight of us including the leonines, of which I am one.' Who are these beings?' 'We are the Lion People. Our home planet is in the double-star system of Sirius.' 'What do you look like?' 'We are very tall, and very, very strong. Although we now walk upright, we are not unlike your lions, in that we have manes, and within the races on our planet there are several colours of skin and mane.' 'And who are the other people with you?' 'They are hominids who come from the large planet that orbits the Blue Star. Our planet, which is much smaller, orbits the Yellow Star.' Having no recall at the time of the true title of these huge, gentle creatures, I created the name 'Paschat'; from an amalgam of the Egyptian goddess, Pasht, and the French 'chat', but have since discovered that they were known as Eyani (nearest spelling to the sonic) and their beautiful hominid companions were the Ishnaans (often referred to as The Crystal People, due to the specifically crystalline structure of their planet). The Eyani shared their original planet with the Na-as, or Plant People, while the Ishnaans co-existed amicably with the Olan, dolphin-like creatures who lived mainly in the water, but who could also negotiate land for short periods. However, the term 'Paschat' seemed to catch on, and those interested can read all about them in my books: *The Lion People* and *The Paschats and the Crystal People*.

From that moment on, those elusive doors of time were finally opened and I was able to recall in some detail the life I had been privileged to enjoy among these gentle giants. As the memories came streaming back, so a strong telepathic contact was forged with two of them in particular, Ka-ini and Mi-kili, a contact which has lasted to this day. But, you may rightly ask, where is the evidence for such a claim? Well, a few days after this session with Pamela, I received a visit from my friends Patsy, Roy and Millie. Hardly had we settled down in our chairs when I noticed that their eyes were focussed somewhere behind me. I asked what they were looking at. 'There is a Being standing behind you, oh so tall, like a lion standing upright. The energies he is emitting are SO beautiful, so filled with love and compassion'. Such were Patsy's words, which were quickly verified by the others. The Paschats had come to stay. I have often channelled them, although perhaps channelling is the wrong word, as I am able to access their data-banks at any time or place, without needing either to enter the silent, meditative mode or to relinquish full consciousness. I do not doubt that they have been the instruments via which H.A. has saved me on more than one occasion.

In the fullness of time, details of my own life as a Paschat came flooding back and I now have almost complete recall. Being so close to these dear beings, it is little wonder that I am so taken with felines of all kinds. I had noticed in the past that when visiting zoos and finding myself confronted by the lions, a strange feeling overcame me, to which the beasts in their cages also responded. The Eyani, or Paschats, started their evolutionary cycle in much the same way as earth hominids, eventually learning to walk upright and acquire some of the skills deemed exclusive to the people of Gaia's domains, plus many more to which the human race has not yet attained.

On one occasion, while taking a seminar in California, I was asked to demonstrate the effect of Paschat energies on wild animals, the lady in question being the owner of a private zoo. An experiment was therefore set up, before an audience, in which I would channel Ka-ini in the presence of one of her ocelots, a particularly aggressive male. I was to be seated in a forward position on the stage, with the ocelot behind me, chained to a large, throne-like chair, but with sufficient play on the chain to allow him to approach me without actually leaping on me. Immediately I made contact with the Paschats, the cat apparently sat bolt upright, making strange little sounds of obvious acknowledgement when Ka-ini addressed it, after which it slowly approached me and settled itself quietly by the side of my chair for the remainder of the connection. Once the link was terminated, however, it moved slowly back to its original position, uttering the usual growls, which signified that it had returned to its own, wild mode. I actually have a snap, taken at the time, of this beast seated on that very throne, but, sadly, it is insufficiently clear for inclusion in this book, although I would be happy to pass it around for scrutiny were I lecturing on this subject.

Paschat society was a very closely-knit one, which also serves to explain how strangely alone I sometimes feel on a planet where the closeness and loyalty of the kind we enjoyed as Paschats is almost unheard-of. They were also great family people, although their couplings, over the whole period of their lives, never produced more than two children, twins. (The same applied to their hominid neighbours, The Crystal People, but since I have covered such information in other publications, space does not permit me to indulge too deeply in this much-loved subject). Unlike the majority of hominids that inhabit the body of Danuih (Earth), the Paschats were a race of old souls, at the end of their physical evolutionary cycle. So, when the time finally came for them to become extinct, they were able to join with a particular group of Angels – the Seraphim – with whom they were destined jointly to carry out the task that had been set for them from 'On High', that of policing this universe and many others. More of that in Chapter 21, when I shall be introducing my readers to the Angelic System and how it works.

Since *The Lion People* was first launched, I have received letters from many countries confirming connections with Paschats, while a T.V. series featuring a Lion Man also reached popularity peak. To prove that I was not the first to recall details of the Paschat planet: an elderly lady with a doctorate in psychology assured me that she and a medical doctor with whom she used to meditate back in the forties, received similar information to mine, resulting in a flow of memories from their Siriun past, when she had been a 'plant-person' and he, a Paschat. Our comparison of notes proved to be highly evidential.

A book was published recently by a leading psychiatrist and his wife, which dealt with near-death-experiences. One thing which struck the writer strongly was the absence of animals from the descriptions given by those who had managed to cheat Hades temporarily of his dues. Surely at least some of these people must have had much-loved pets, in which case why were those dear animals not also there waiting for their loved ones to greet them? There is, of course, a simple answer. Those souls, or 'fields' as I prefer to call them, who have not as yet individuated from the hominid collective tend to see only their own kind when they pass over, because they are still imbued with hominid programming of the earthly variety. I have explained all this in my book *Cosmic Connections*. The cerebral programme with which the brain is imbued at the point of death is carried over by the field (soul/essence), and so, depending on the closeness of that soul/essence to the hominid collective-experience, so will those images appear again in the dimension immediately above the one in which we exist at present on this planet. Not belonging to this collective, when I finally shed this body I will eventually return to my own kind, where I will meet up with those Paschats who are also serving the Angelic Hosts. And of course, being once again in my own element, Time, I will also be reunited with Nanny, Win, and other dear friends – within their time frames – with whom I have effected deep bonds of love during my sojourn on the body of Danuih.

As time progresses, the peoples of Earth will become accustomed to meeting beings from other worlds, who, although they do not resemble them in appearance, are considerably more advanced both technologically and spiritually. In other words, they are older souls – their field bandwidths are considerably wider than those of the average hominid. Of course, not all those races that have achieved technological advancement are necessarily spiritually advanced, but then that is a lesson, and rather a hard one, I fear, that Earth hominids have yet to learn.

Among the cats which now grace my humble abode, some are older souls than others. For example, that beautiful essence who used to be Woodwee – the little black-and-white cat about whom H.A. commented in an earlier chapter concerning his highly evolved soul-status – has returned in a new body as Tami, to share my final years. She was my partner when we were Paschats, and when we finally vacate this area of the galaxy for the higher frequencies, we will once again assume our flights together through time. Devas often take on the bodies of animals for one reason or another, the main one being out of love and loyalty, as in the case of Woodwee/Tami and myself.

People often ask me to confirm whether or not they are an 'old soul'. Status being essentially a young soul (narrow field bandwidth) phenomenon, those requesting such reassurances are advertising blatantly the stage at which they really are. In the same way, people betray their former lives in their interests; those who belong to the 'Sealed Knot', for example, having obviously lived through the days of the Cavaliers. Or it could be old U.S. cars, Indian gurus, African dances, WW1 aeroplanes, Red Indian rites or, as in the case of Jean Playdon (see Chapter 8), cowboys in the early American pioneering days.

As far as my Paschats are concerned, psychologists would undoubtedly dub them 'compensatory', which is ironic, since the incident I related when as a small child I looked into Nanny's high mirror for the first time, occurred long before life had dealt me those bitter blows which could possibly justify such a comment. In fact, I was aware of both my spiritual ancestry and the existence of the Paschats long before I ever met Tony, although at the time I did not possess the terms of reference essential to the expression of such 'memories'. And it was not without reason, albeit intuitive on their part, that when I was in the WAAFS and the boys in the Signals Section gave all of us girls the names of animals, which they engraved on our drinking mugs, I was 'Moggy the Cat'; while the comment was often passed among them that if I ever give birth to anything it would have four legs and a tail!

Of course, to the average person, Paschats will be viewed in the 'alien' context and I am sometimes asked, 'Have you ever been abducted in a UFO?' Let me state categorically that as of the moment I am writing, I have never seen a UFO, let alone been abducted into one for experimental or other purposes. Such a situation, if it were ever to arise – and that is highly doubtful – could be likened to a burglar who is about to break into a house, suddenly seeing a police car coming straight towards him. And were such beings to have the temerity to approach me for cosmically illegal purposes, I would immediately switch to either my elemental or my Paschat status, which would probably frighten the life out of them and send them on their way with the proverbial flea in their ear. As I have said throughout this book, in matters relating to survival, or to interference with the 'work' which some of us have entered hominid bodies to undertake, we look after our own. After all, I am an alien myself!

The nearest I have ever got to being approached by a UFO occurred in a dream in which I had arranged a special meeting with a Paschat at a given place and time. After waiting around in the dark for what seemed to be an age, I thought to myself, 'What a load of self-delusion. No-one is coming, and no-one ever will'. And then, suddenly, I became aware of a presence behind me. Perhaps a UFO had landed after all. A voice spoke, clearly and precisely: 'Keep walking, and I shall always be behind you'. It was once again that special voice I had come to know as 'Father'. But as I looked ahead there was nothing substantial upon which to tread, only the blackness of Eternity. Tentatively I extended a foot into that emptiness, but before it reached the point of fall, a stepping-stone appeared immediately beneath it. Likewise with the next step, and so forth. And always there was this kind but stern voice, saying, 'I shall be behind you all the way, I shall be behind you all the way ...' I awoke repeating his words over and over again. At the time I did not fully understand their meaning. I do now. In renewing my contact with the planets, and the Universe in particular, the memories of my own cosmic roots have come flooding back. For many years I had known only the Sun and Danuih as my spiritual adopted parents, but, as is the case with many adoptees, I have always been fired by a burning desire to discover my real cosmic ancestry. Now I have.

To return to the Paschats. From the point of view of our present position in space-time, the Paschats (Eyani), the Crystal People (Ishnaans), and all those creatures that enjoyed life cycles in the Sirius system, have long since passed on. But since at least two of the races concerned have learned the art of moving through time, they are able to adopt the appearances they once had in their past and to project into our present without any problem. That is one of the perks of being able to negotiate the myriad levels and speeds of time.

As anyone who has read those of my books which cover the Paschat material will know, Paschats did land on this planet many centuries ago. Evidence for this is given in *The Sirius Connection*, in addition to those works which deal specifically with the Paschat phenomenon. According to Ancient Egyptian sources, they landed in southern Egypt; folk memories of their arrival, and striking appearance, featuring strongly in Egyptian iconography: several of the great Gods of Egypt are of decidedly Paschat appearance, notably Sekhmet, Bast, Tefnut, Maahes and Wadjet.

When it comes to extraterrestrials, why do we look to the skies for them, when the hominid soul (field) is itself alien to this planet? I repeat, Danuih's (Gaia's) *real* children are the plants, animals and elementals, whose good offices, plus those of their 'mother', came to make this planet what it is today – a suitable place for hominids to exist (until such time as they destroy it). The renowned astronomer, Heather Couper, completed her commentary at the London Planetarium with the words, 'We are all the children of the stars'. Some of the genetic material of which our bodies are composed was undoubtedly conveyed to the body of Danuih by what Professor Fred Hoyle has described as 'The Panspermia Theory', which conceives of alien micro-organisms, distributed throughout interstellar space, penetrating the Earth's atmosphere. Hoyle's answer, when questioned as to whether life originated on Earth, was a resounding 'No'! But this is only half of the story – genes have to be externally manipulated by higher intelligences before the required mutations can take place – as above, so below!

Why all aliens should be conceived of in the hominid form, albeit it with strange ears and bumps on their heads, has always puzzled me, since I have been around in both time and space sufficiently to know that intelligent life comes in all shapes, sizes and colours, depending on the conditions prevalent on the planets concerned. When considering the Earth hominid mode, it should be borne in mind that the human brain was designed to accommodate the whole cycle of hominid experience, each area being externally activated from a higher source at times of great change. After all, it was not so long ago that people were put in the stocks, or drowned in the millpond, for beliefs that are both commonly accepted and actually endorsed in this day and age. Virtual reality would have been dubbed 'witchcraft' in the reign of Elizabeth I, but today it is accepted as a fact, and an entertainment to boot. For Danuih and her inhabitants, time is gradually speeding up. It has to, in order to accommodate the next stage in the development of both the Planetary Genius herself and all those life forms that rely on her for physical sustenance and the spiritual evolvement experience. (I prefer the concept of 'field expansion', as the word 'spiritual' can tend to carry either 'holier-than-thou' or dogmatic religious connotations).

Germane to the 'alien' theme are, I feel, the many theories that have recently surfaced regarding the use of advanced mathematics among otherwise primitive peoples. To me, as a deva, mathematics encodes universal principles from advanced frequencies which can be translated, via left-brain logic, into a series of comprehensible equations. However, this process can easily be by-passed by the right brain, while the problem will eventually be resolved as new knowledge regarding the functions of hitherto unused areas of the human cerebral mechanisms slowly come into scientific focus, the recent discoveries concerning the striatum being one example. These, and other 'by-passes', were taught to the early Atlanteans by their Siriun contacts and practised to within years of the final inundation, after which such skills became lost in the obscurity of chaos. They re-surfaced more recently in discoveries relating to the proposed mathematical content of the Bible, and to pyramid geometry, Mayan prophecies and similar observations, which have been found to contain positive information of a prophetic nature, conveniently encoded in mathematical analogies. In his book, *From Atlantis to the Sphinx*, Colin Wilson renders a cogent explanation for such anomalies, but since this spans several chapters it would be impossible for me to condense it into a few sentences.

Those interested are therefore referred to the work in question.

An interesting corollary to the above, which could possibly be interpreted by some in the 'greys' context, is a dream I had in my thirties in which my Atlantean brother, Pera, cut open a portion of my skull and effected some insertion, change, or possibly 'release' therein. However, I felt no fear or discomfort, only the wonderful love that Pera and I have always sustained as cosmic brother and sister. In one particular meditation to music, I found myself out in deep space, but *very large*, so much so that the stars (suns) were mere stepping-stones, across which I walked with ease. From the distance I saw Pera approaching. He was also stepping lightly on each star. We ran towards each other, and the moment we met – well – there are no words to describe that moment of sheer ecstasy.

For the benefit of those readers who may not be familiar with the term 'greys', these are strange, extra-terrestrial androids who are believed to abduct humans for experimental purposes. People who claim to have undergone such experiences usually describe them as being grey in colour, with strange, black, slanted eyes. Amusingly, a friend of mine recently commented that the headlights on the front of my car (a Ford Puma) were exactly like those of the 'greys'! Well, what would you expect an E.T. to drive?

But to return once more to Earth and the dimension in which my present body is now encapsulated. The human brain has the inbuilt mechanisms for dealing with complex mathematics at a purely mental level, thus by-passing the need for lengthy equations. I know this is so because I have done it myself when working with Professor Peter Stewart.

For example, employing the visualisation method, I have been able to slow down the reaction which takes place when a positive particle is annihilated by its anti-particle, the annihilation process resulting in a discharge of energy in the form of a gamma ray. I have made similar observations in the field of quantum mechanics (at one end of the scale) and the physics of relativity (at the other). Time, as I have already explained, can be both telescoped and expanded, each 'band' being relative to the evolution and experience necessary to those life-forms encapsulated therein. The slower the time band, the heavier the matter/mass. Conversely the faster time moves, the lighter and more subtle the nature of those intelligences utilising those particular frequencies. Moving from band to band can, I assure my readers, be highly instructive.

The interaction between human and alien psychology is a fragile affair and consequently I exist in a sort of no-man's land, in that although I communicate with those involved in what is broadly termed the 'psychic scene', I do not necessarily qualify such experiences in the spiritual or supernatural category. Equally, although I accept the logic of science, I am all too aware that in our present time its 'discoveries' represent only a minuscule part of the true cosmic picture. Although I have been broadly labelled a 'psychic', I do not 'see' or 'hear', in the strict understanding of these words. I am simply 'aware', and that awareness incorporates not only my visions of events past and future, but also the feeling of alienation that I experience in a hominid body – the agony, joy and pain, but mostly the sense of being lost. However, in spite of all this, I am grateful for the presence of my beloved cats, and of those dear friends who have understood and accepted me for what I really am.

Which brings me round full circle to the Paschats, who, along with their Ishnaan friends, managed to crack the time code at a purely mechanical level during that period of our planet's history labelled 'Jurassic'. This enabled them to pass through certain time-bands in true Star-Trek fashion, although I feel it essential to point out at this juncture that *there are bands of time, the frequencies of which are so fast, so subtle, that no mass/matter could possibly exist within them.* These are the spheres of the Higher Angels, and of those fields (souls) who have long since left the worlds of base matter far behind. But remember – finer frequencies can always penetrate those that are denser, even though such excursions may cause them some discomfort, whereas denser frequencies are limited to their own time-bands, and those immediately below them.

CHAPTER 20

Doubts, Dreams And Disillusionment

Here we go, back to Earth with a bump, and down to the nitty-gritty of living on a small and somewhat chaotic planet. But life must go on, and so must my narrative. Let us therefore take a journey into the more recent past and see how things developed in the mundane life of Murry Hope.

Life with Jed was entirely different from anything I had ever experienced with my previous partners. Mind you, my astrologer friends were quick to point out that the combination of an energetic, extroverted and restless Gemini and a serious, introverted, stay-at-home Virgo, no matter how brightly it might glow to start with, would inevitably burn out. And that is exactly what happened, but not until the effect of Jed's natal Sun, conjunct my Jupiter in Gemini, had served its starry purpose. However, the 'bright glow' bit certainly worked for several years, until yours truly started to feel the strain, plus the need to withdraw for a change.

One interesting thing about all my ex-husbands is that, in all honesty, I never really trusted any of them. But I did learn from them, and the experiences I underwent with them were undoubtedly valuable to me, in that they added to the data-banks of my kind thus helping to build a more comprehensive picture of the framework of hominid psychology. As I have explained previously, I always saw the end of a liaison well in advance, and usually before I had actually decided to embark on it. These remarks apply to Jed in particular, as I noted, even before I married him, that there were certain inconsistencies in the relationship that would inevitably lead to separation. And yet I was also very aware that, with his help, I had some important work to do which I could not carry out alone.

It was during the early days of our marriage that those who had taken over The Atlanteans when I left decided they would like to forego the Atlantean tag once and for all and to rename their organisation The Pegasus Trust. They therefore requested my assistance to close down the Old Atlantean Ray and to initiate them into the new one, which is what we occultists would describe as the Greek Ray. For this purpose, and so that a whole group of their members could join in the process, I wrote a psychodrama entitled *The Birth of Pegasus*, which was duly performed and greatly enjoyed by all present. Prior to this point in the proceedings, I was allowed to sit alone in a small room so that I could take the action necessary for the closing down of the Atlantean connection. While I was doing just this, H.A. came to me very strongly, saying, 'My dear child, you have now disconnected my old Ray from the group in question and supplanted it with a Greek-type energy. But what are you going to do about the Ray you are now holding?' 'And what would you have me do with it, Father?', I asked. 'Will you keep it for me, as it is imperative that it is not withdrawn from the planet at this crucial stage in the evolutionary pattern of Danuih (Gaia) herself, and of all life forms extant on her body.' 'If that is what you wish, Father, then it shall be done.' 'Thank you, my child. However, I must give you a warning: carrying this Ray will prove a tiresome burden to you, especially in the years lying directly ahead. Do you feel you can cope with such a daunting mission?' 'Do I have any choice in the matter?' I questioned. 'Not really,' he replied, 'Since that was one of the tasks you came here to do.' And that is how I became Custodian of The Atlantean Ray, in the country where it was originally 'hidden' by the last Arcanophus, just prior to the Old Country's submergence beneath Poseidon's mighty waves.

In addition to shepherding me into mainstream writing, Jed also encouraged me to take up my singing again, coaching with the eminent musician Dr. Herbert Sumsion helping to give me sufficient confidence to appear once again as a soloist. Jed and I together made two appearances at the Cheltenham Music Festival, the first being a Lieder recital and the second a Baroque Concert with orchestra. In addition to undertaking the bass solos in Handel's 'Messiah', he also appeared with the Highnam Opera Group, while I enjoyed the odd local church job.

On the writing side I received two more commissions from Thorsons/HarperCollins, one of which I was able to complete while we were still living in Cheltenham, and the other once we had moved to Devon in the December of 1985. The property we had bought in the West Country was a former farmhouse surrounded by a large plot of land, the previous owners of which were obviously used to a much rougher life-style. We spent a fortune on central heating, double glazing, cavity wall insulation, the installation of a modern en-suite bathroom, new kitchen and many other up-dating innovations. By the time we had it all finished it looked really good. The trouble was, however, that we had run out of money, while also discovering, to our cost, that none of the locals wanted anything to do with us. And by that time Jed had become bored with the whole situation and longed to return once again to the bright lights of the east. The good thing that did come out of the Devon episode was that living in isolation (a mile from the nearest neighbour), and with Jed's help, I was able to produce several more books.

It was while we were living in the Devon area that Jed persuaded me to apply for a place at Exeter University to read psychology. After completing the necessary application forms, an interview was arranged with the head of the psychology department. Having made mention in my application that I had already written books on the subject, copies of these were sent in advance, their contents possibly giving the staff some idea as to who and what they were dealing with. My interviewer turned out to be both charming and sympathetic. He could certainly find me a place for the following year, but, since the first two years of the course were taken up mainly with statistics and one did not progress to the sort of material I had been writing about until later, he felt my best line of action would be to do a year at a U.S. University, where I could get through the degree course quickly, my books *The Psychology of Healing* and *The Psychology of Ritual*, constituting doctoral thesis material in themselves. He was quite right, of course, while his 'let-out' was a boost to the jolly old ego, if nothing else. But the prospect of a year in the States away from my darling cats did not bear thinking about.

We eventually managed to find a buyer for our farmhouse and moved yet again, this time to the Bognor Regis area, at the request of Betty Hope, an elderly lady and former member of The Atlanteans, who felt that she was definitely a distant cousin of my late father, her family having hailed from the same town as my paternal grandfather. Even the photographs she showed us emphasised the likeness between her family and that of my father and his father. After taking on a short rental we found a spacious bungalow in a place called Rose Green, and once again the commissions poured in, so I was kept very busy indeed. When I first started writing, Jed would help me with the computer work, but after a while he taught me how to use it for myself. Mind you, to this day there are still complicated commands that I would never risk using, for fear of obliterating all! That dear old piece of equipment which was born in 1978 (purchased by Jed second-hand), and to which I have given the name 'Beryl', is being typed on as I write. And her 'accompanist', my printer, 'Eileen', will run it all off for me, as she has done for the past fourteen years.

Writing was not the only activity in which I engaged over this period. A visit to Australia, under the auspices of Angus and Robertson, to promote *The Way of Cartouche*, proved both interesting and rewarding. This involved several T.V. appearances and radio interviews, and the P.A. allotted to me was more than helpful. While in Sydney I was greeted warmly by my step-sisters, Freda and Wendy, Freda having made the journey from Cairns specially for the occasion. From Sydney I was flown to Perth to repeat the promotion routine for West Coast viewers. Aside from my home here in England, the only place abroad I have ever liked was Australia. But perhaps that was because everyone I met was friendly and helpful, while all the T.V. programmes I watched in my hotel room were British – the Two Ronnies, Inspector Morse, etc. Home from home, in fact.

During the preceding years, I had been privileged to effect a congenial correspondence with the eminent American psychologist/metaphysicist and author, Nancy B. Watson, who was resident in a suburb of San Francisco. Nancy suggested that I visit California and effected a connection for me with a prestigious group in that area, for which I undertook two seminars in consecutive years, plus supporting media work. It was during the latter of the two that the ocelot experience, as described in Chapter 19, took place. These were quickly followed by further introductions and subsequent bookings for lectures and seminars on the subject-matter of my various books. Meeting Nancy in person, and staying as a guest at her home, proved an enlightening and stimulating experience and we have remained good friends to this day. It was during my last Californian visit, in 1988 if I remember rightly, that I founded the Institute for the Study and Development of Transpersonal Sensitivity. Although on my return to this country I continued to teach along those lines, I eventually handed the whole project over to a psychologist I had met over there who had become particularly interested in my paraphysical approach, the strain of working with groups once again proving all too much for me.

But it was not only abroad that I was in demand. Lectures, seminars and consultations came my way, especially in the North of England, where I regularly attended the large gatherings at the 'Happiness Symposia'. This was fine while I had Jed to drive me around, but, to be honest, left to my own devices I would never have gone anywhere.

The use of my extra-sensory faculty was, of course, not limited entirely to writing, although I have always 'heard' what I have to write. One interesting story thus related occurred more recently, when I was required to produce some scientific material, but found myself sadly lacking the correct terminology critical to its succinct expression. I clearly heard a man's voice dictating the facts to me, which was all well and good until he gave me one word, the meaning of which was lost to me. 'I must look this one up in the dictionary', I told my helper, which seemed to annoy him. 'Can't you take my word for it?' he rejoined, somewhat impatiently. 'It's not that I doubt your word, but if I am ever asked for an explanation once the book has been printed, I would look pretty stupid if I fell down on this one.' There was a slight pause, as though, had he been in a physical body, said gentleman would have scratched his chin. 'Fair enough. But hurry up, and let's get on with it.' Being aware of the name of the scientist with whom I was dealing, I mentioned the matter to Professor Peter Stewart, describing the kind of personality traits my helper was showing, which he had probably carried through from his last life. 'Did you ever know a scientist named Haldane?' I asked Peter. 'Know him, I actually worked with him. An irascible old so-and-so if ever there was one.' It seemed I had described the late Professor John Haldane to a 'T'.

By now, as many of my readers will have guessed, the rift between Jed and me was widening. I could no longer keep up with his pace and, to be fair, I was, to an extent, holding him back. But the main problem between us was always money, and, try as I may, I was never quite able to come up with the goods. But then Jed always had been both money and 'big-time' orientated, whereas I am more interested in the security of a quiet and peaceful home life. Besides, there were other levels at which we did not gel, his libido often proving a stumbling block in our relationship. I have always been obliged to accommodate my husbands, until the very act of playing such a rôle for an extended period started to affect my health. So I cannot lay all the blame for our break-up on Jed's doorstep.

Being under the mistaken impression that he had potential as a businessman, Jed tried all sorts of different enterprises, each of which folded, leaving debts in its wake. In the May of 1990 we were obliged to sell our bungalow and go back into rented property. Around the same time, Jed was having some medical problems which necessitated surgery, as a result of which he went into a private hospital to have the matter attended to (his U.S. insurance covered private treatment). It was around then that our marriage slowly ground to a halt. Jed was missing his U.S. lifestyle, I was feeling trapped, and the two of us were rapidly getting on each other's nerves. Once again foregoing the sleaze, our divorce went through on incompatibility grounds. But in order to facilitate matters, and as he had done so much to get the project off the ground, on the advice of my solicitor I decided to let him take over my Cartouche royalties, little realising at the time that the production of said package would go on for so long, and attain such phenomenal sales figures.

He took off early in the first week of April 1991. I was left in the rented property with my five cats, a pile of debts, and little or no income with which to meet the rent, and I went down with the old renal problem. Fortunately, I received financial help with the debts from two charities, plus loans from friends, which enabled me to avoid bankruptcy. However, I was soon faced with another move, my landlady and her husband having found a buyer for their property. Being decent folk, they went to the trouble of finding me a replacement home, a small lodge in a village called East Lavant, on the outskirts of Chichester.

End of that saga. But hardly the end of my tale or of my experiences in the world of the paranormal. Apart from the methods of 'communication' already discussed, there are other ways in which the prescient faculty can be exercised: dreams, for example – I have received an enormous amount of information while in the sleep state. But, you may ask, how can one distinguish between those dreams that have psychological rather than mystical relevance or esoteric content? As this is such a personal matter, each one of us must obviously define our own criteria when effecting judgements on the issue of out-of-the-body dream phenomena. In my own case I usually wake up 'knowing', experience having taught me that if one's communicators wish one to remember the message encapsulated within the dream sequence, or one has witnessed some event, or received some warning of great importance, this will always occur just prior to waking. My cats, being all too familiar with this rule (and much to my annoyance at times!), will often wake me when I am experiencing what the hominid side of my nature might consider to be a good time, whereas they are always silent in the event of my receiving a message of some import which needs to be surfaced from the unconscious. May I therefore bore my readers with a few instances of prophecy via the agency of dreams on the one hand, while also illustrating the powerful influence exerted by the soul (field) via the unconscious on the other.

I often shape-shift in my dreams, usually to the elemental or feline modes. In one instance I found myself walking down a narrow lane, at the end of which I knew there was an enemy waiting to attack me. Shape-shifting into a massive tiger, I trekked across a piece of grassland and crept up behind her, uttering a mighty roar, whereupon she took off, frightened out of her wits. A few days later I overheard this (real life) enemy telling some friends about her 'terrible nightmare', in which a huge tiger had crept up behind her. One of her audience enquired as to whether the beast had actually hurt her in any way. She replied in the negative, but assured her questioner that it had nevertheless scared the daylights out of her.

Over the years I have often seen fit to criticise the abominable behaviour of that savant of evil, the late Aleister Crowley. He must have been waiting to even the score, as in the next dream he had me prisoner in such a way that I was unable to move. I tried calling on every Being of Light I could think of, but to no avail. Obviously enjoying his moment of power, he told me, 'Don't waste your time with your stupid prayers. I am far more powerful than you, and intend to have my will with you before I finish you off for good.' Searching desperately for a solution, I suddenly came up with an idea. 'You are supposed to be an occultist who obeys The Law, be it for darkness or Light, right?' 'Correct', he answered. 'Then will you obey that Law which allows a condemned person to offer a final appropriate supplication to the god or goddess of his/her choice?' 'If it amuses you', he replied. 'But hurry up, as I am anxious to be about your destruction.' I knew that were I to call the wrong name I would be damned forever, so it was essential that I make the correct decision. Taking a deep breath, I shouted,'Artemis', with all my might. Suddenly there was a rush of wind, and She appeared in her full hunting gear, surrounding by her pack, which immediately fell upon him, whereupon I woke up, free, and back in The Light. To this day I have always had a deep love and respect for that Archetypal Being who manifested to the Greeks as The Patroness of Cats, while one is also reminded of the myth of Actaeon on the one hand, and the fact that Artemis was also revered as the Protectress of Women on the other. I have never since had a squeak from the Crowley direction.

The next dream concerns my cat, Athene, who passed away following a heart attack. I was with Michael at the time and we were both convinced that she would reincarnate and find her way back to us. Then one night I had this dream: it was morning and I had gone down to open the post. Among the letters was a leaflet from the Governing Council of the Cat Fancy, to whom I had written to find out if there were any local Siamese breeders they could recommend. Upon looking down their list I noticed one that was underlined in red, but it was in Wales. As is usual in dreams, I then found myself in the house of a Welsh lady who was showing me a litter of apricot-coloured kittens, one of which came towards me and, addressing me in perfect English, said, 'My name is John, but you can call me Horus – I have been waiting for you to come.' But immediately I showed an interest, the lady told me I could not have that one, although she would not say why. And then I woke up. Sure enough, in the morning post, there was a communication from the Governing Council of the Cat Fancy, with the name of a recommended breeder underlined in red.

At that time I was working as a temp on my friend Val's switchboard in London. Upon arriving at the office that morning, I told her about my dream and the subsequent arrival of the post. Val suggested that we ring the breeder: the 'phone was answered by a lady with the lilting accent of the Welsh. 'I understand that you have some Siamese kittens for sale?' 'No, not Siamese dear, my kittens are red Burmese.' 'What exactly is a red Burmese like?' I asked. 'A sort of apricot colour, very pretty', she replied. I was interested, and Val, who was listening in, was sitting there with a broad grin on her face and her fingers tightly crossed for me. 'I have only two left now', continued the woman, 'one is already spoken for, while the other is ear-marked'. My initial reaction was one of disappointment, but I was determined not to give up at this point. I asked what she meant by 'ear-marked'. 'He has a little mark on his ear which tells me there is someone special he has to go to.' I asked when he had been born. The date of his birth in February just happened to fall exactly on my Aquarian ascendant, which I hastened to tell the lady at the other end of the line. 'Are you an astrologer by any chance?' she asked. 'Yes, I am,' I replied: and so, apparently, was she. From that moment I knew I had contacted a kindred soul. Our conversation ended with the lady, whose name was Avril, saying that the kitten was obviously earmarked for me. And so a small red Burmese kitten, to whom we eventually gave the full name of Horus J.(for John) Mancat, (he was so butch!), came into our lives. On entering the house for the first time, he went straight through to where the food bowls were kept, and then round the corner to the litter tray, just as Athene had always done. He stayed with me for fourteen wonderful years.

My final dream tale concerns a young woman in distress. In this dream sequence I found myself standing in a small bed-sitter-type room, which I judged to be somewhere in the Streatham area of London. Seated on the bed was a girl of about eighteen, with a bottle of sleeping tablets in her hand which she was about to take. Searching her mind for the reason, I realised that she thought she was pregnant, which in those days (1950's) was anything but an ideal situation for a teenager to find herself in. As I looked into her body I realised that she was not actually pregnant at all, but how could I tell her? Many are the times when, in sleep state, I have endeavoured to attract the attention of some person in danger, but without success, my etheric hand usually passing straight through their frame as I have tried hard to tap them on the shoulder or make a similar gesture of warning. This time I knew I had to take an alternative action, so, just as she had lifted the glass of water and was about to shake the tablets on to her hand, I switched to my elemental energies and created a vortex of energy which I directed at her hand, knocking it sideways and causing her to drop both the water and the tablets all over the floor. In sheer desperation she cried out, 'I can't even do this right', and promptly collapsed into a flood of tears, hiding her face in the bedclothes, whereupon I drew her spirit away from its shell and she promptly fell into a deep sleep. I knew that when she awoke the next morning her period would have started and her problem would be over.

Now here is the corollary. A few years later, when I was living at Mulwarrie House with the old Atlantean gang, I met a girl at an audition whom I felt sure I knew from the past. Although at the subconscious level the recognition was mutual, Ellen (shall we call her) could not place me. Later we had a coffee together, as was the usual custom when one failed an audition, and I congratulated her on her excellent singing voice. 'It wasn't always like that', she told me. 'In fact, a few years ago I almost took my own life. I had been with this boy, and when my period didn't come I thought I was pregnant. My father would never have had me home in that state, so I got hold of these tablets from a friend and decided to do the deed. But when I sat down to take them everything went wrong. I think that room must have been haunted, because something definitely knocked my hand and caused me to drop the lot, tablets, water and all. All I remember after that was feeling suddenly very tired, and falling asleep. And when I woke up the next morning my period had started. 'Well', I told her, 'That is all in the past now. Good luck with your next audition'. Of course, I had recognised her straight away, but the confirmation had to come from her.

CHAPTER 21

The Kingdom Of Elements, Devas And Angels

Let us take a temporary break from the mundanities and woes of your author's life and direct our attention to more pleasant areas of enquiry, which are nevertheless germane to her devic origins. At the commencement of this book I touched briefly on the evolution of the devic kingdoms and the fact that, contrary to what certain religions would have us believe, angels did not commence their evolutionary cycle as 'perfect beings': nothing ever does. The difference between the hominid experience and the world of devas is quite simple – they are totally different species; alien perhaps, but not in the 'planetary visitors from outer space' sense.

I also feel it important at this point that we sort out our semantics, there being some confusion of terms where elementals and *elementary spirits* are concerned. In my terms of reference, an elementary spirit is a lesser evolved entity (miniature field), probably from the sphere of pre-human existence or some time-frequency that has not yet offered it the opportunity for experience in the worlds of matter. I realise that some occultists employ this term when describing thought-forms generated by their use of magical invocations plus will, but I am not, nor ever have been, included in this category. In my understanding (and the light of my personal experience, of course), *elementals* are the spirits of the four accepted elements, plus Time. Tradition ascribes specific qualities to each element. The Salamanders (fire) are associated with creativity, ardour, raw energy, valour and loyalty; the Sylphs with intellectuality, speed, communication, detachment and inventiveness; the Ondines with emotions, feelings, receptivity, understanding and sympathy; and the Gnomes with thrift, acquisition, wealth in all forms, conservation and practicality. Likewise with music and medicine, where Fire is the stimulant, Air the tonic, Water the narcotic and Earth the sedative. The four 'humours' or psychological types, as outlined by Hippocrates, are also associated with the elements thus: fire – the sanguine, air – the bilious, water – the phlegmatic, earth – the melancholic. Even the scriptures align them with the four great Archangels and their respective beasts: Michael – fire (symbol, the lion), Raphael – air (symbol, the eagle), Gabriel – water (symbol, Man) and Uriel – earth (symbol, bull). So while the priest in his church may invoke in his litanies the assistance of Michael the Archangel, the occultist may be busy with his/her Rite to Gabriel, Uriel or Raphael. Where's the difference?

Each Elemental Kingdom has also been accorded a ruler – Djinn being 'King' of the Salamanders, Paralda – 'Queen' of the Sylphs, Necksa – 'Queen' of the Ondines and Gob – 'King' of the Gnomes. These names and titles are, of course, purely arbitrary; tradition is simply telling us that all those beings who inhabit these 'Kingdoms' are subject to strict sets of rules, which have to be adhered to by each entity if it is to proceed along its correct evolutionary path.

Having acquainted my readers with the Elemental Kingdoms, where does the term 'deva' enter all this? The term 'deva' (Persian *div*, Latin, *divus*), comes from the Sanskrit and should not be confused with the Persian *Daeva* – an evil spirit. Devas featured strongly in the Hindu religion, certain benign deities, notably Indra, being counted among their kind. In recent times, however, it has become commonly used in describing elementals or faery folk generally. Regarding its use in Theosophy, in his *Encyclopaedia of Occultism*, the late Lewis Spence defines it thus:

'Devas constitute one of the ranks of orders of spirits who compose the hierarchy which rules the universe under the Deity. Their numbers are vast, and their functions are not all known to mankind, though generally these functions may be said to be connected with the evolution of systems of life. Of Devas there are three kinds – Bodiless Devas, Form Devas and Passion Devas. Bodiless Devas belong to the higher mental world; their bodies are composed of Mental Elemental Essence, and they belong to the first Elemental Kingdom. Form Devas belong to the lower mental world, and while their bodies are composed also of Mental Elemental Essence, they belong to the second Elemental Kingdom. Passion Devas belong to the astral world, and their bodies are composed of Astral Elemental Essence. Devas are creatures superlatively glorious, of vast knowledge and power, calm yet irresistible, and in appearance altogether magnificent.' *(Page 122 in the above-mentioned publication.)*

While I cannot, in conscience, go along with the latter superlatives, the whole concept does seem to tie in with both Christian and pre-Christian concepts of angelic beings. But taking all this into consideration, why have I seen fit to place myself in the devic category, rather than staying with the 'elemental' tag? There are two main reasons: the first being that the term 'elemental' itself, having magical-cum-occult associations, could render a false impression of the way I function, and, secondly, because the term 'deva' has been applied to me by those in the know, and I was actually introduced as such at a recent seminar that I gave at the Theosophical Society's headquarters in London.

I owe my first knowledge of what are known as 'Angelic Choirs' to my childhood indoctrination into Roman Catholicism, the basic catechism teaching being that there are nine choirs of angels: Seraphim, Cherubim and Thrones, Dominations, Principalities and Powers, Virtues, Archangels and Angels; each having specific duties in the heavenly (or otherwise) scheme of things. This dogma was based on the writing of St. Thomas Aquinas (c1225-1274), who thus earned himself the title 'The Seraphic Doctor', and who was also, albeit on the quiet, an occultist of some distinction, his tutor being the great occultist Albertus Magnus. In fact I spent a deal of time studying his life and came up with some highly interesting observations, which I presented in lecture form. In addition to information supplied by Magnus, when it came to the study of angelology, both men probably owed much to the writings of Dionysus the Areopagite – sometimes known as St. Denis – who lived in the sixth century and was deeply influenced by the Neoplatonic philosopher Proclus (c411-485).

Like Proclus, he sought to combine Neoplatonism with Christianity. Dionysus produced four books on the subject of angels: *The Celestial Hierarchies, Ecclesiastical Hierarchy, Divine Names* and *Mystical Theology*. The angelic theme was taken up later by Hildegard of Bingen (1098-1179), a renowned mystic of her time who was also a skilled writer, poet and musician.

However, angels are by no means the sole property of Catholicism, the scriptural tradition of pre-Christian Judaism featuring as many, if not more. In his *Dictionary of Angels* (Free Press, New York 1967), Gustav Davidson offers a comprehensive list of angelic nomenclatures, accompanied by descriptions of the specific areas of influence designated to each. The Hebrew for 'angel' is *malak*, while it is actually the Greek *angelos* from which the term *angel* appears to have originated. During certain periods of history, angelology became a serious ecclesiastical and mystical study. In his classic, *The Occult Sciences*, the eminent Victorian scholar A.E. Waite tells us that in general literature, perhaps the most curious work along these lines is Heywood's *Hierarchy of the Blessed Angels*, which he describes as 'a storehouse of curious research', while other writings he recommends on the subject are *De Apparitionibus Omnis Generis Spirituum* by the Jesuit Peter Thyraeus (c1600), *Pneumatologia; or a discourse of Angels, their nature and Office or Ministry* (anon. 1701). Moving into our own times, one of the best books on the subject available at the moment is undoubtedly *The Physics of Angels (Exploring the Realm where Science and Spirit Meet)* by Dr. Rupert Sheldrake and Matthew Fox, in which the former describes the Field Theory, as applied to angelic beings, in a way that I could not hope to better.

Germane to this theme is, of course, the fact that all elementals commence their evolutionary cycles as minute particles, which is why I, as a Time deva, find it easy to relate to both particle physics and general theory of relativity. I have often insisted that the birth of this universe commenced with a single, specifically-charged, cone-shaped particle, programmed by Time to kick-start its strident nativity. Needless to say, such a proclamation was received with polite disdain by those qualified to comment via their appropriate disciplines. However, the tide has now turned in my favour. In an article featured in the *Weekend Telegraph*, March 14,1998, Professor Neil Turok explains Professor Stephen Hawking's new theory regarding the birth of our universe. In simple terms, the Singularity (Big Bang) was initiated by a single particle which Hawking has called as 'instanton'. I hand over to Turok:

'You can think of space and time as constituting the surface of a cone. The cone is placed vertically with its sharp tip down. Time runs up the cone; space runs around it. Time and space end at the sharp tip.

... Think of inflation as being the dynamite that produced the Big Bang. Our instanton is a sort of self-lighting fuse that ignites inflation. To have our instanton, you have to have gravity, matter, space and time. Take any one ingredient away, and the instanton doesn't exist. But if you have an instanton, it will instantly turn into an inflating infinite universe.'

Well, well, here we have all the elements present, *including time*. So why did I choose to subsume this interesting and highly instructive piece of scientific discovery in a chapter about angels? Because such beings were the intelligences behind the creation and programming of that instanton. Consciousness inevitably preceding matter, the quality and purpose of any new universe is designated by those angelic forces responsible for its genesis. As I demonstrated in a little experiment I carried out for Professor Peter Stewart, movements from one frequency to another are always negotiated via a vortex (cone), and the birth of a universe is no exception to the rule. The manifestation of mass, as in the birth of a universe, has ever been contingent upon space-time co-ordinates requisite to the purpose/function of the creation in the process of formation. Hawking's single instanton would therefore have contained the blueprint of, and the entire programme for, every species destined to experience within our universe.

Well, so much for the academic side. My own approach is from a very different angle. As I said earlier in this chapter, angels, contrary to Christian tradition, are certainly not born perfect; far from it, in fact, and, as I hope to illustrate, they have, and always will have, free will. Like everything else in this and every other universe, they commenced their life-cycles as what I would describe as miniature fields of energy which, as they expand and accrete, slowly acquire knowledge which in turn results in further field expansion. To put it into simple terms, their evolutionary journey commences as a minute, elemental particle – Fire, Air, Water, Earth or Time. Take my own case, for example. I know I existed as a neutrino, but that is only one 'tag' that happens to be appropriate at the moment. Scientists working in the field of quantum mechanics continue to find smaller and even smaller particles as their researches progress. As each elemental field (spirit, if you prefer) evolves, so it becomes aware of, and therefore imbibes, the energies of the other four. The process works as follows: a single Time elemental will first of all be drawn to the nature of Fire, since the compatibility between Salamanders and Time beings is very strong. These two elements are not usually comfortable with Earth or Water, so those are likely to be the last two elements to which they attain before they become five-fold or, in other words, a junior angel.

One of the interesting facts about the Aquinas angelic divisions is that the Seraphim, Virtues and Powers are believed to be of a fiery nature; the Thrones and Archangels – Aquatic; the Dominations and Principalities – Aerial; and the Cherubim – Earthy. (In Ezekiel, Satan is described as a Cherubim). In other words, we are back full-circle to our four elements, to which I have now added number five, which is Time. But why should this 'new' element suddenly appear on the scene? It is because Earth hominids are on the verge of recognising, coming to understand, and eventually learning to manipulate, that final Element – Time which in devic terms means that the Higher Powers are ready to pilot the human race into its next evolutionary cycle. Anyway, the concept of five elements is hardly new. In certain Eastern countries, for example, the fifth element is known as Aether (or Ether), while the belief in a five-fold power as far back as the time of Ancient Egypt, and before, may be evidenced in the Five Epagomenal Neters and the Ancient Egyptian symbol for the star Sirius, the 'Time-Keeper' for this neck of the galactic woods.

So, while I cannot hope to match the scholarship of those

great minds mentioned above, what I can do is tell the story from the other end of the scale, as a devic Essence who has actually trodden that particular evolutionary path, and thus gained its Five-fold Nature. I have known what it feels like to exist as a particle without mass and therefore unattached to the physical – up to a certain point, that is, since no particle remains in any one state forever. Everything changes, alternating between the chaotic and the stable. The quantum worlds may be chaotic, but rest assured that even within that chaos lie the seeds of order. Einstein never accepted the 'chance mode' so often favoured by scientists specialising in quantum physics. In fact, he stated, 'Quantum mechanics is certainly imposing, but an inner voice tells me it is not the real thing. The theory says a lot, but it does not really bring us any closer to the secret of the "Old One"'...'God,' says Einstein, 'does not play dice.' In other words, there is no such thing as coincidence, in spite of those periods of chaos through which all evolving life-forms must inevitably pass.

One radical difference between the devic kingdoms and the hominid evolutionary pattern is the death syndrome. Not normally possessing solid form as such, even when their evolutionary journeys take them through the atomic structures of mass, elemental spirits do not 'die'; they simply change by a process of accretion. It can be argued that the human field (soul) does likewise, although its body (mass) has a limited span of existence which, once again, is ordained by the physical conditions prevailing on the planet in question.

So what role, you may ask, does a Time deva play in all this, assuming it has gained its Five-fold Nature? Although I am able to enjoy concourse with the planetary and stellar devas, my kind are NOT planetary genii. We are the movers and shakers of the Cosmos. Do not think of us in terms of a 'single unit': we are legion. During our periods of travel we assist other angelic beings in the process of effecting genetic mutations of all kinds, not just on Earth, but in this and every other universe: and these, too, are legion, but as yet I know them not, as I am but a child among my kind, with much still to learn and unending tasks to perform. What I can tell you, however, is that certain Stellar angelic genii are responsible for the collective evolution of our solar system and all life experiencing therein, *in addition to its parallels in other areas of space-time.* And this is but one small area of our universe. Likewise, as mentioned above, there are those angelic beings to whom falls the task of actually creating new universes by producing the instanton and resulting singularity, essential to the manifestation of matter or mass at a given frequency. And it is with this latter task that the co-operation of the Great Time Entities is needed.

I am sure that some readers will want to know how devas feel about the subject of God. In my conversations with those planetary genii and senior angels with whom I have been privileged to converse, all were in accord, in that their view on supposed 'hot lines to God' was that they were simply not on, such assumptions constituting the sin of pride. While they all agreed that there is a 'single, infinite and timeless Source', they felt that calling on It willy-nilly constituted an impertinence generated by pure ego. And as to the 'holier than thou' approach, may I refer my readers to the parable of the Pharisee and the Publican. So, while the proverbial infant may be destined to attain to professional achievements *in the fullness of*

Time, the ascent to that position cannot be instantaneous (even by the laws of logic and physics), and the Laws of the Creator are nothing if not logical.

But let us return to our angelic friends. Angels, more often than not, are looked upon as being beautiful, benign beings, whose only task (aside from providing voices for the heavenly choirs, and orchestral players to accompany them) is to guide humans through the dark days of their evolutionary cycle. But hold on a minute – all angels are not on the side of Order. There are also angelic agents of chaos, or darkness, as some might prefer to call it. Take the story of Lucifer, for example. Now there is a classic case for the evidence of freewill among the angelic hosts. His sin was Pride! And he was a cherub – which tells us that he commenced his evolutionary cycle as a gnome. Gnomes have always been associated with money ('Gnomes of Zurich') and in my humble capacity as an observer for my own kind, I cannot help but notice the hominid preoccupation with possessions: possession of money, property, land – each other, even! All very Luciferian. There is a legend which speaks of Earth as being a fallen planet and yet Danuih herself is by no means off-track, so from where did this unwelcome devic influence hail, and why are we stuck with it here, on Earth?

I recently came across a short article in the *Daily Mail* (12/6/97), which reads as follows:

SISTER PLANET THAT MAY HAVE BEEN PIG-IN-THE-MIDDLE

'The Earth may once have had a sister planet which was flung from the solar system, scientists claim. A computer model of the creation of the planets has discovered a 'hole' between the Earth and Mars where a body once existed...'

Many years ago, during my days with the Atlanteans, when H.A. was addressing us through Tony, he told us that our Moon was once a planet in its own right which was flung from its orbit and captured by the gravitational pull of the Earth. Interestingly enough, it has recently been observed that, taking weight and size into account, our nightly 'light' has been deemed to be far too large to fit into the normal pattern for moons, while from a devic standpoint the energies it emits can sometimes have anything but a beneficial effect on the *minds* of humankind, as anyone who has worked as a psychiatric nurse will, no doubt, be happy to confirm. What I am therefore suggesting is that our 'captive' is a devious character who has found the ideal outlet for his[1] wayward energies among that species known as *homo sapiens*. Think about it.

For every deva of Light, there is believed to be an angel of Darkness. We are back full-circle to the chaos-versus-order scheme of things. And yet both are absolutely essential to the progress of all life, at every level. If we do not learn to cope with the inconsistencies, inconveniences and adversities of chaos, our fields will never expand; or, to use more popularly accepted semantics, our souls will never experience spiritual advancement. Besides, chaos is the child of order and order the child of chaos, the excessive build-up of either inevitably exploding into the rebirth of the other. All schools of magic

---

[1] (*Although lunar energies are now viewed in the feminine context, the planetary deva is, by nature, positive. I have dealt with the subject at length in my conversations with the devic entity in question in my book *Cosmic Connections*.)

acknowledge the existence of the eternal battle between Light and darkness, good or evil, as indeed do all religions. After all, it is all there in the Gospels.

But what about fairies, and where do they fit into the devic scheme of things? There was a full centre-page spread in the *Daily Mail* of September 5th, 1997, which featured the headline *HASN'T EVERYONE SEEN FAIRIES?* Among the comments made by several of those believers who had been interviewed for the article, one sentence, from Brian Froud, a 50-year-old artist and illustrator, caught my eye. It read:

'I think angels are grown-up fairies, part of the hierarchy we call the supernatural, but it is natural to me. They are the hidden agencies of nature, and the energies underneath it all'.

Congratulations, Mr. Froud. He was also sensible enough to realise that the 'wings' usually associated with our devic friends were nothing more than the manifestation of 'the energy flowing through their bodies'. After all, at the time when most of these angelic essences made their appearance in religious iconography, it was generally believed that wings were the only way anyone (or anything, for that matter) could ascend to the heavenly vaults that surround our beautiful, but sadly ill-treated, planet. Fairies, gnomes, goblins, trolls; all these are but the nomenclatures allotted to the various denizens of the elemental kingdoms by successive cultures over the ages. Doubtless these have their equivalents in other languages worldwide. Before 'civilisation' and the hardware of its accompanying technology took control of our planet, hominids were much closer to the natural children of Danuih (Gaia). In fact, to this day, in certain isolated country areas, there are still people who put out bowls of milk or other small offerings for the 'fairies', *sidhe*, or 'wee folk'. Animals are much closer to the devic kingdoms than hominids, although there are still those who have carried forward the old ways, such as 'horse whispering' and 'talking to the crops'.

Before I forget, there is one other question that I am bound to be asked. Of the nine choirs of angels named above, which, if any, represents the element of Time? Take a brief look at the aforementioned elemental categories into which the ancients placed them, and you will notice that there are three Fire (the Seraphim, Virtues and Powers), two Air (the Dominations and Principalities), two Water (the Thrones and Archangels), one Earth (the Cherubim) (plus the ninth choir which are simply labelled 'angels', as I learned at school, which is believed to include what are popularly viewed as Guardian Angels). Now, which of the 'Fire Angels' is the odd man out? – Go on – have a guess! All will be revealed!

Since I have 'come out' as a deva, I am constantly being asked what it actually feels like to be in a hominid body. Shall I or shall I not tell the truth? A lot of rubbish has been written about elementals, probably by people who have never had the opportunity to meet one and hear his/her story first-hand. My anguish at my separation from my own kind, and my understanding of their nature and purpose, is encapsulated in the following poem, which I wrote one lunch-time in the early fifties when I found myself alone in the office at 28 Belgrave Square, and which my publishers have insisted that I include in this book. So, rather than spoil the magic of this moment, I will forego the more mundane aspects of my earthly sojourn until the next chapter.

THE SERAPHIM

Hear me – for my voice is golden as the wings that bear me.
Stark is my message, yet cloaked in the shrouded corpse
    entombed in repose,
Oblivious of its accelerating transition.

My wings beat a message – fleet as the Griffon's featherless
    drumming,
Silent as the glide of Pegasus, alone on his
    riderless journey to Olympus
Where my seat awaits my return.

Hot is the flame of my sword, but fiercer burns the weapon of
    my brother,
In whose militance I present my arms in the cause of the
    Lost Ones,
Who are blinded by the darkness.

White visions are my gown, but blue is the auric flame of my
    head,
My adversaries are dim spectres, in whose presence I am awed,
But not subdued.

Fast is the speed of my light, but faster moves my body
    through the stars
Which are my children; yet I, in turn, am child of the
    Lords of Timeless Infinity.

Stirred are the aqueous depths when I touch those beclouded
    souls
Which stagnate in deep confusion, knowing neither
    origin nor ultimate form;
For the unused limb withers.

Seared by my glowing sword are the fetters of the
    self-imprisoned,
Enfeebled by the stupor of displacement.
    For to live they must move –
But to move is to suffer.

The inhalers of my exuded fumes breathe freely.
    Silently drop
The slime from their withdrawn feet, motioned
    purpose stirring
To memory progress overdue.

Heed me, oh tired ones, and warm your stiffened limbs in my
    golden heat.
Thaw your restricted minds, and with Prometheus
    enjoy the gift he first bestowed,
Before Light flees the vulture.

Shrink not in terror at my approach, but hark my heraldry –
    shrill as
The summoning wind, yet voluptuous as the lay of
    the maned Lion
Hailing his evening mate.

Concealed in my flailing arms lie deep caresses –
    the Healing Waters of Day.
Yet scalding are their torrents, glistening unbeholdable
    as the
Fire of which I am – for the Harbinger is come.

CHAPTER 22

Will The *Real* Murry Hope
Please Stand Up!

Oh, dear, must I? I suppose I had better descend, albeit with a
bump, from the celestial heights, once again to pen what
remains of my adventures to date. I shall therefore pick up the
story at the point at which I took over the tenancy of No. 14
Pook Lane. At that time I had five cats, although since my dear
Nephthys died in March 1988, I have consistently lost cats one
after the other, all in rather strange circumstances. Some died
of illness or had to be put to sleep. Others simply disappeared
and, sadly, the same was to apply to my new abode, the
pattern continuing right up until the end of 1996. Then,
following a break of two years, my darling Purrdi died in
August 1998, but a fragment of his spirit was soon back with
me in the persona of Pearl, who is also a silver Chinchilla, but
this time a little girl.

This was a period in which I was struggling with debts of
all kinds. I received some help from my Union Benevolent
Fund, who have kept my car on the road for me among other
helpful contributions, while friends also rallied round to see
that my cats were not denied essential veterinary treatment.
Finally, when the last cheques dribbled through from the sale

of my books, I was forced to go on to Income Support. To help with the cats, if nothing else, I decided to take a monthly class at my home. My Income Support precluding me from exacting a fee, I used to place a covered bowl on the table for any kind offerings that might help with the occasional bill, or tin of cat food. As the classes usually lasted all day, I did not feel this was too much to ask. Sometimes we would miss a month, especially around Christmas time and during the summer holidays, but somehow the Universe always managed to provide, albeit only the bare necessities.

It was while I was living at the Pook Lane lodge that I received a visit from an American psychologist who had been commissioned by a major university (and, I found out subsequently, the U.S. Government) to check out all those people who were claiming to be some sort of alien. He was also interested in the material given during channellings which he told me could be divided into two main categories – an excuse to say one's piece without accepting responsibility for same and the relinquishment of conscious control to a mind external to that of the channeller. He placed me in neither of these categories however, his studies of the subject matter of my books suggesting that I was probably part of an alien 'group mind', which spoke not only for myself, but for certain 'observers'. The Paschat material he found especially interesting as it contained so much accurate scientific knowledge. There was lots more, but does it really matter? I think not. One interesting question he asked me, which seemed to clinch the matter for him, was, 'How do you react to low-voltage electrical fields, a vacuum cleaner for example?' I told him I hated the things. In fact I dislike all electrical gadgets and have done so since my earliest childhood. On one occasion when Nanny took me to have my hair cut, upon the stylist producing a pair of electric clippers to trim my neckline, I leapt out of the chair and took off down the street, to the consternation of both adults concerned. The fact that I am now obliged to work with a computer does little to lift my spirits, but, as the saying goes, 'needs must when the devil drives'.

In 1993 I received notice from my landlords to vacate their property, the conditions of my contract stating that, should the use of the property be needed by any of the owner's family, I would be required to leave. Due to the arrival of some relatives from the States, that necessity had now arisen. As I was already on the Council's housing list they found me a small flat in a converted railway station about half a mile up the road from Pook Lane. I moved in the January of 1993, and darling Purrsi (Korat) was run over on the main road a few days later. Shortly afterwards, my seven-month old Persian, Ptah-Ptah, had to be put to sleep, suffering from incurable feline infectious peritonitis. The station abode was a disaster area from the beginning. It adjoined a large council estate, of the kind where gangs of youths and unruly children make life a hell for the orderly and the elderly. I made the fatal error of asking some skate-boarders to desist from using my small verandah to practise on, which evoked an angry response from one of the fathers, who assured me that he would, 'have you old biddies out of here in six months, or you won't recognise your face in the mirror by the time we've finished with it.' Could it be pure coincidence that after making this threat and returning to work on his chain-saw, said person accidentally severed several of the fingers on his right hand? Not guilty!

I reported his threat to the police, but it seemed there was little they could do, no actual assault having taken place. Another family who had moved in at the same time as myself, and who saw fit to stand up to this man and his cronies, had their car smashed, their front door knocked in and several other damaging incidents. Over the following weeks I was persecuted by a group of youngsters who would stand outside my window chanting, 'Out, out, old biddy, out, out, old cow'. In the end I resorted to crawling past that window to avoid them seeing me there. By the May of '93 I could take no more, and so, on the advice of a social worker friend and my doctor, I sought alternative accommodation. Not that this proved any better, but at least there was no violence. On the day I moved, I was helped by a local friend and one of the old Atlantean members, a former nurse. As we loaded my bits and pieces on to the van, a crowd made up of both children and adults gathered outside. And when we drove off, they ran behind us, making obscene gestures and shouting, 'Good riddance, old cow, we won, we won!'

The only event that served to highlight those few months at the old railway station flat was my being invited as guest speaker at the annual MENSA meeting at Worcester College. My subject was 'The Field Theory'. Much to my amazement, I received a standing ovation! It helped me through the following weeks of torment and misery.

My next abode was a converted stable on a small estate: all very fine in the summer, but the only heating in the enormous, barn-like living room was a wood-burning stove, and I am allergic to coal and wood dust! But once again some higher power stepped in. I received a letter from the planning department of the local council, telling me that since no planning permission had been given for the conversion I was an illegal tenant. I promptly rang the Housing Department, with which I was still registered for a council tenancy in a country district, and put the two departments together. And, by the strangest of coincidences (but is there really such a thing? I still think not!), it so happened that a vacancy was about to arise in the small village of Singleton, where I now reside.

I moved there (here, as I write), on 11th October 1993, my third move that year. My little bungalow is pleasant enough, but regrettably it only has one, small bedroom, which means that in addition to my small bed, wardrobe and dressing table, I am also lumbered with a computer desk, enormous bookcase and filing cabinet. In other words, the room is grossly overfilled. But I have little option as the council are not obliged to provide a second bedroom for a single person. However, my doctor has now asked them to move me as soon as one becomes available, on the grounds that I have no-one to look after me when I am ill. Several of my friends would be only too happy to spend some time down here under such circumstances, so we shall just have to wait and see what comes up.

I tried taking the classes again but the strain of a whole day's teaching started to affect my health, and I was obliged to give it up. In 1995, Element Books decided to revise and re-issue a title I wrote for them in the Eighties, *Ancient Egypt: The Sirius Connection*. I completed the rewrite, and Professor Peter

Stewart kindly spent a whole day with me, going over the page proofs and checking the scientific input. And so the new edition finally went to press, to emerge as *The Sirius Connection – Unlocking the Secrets of Ancient Egypt*. Although I cannot claim it to be a world best-seller, it certainly took off and my subsequent royalties enabled me to clear most of my debts, and to purchase a decent car.

So much for the history to date. But what of this strange female who is a combination of genetic inheritance, current social programming and an alien soul? As my readers will have gathered, I am no social animal and would possibly describe myself as something of a recluse. I don't 'do' holidays and my other dislikes include large gatherings of any kind, and being 'dropped in on'. I am quite happy to lecture, however, in the comforting knowledge that I will soon be on my way back to the silence and peace of my own pad. I used to say that the things I hated most were the 'four 'P's' – parties, pubs (of the noisy, beery kind), politics and pop music, whereas my favourites are all 'C's' – cats, cars, clothes and chocolate. Unfortunately my health precludes me from indulging too heavily in the latter, severe migraines and digestive problems resulting if I ever allow myself too many lapsed moments. I also hate dealing with food in any form, cooking proving an anathema to me. Were it not for my awareness of the needs of the physical body, I would exist solely on cups of tea and milk-chocolate bars. Even the simple act of making cups of tea for more than two people is guaranteed to put me in a flat spin. I can never recall who does and who doesn't take milk, sugar, herbal tea or whatever, and usually end up begging my friends to come and take over. It is not that I can't cook, but simply that I would rather not engage in that practice. Cars, now that's another ball-game; fast, sporty models in particular. I drive a Ford Puma at present – although, if I am honest, I am (to my deep regret) getting too old for all that speeding about. As to my musical tastes, I think I have made these abundantly clear in earlier chapters. I adore baroque and, of course, my beloved Mozart, although I am none too keen on contemporary classical music. As for this so-termed 'New Age' stuff, being totally unstructured and going nowhere it reminds me of the Ooslam Bird, which goes round in ever-decreasing circles until ... oh well, I think I'd better leave that one there! After all, the Universe *does* have structure, and it *is* going somewhere!

More than anything else, I hate NOISE. It was exactly the same when I was a child. The sound of other children screaming and yelling would send me running back to the peace of Nanny's kitchen. Silence I adore. People often ask me how I can sit for hours in utter silence, apparently not doing anything. But it is in those precious moments that I am able to expand my consciousness sufficiently to effect a contact, not only with my own kind but also with other, timeless realms of infinity. The telephone analogy I used in an earlier chapter begs repetition: how can those Beings of Light from more exalted regions of consciousness get through to us if our line is continually engaged? Besides, I have always felt that people who rely on a constant output of noise, of any kind, are somehow lacking in either self-esteem or some other psychological quirk that precludes them from facing their real selves.

Contrary to what some readers may think, I am not all

doom and gloom. In fact, I am something of a comedienne, and on one occasion actually appeared as a stand-up comic. Also, those theatrical roles in which I excelled were always of the comedy variety; but then, comedy and tragedy have always walked hand-in-hand, many comedians having a darker or deeper side to their natures. And although I may write about the past I am by no way obsessed with it. My concern with its patterns is related solely to its influence on the future, since history inevitably repeats itself, albeit sometimes in lengthy cycles. As the popular saying goes, 'What goes around comes around'!

It has often been pointed out to me that had my father lived, and offered me the advantage of a University education, I would probably have read medicine initially, but then drifted into anthropology or the classics and ended up in some academic backwater, having eschewed the world. In fact I would never have done the work I was destined to undertake. So the lack of parentage has proved an advantage in the long run.

A friend whom I allowed to read what I have written so far in this chapter rebuked me with the words, 'But you haven't actually said anything about your attitude towards the ordinary, everyday things of life, what you look like, your choice of clothes, your favourite colours, decor, etc. And what about your home, your garden? Do you like sport? Debate? Do you still sing?' All right, all right. I'll get there eventually, but it's all rather boring.

I am 5'6" tall and I weigh 7 stone 10lbs. My eyes are a dark teal blue. Although I have freckles, there is no pink in my skin tones; I never burn in the sun, but turn a strong shade of yellow-gold (a dermatologist once told me that I had a predominance of green-pigment in my skin – no, I'm NOT a Vulcan!).

When it comes to clothes I am positively 'square'. I dress in Aquascutum and Daks when I can afford to, which means I have few of these excellent labels in my wardrobe at the moment. I favour Calvin Klein jeans and denims, and religiously avoid anything flowery, flimsy or frilly. Very Virgoan, one supposes. The same goes for scents – the woody ones being most favoured. My favourite colour? Blue, blue and more blue, interspersed with white and the occasional dash of orange. I am useless at sport of any kind, my poor co-ordination often making me a laughing-stock when I was a youngster, although I would love to swim regularly were there a heated pool near to where I live. I like walking, but not alone, which means I never go anywhere these days. Sad! Gardening I positively adore. As for debate, well, as I commented in an earlier chapter, the least said; it always strikes me as a platform for those anxious to lord their views over others under the democratic guise, while also affording listeners with no views of their own an opportunity to jump on an appropriate bandwagon. The lack of opportunity to express my musical vocals skills does cause me some concern however, my last public concert being almost two years ago, so my New Year resolution for 1999 is to get back into practice once again, assuming that the instrument is still functioning, and I rather think it is.

I don't attend many lectures these days. As the current expression goes, I've read the book, seen the film and got the tee-shirt. I also refuse to subject myself to appearing in any sort of public entertainment masquerading under such titles as 'research', 'investigation', 'curiosity', 'searching for the truth', etc. I've been along that corridor – a painful journey, from which I escaped, but not without battle scars both mental and physical. Hominid reaction? One sees it coming! Children discard toys when they become bored with them. By the same token, young souls discard ideas, always aiming to keep with the *de rigueur* of current crazes, be these political, social, esoteric or whatever. If I do not feel the ways of the times to be right, I will not keep up with them, and to hell with those profit-making schemes that shelter behind fancy, New Age titles.

Perhaps I should try to describe psychologically and analytically how it feels when someone is putting me to the test, either in debate, question time, or purely out of curiosity. At times my left brain experiences a clarity – everything is easily explained. Complex matters I hand over to my right brain, which knows the answers because it has direct access to my 'field'. The problem only arises when the right brain presents the left with information which it does not have the software to process. This tends to produce a frustration, especially when there is cross-questioning and debate involved. However, I am usually able to sort it out later into terms appropriate to the subject matter, and currently acceptable to the questioners. In simple terms, my right brain accesses cosmic frequencies and my left brain interprets the information received therefrom into recognisable referentials. Thus any pressure of the kind usually brought about in debates inevitably affects reception.

As for my home, had finances permitted, it would harbour

antique furniture in medium oak, soft blues and browns, a grandmother clock ticking away happily in the corner (I adore clocks!), and the usual sort of things that those of a generation before me held sacred. But sadly I have not been thus blessed, so I have had to make the most of a few reproduction pieces and a cheap carriage clock! With several active cats around, it wouldn't do to have the real thing, now would it? I am, however, VERY houseproud!

People have often commented on my supposed phenomenal speed of writing. But why isolate 'writing'? I work at one speed only, and that goes for *everything*, from washing up to writing books. So when I am asked for more there is none to give, and, if pushed, I promptly collapse, my field effecting a visibly, clinically diagnosable somatisation.

Chameleon-like, I have, over the years, hidden behind many masks, endeavouring to be all things to all people. This has constituted an essential part of my survival programme. Nobody loves a misfit, so one tries awfully hard to *appear* to fit in. But it simply doesn't work. Sooner or later one meets up with those of opposing views whom one has diplomatically placated in the past, and the cat is out of the proverbial bag. So, let me state categorically that I am not in anyone's metaphysical camp. New Age psychobabble I abhor. Myth I view in much the same way as Jung – primitive explanations for cosmic phenomena and the complete psychological history of mankind in story form. As for meditation, pathworkings and similar techniques, their validity surely lies in their psychological/therapeutic effect on the practitioner, possibly manipulating the mind to accept an alternative pattern. Any psychologist worth his/her salt could achieve the same results. As I have said previously, I never meditate in the accepted understanding of the word, and on occasions when I have been obliged to try I either go to sleep or whizz out into the Cosmos and connect up with my own kind; great moments of inspiration inevitably coming to me when I am not expecting them.

I am reminded of an instance at a major London psychic festival when I was approached by a venerable Chinese gentleman who sought my advice on a private matter. He must have been satisfied with the little help I was able to give him, as he thanked me and added: 'I know that you, too, have many problems to face in the future, but you are fortunate in that you have powerful ancestors, who will help you to overcome them'. So, it would appear that help comes from both spiritual and genetic sources.

My poverty status has often been criticised by my contemporaries, on the grounds that, with all my knowledge (what knowledge?), if I pulled myself together I could accept the many well-paid lecture tours that I have been offered over the past few years. But I am all too familiar with the pattern. Once one has said one's piece from the platform, one is then expected to keep it up for hours after, for the benefit of individuals hungry for information who don't care a damn whether one is tired, ill, or whatever. If pushed beyond a certain point I inevitably vacate my shell (pass out), as both Jung and Freud did in similar circumstances. I can handle the occasional public lecture or seminar, but I always pay for it later.

Several of those members of the Atlantean Society who left at the same time as me have often asked me why I don't take up channelling H.A. The answer is that I have no need to. As I have already explained, the five of us (I, my three devic brothers and my sister) are one unit, and he is the fulcrum, the term 'Father', being purely for convenience. I therefore have instant access to the 'family' mind without the need to present myself as a medium.

The fact that I have no interest in old buildings, visiting the pyramids or seeking the history of this planet in similar ways, has often been commented upon, and I touched briefly, in an earlier chapter, on an unpleasant experience I had when visiting an old castle where deeds of unimaginable horror had taken place. I have often undergone similar experiences in churches, on old battle fields and at locations of cult ritual or brutal abuse. There have, of course, also been holier, more sacred events, which brings to mind an amusing episode in which a 'skill', similar to my own, surfaced in a complete stranger.

A group of us, consisting of Jed and me, Patsy, Roy and their son, Marcus, and the late Nerys Dee and her husband, decided to attend the Padstow Festival in Cornwall one 1st May. We stayed the night at an hotel so as to be there in time for the start of the ritual the next morning. Unfortunately it was a drizzly day, although not too cold, and as the procession started on its regular course we stood among some thousand or more other rain-coated spectators who lined the narrow streets. In addition to the two horses, the procession also featured a large drum called 'Brenton' (believed to have been brought home from Waterloo in 1815), which makes an appearance once a year and is handled by someone special, who knows the exact beat to use for the occasion. There were only two lines of people in front of our little group as the procession passed us, and as it did, the drummer suddenly stopped and, reaching behind these, beckoned me to join him. He then handed me the striker and motioned me to continue as he had done, which I did, subconsciously observing the correct interval for the beat. And so, side by side, we walked in procession to the stopping-point, whereupon I handed the piece back to him. Looking him straight in the eyes, I said, 'Why did you do that? Why me?' He leaned towards me in a confidential manner and whispered, 'Well, you knows, and I knows', whereupon he rejoined the rite and I returned quietly to my friends. You see, we can sense the presence of one of our own kind, even among a crowd of strangers.

I think I have already covered my views on travel in an earlier chapter, so all I can add is that I shall sustain in my data-banks a fond memory of the England in the Thirties and Fifties. As for the sixties, I would appear to be out of step with the view shared by many, that this period constituted a major turning-point in the journey towards the Golden Age. For me, I see only the acceleration of chaos that will eventually precipitate Danuih's essential culling. But then, as I have already explained, Order is inevitably the child of Chaos, and, as always, Time will be the ultimate judge. Perhaps one should take heart in the fact that there is no longer the need to cloak one's prophecies in allegory in order to avoid the wrath of the current religious, New Age or scientific establishments. The icons of the latter are just as prone to making their forecasts as were the seers of the past, the only difference being that they are not so ready to admit to their mistakes, and to accept responsibility for them. I have always tended to be ahead of my time, but for the benefit of future generations, if not this one, I have told my story, in all honesty, inasmuch as the limitations of my physical brain and its current software will permit.

Epilogue

Regretfully, (from my readers' standpoint, anyway), I am no novelist and putting this book together has proved an onerous task at best. As I read back over the preceding pages I find myself thinking, 'what a jumble', and wondering how much better a job a professional biographer could have made of it. In fact, when discussing the periods in question with two close friends, to whom I have allowed a peek preview, they have both commented on the humour that has somehow crept into my description of events, including those that could be easily labelled as being highly upsetting. My pain, in fact, has come in the later years, when upon viewing my life from the age of 35 onwards, I have been able to see clearly, in hindsight, that dark and seemingly unending tunnel of despair through which I have travelled towards the final discovery of the light at the other end. However, in the words of the song, *'Non, je ne regrette rien'*.

Not that all is roses at present, but at least I now *understand* and can therefore distance myself to a degree from the discord that constitutes modern-day life. As an observer of human behaviour I cannot help but observe the dominance of the

Element of Water in the hominid psychology. But then, wiser folk than I have noted the same thing, which is undoubtedly why the symbol of The Man was used by the Ancients to denote that element, both in pagan and Christian iconography (The Angel Gabriel – Water – Man – see Chapter 20). As far as humanity is concerned, this element constitutes both its weakness and its strength, the former lying in the fact that people can be emotionally manipulated into believing anything, about anyone; the latter in that the watery element can generate those precious virtues of compassion and caring.

Standing back and viewing the history of human life on this planet, I note the ever-changing tides of chaos and order that have dominated society since hominids first endeavoured to take control of their destiny. For example, there is the 'chaos through freedom' syndrome: people feel the need for self-expression, but inevitably end up going 'over the top'. The result – anarchy. But after a while they become dissatisfied with the lack of security that the freedom to destroy willy-nilly has automatically licensed, and so the pendulum once again swings to Order, and even tougher measures than those previously used are employed to redress the balance.

I discern periods of economic and social stability shattered by the impact of two world wars, their final demise hastened (weakened), by the sinister, destructive strides of technology, which have surreptitiously undermined and outstripped its very foundations. I watch this slow and insidious disintegration, and, to use a currently popular turn of phrase – it freaks me out. But then, I am sufficiently well-acquainted with the sine-wave currents of chaos and order to know that one is inevitably born of the other, so I take what little solace I can from the knowledge that the next period of order will be directed by my own kind – the devic forces – which control the ebb and flow of mass/matter. But then, have I not seen it all before? In Mu, Atlantis, Antarctica, where humankind has placed its proverbial foot on the accelerator of doom, thus invoking – albeit unconsciously – the elemental wrath which is the natural outcome of this fateful joy-ride? Once again my kind are forced to show their true power and absolute authority over Danuih's errant brood.

You want a prophecy for the future? Then you shall have it, although I have already committed myself in several of my earlier writings, notably *The Gaia Dialogues* and *Cosmic Connections*. The writing is on the proverbial wall. If you don't believe me, look to the discoveries that have recently emerged concerning prophecies and warnings, given by advanced races from the past which are only now surfacing. Of course the planet will change. Change is as much a part of her natural life process as it is of all that lives on the space-ship that is her body. And these changes will be drastic. Millions of lives will be lost. Coastlines will alter so much as to be unrecognisable. Global warming? That is only one of the symptoms of the malaise that is afflicting the body of Danuih, and, as Professor Sir James Lovelock so wisely pointed out, when we are suffering from a virus our bodies produce a fever with which to drive it out. And so it is with Danuih. I have stood afar and watched such things happening – heard the cries of the suffering and wept with those who have sustained great losses, for such is the lot of we whose evolutionary paths lead us through the labyrinths of Time. Of course, hominids will eventually encounter other species, the denizens of different worlds, both in this Universe and others parallel to it; and to a degree, their own technology will launch them into that transition – Nature will do the rest.

In the light of the above it is little wonder that I am not popular with many groups, especially those which have opted for the cosy approach, the 'if we all meditate together we can stop these events taking place' attitude. Well, I put it to you this way: if your meditations possess such powers over the elements, why do you not apply them to earthquakes, volcanoes and other elemental phenomena which disregard all that is sacred to humankind, including life itself? I put this argument to a lady at a meeting I was addressing, who assured me that if her group and others like it put out their thoughts they could control *anything*. 'Then why did you not', I asked her, 'prevent the earthquake at Kobe?' 'Oh, they're Japanese. That's probably a karmic punishment for the atrocities of the second world war.' Excuses, excuses.

It is not only my prophecies for the future that seem to put some people's backs up. I have even been criticised for my apparel – too square for some, it seems, while on another occasion, when a friend was trying to interest a stall-holder in one of my books, he replied, 'Murry Hope – get real, man. She doesn't do drugs, dresses like one of them (?) and doesn't have a clue what real life's about.' Well, don't say I didn't warn you. But then my energies can have a strange effect on some people, and, although those who function well below their frequency are seldom bothered by them, others find their accelerating impulses disturbing. Such people are aware of the difference but their inability to comprehend, communicate with, or gain control over the situation tends to make them feel threatened, and a threatened hominid is someone best avoided.

But what of my own future in this body? My circumstances will, I know, change considerably over the next two years, and for the better in some respects, although the acceleration of chaos is obviously a factor with which we shall all have to live, no matter what is going on in our private lives. I hope to enjoy the company of my beloved pedigree cats, Hattie (sorrel-silver Somali), Tami (golden Chinchilla Persian) and Pearl (silver Chinchilla), for some years to come, in the sure knowledge that even if the older one, Hattie, leaves before I am 'called', we shall meet up again in another, happier and more exalted dimension. The same goes for my friends. I also have a feeling that I shall not be 'alone' here for that much longer. Well, as they say, Time will tell.

Viewing the foregoing chapters through the eyes of a modern psychologist, the word 'compensatory', as I mentioned earlier, immediately springs to mind: but surely every aspect of living is based on compensatory factors? We spend most of our lives compensating for one thing or another, but this does not make us 'psychological cases'. Likewise the (questionably!) normal, cynical appraisal of anything paraphysical is to condemn it on the subconsciously fear-based grounds of illogicality, when an unbiased approach would serve to show that it is, in fact, logic *par excellence*.

In explaining my reason for being here, I have indicated that I am in the 'observer' mode: watching, listening, taking in all and everything within the limitations of my human brain, and transmitting *instantaneously* to the data-banks of my own kind. My meagre offering is therefore nothing but the true story of an alien entity encapsulated – nay, trapped – in a human body which limits drastically the self-expression of its true beingness, or 'field' as I prefer to call it. Consequently, there is a lot I cannot – nay, dare not – say in this book if I wish my last few years to pass in peace, but rest assured that I shall leave such knowledge when I die, so the truth will out in the end. And as to the 'Hallmark' of a changeling – well, that all depends on why any of us are here; although I can guarantee my readers that, like bad pennies, our kind inevitably put in an appearance prior to the advent of chaos on a large scale. But take heart: in spite of my comments at the end of the preceding chapter, as I have also viewed, with joy, the post-chaotic period, when humankind will finally achieve that mythical Golden Age.

But, you may ask, have I as an individual lived up to the changeling myth, or any other legendary tale, for that matter? Students of the psychology of allegory will doubtless have detected a parallel, and not dissimilar apologue, encoded within the web of my tale. I refer, of course, to the age-old fable of some regal personage, who is slaughtered or deposed by a rival, but whose infant child is, like the changeling, smuggled to safety by a menial and raised among the poor until such times as he/she is alerted to his/her rightful heritage.   In spite of the fact that such considerations as breeding no longer count in today's world, these myths still persist, and I am living proof of them. My Nanny used to say, 'Send a pig to school and it will come back a pig', so one supposes the converse also applies. It certainly appears to do so in my case. As with both the mythical changeling and the progeny of the deposed, I was rejected at birth and left to discover both my spiritual and social backgrounds in the school of life. Although raised with love in the ways of ordinary folk, I have frequently been spurned by the *nouveaux riches*, due to either my lack of formal education or material wealth. Only in my latter years have both my cosmic *raison d'être* and true genetic/social identity been revealed to me, finally affording me a degree of confidence which I have sadly lacked in the past. All right, so I may appear to many as 'a bit strange', but then a certain section of British society had ever been noted for spawning eccentrics or oddities!

Like its fabled parallel, the changeling story is classified as a myth, but what is a myth? A statement of cosmic fact, perhaps – cyclical, immutable, abiding – which the great Jung expressed as follows:

> 'What we are to our inward vision, and what man appears to be *sub specie aeternitatis*, can only be expressed by way of myth. Myth is more individual, and expresses life more precisely, than does science. Science works with concepts of averages which are far too general to do justice to the subjective variety of an individual life.' (*Memories, Dreams and Reflections*, p.17)

This theme is re-echoed in the words of Russia's Professor Ivan A. Efremov, who insists that 'historians must pay more respect to the ancient traditions and folklore', and accuses scientists of the West of 'a certain snobbishness when it comes to the tales of the so-called common people'.

Taking into account the very first sentence of this narrative, I feel that I am entitled to end it in similar vein, with the words: 'And they all lived happily ever after'. After all, it *is* a *Faery* story!

Some other titles from
LIGHT PUBLISHING

SPIRITUAL REALISATION: INNER VALUES IN EVERYDAY LIFE
Communications by Chan, spirit guide of Ivy Northage
Chan's suggestions for handling life's problems carry spiritual authority but are never over-assertive. A book to treasure.
£7.50 paperback, ISBN 0 903336 21 9

MEDIUMSHIP MADE SIMPLE by Ivy Northage
Widely regarded as one of the classic texts on practical mediumship. Ivy Northage draws on forty years as medium and teacher, giving clear descriptions of psychic development and its practical applications.
£7.99 paperback, ISBN 0 903336 19 7

WHILE I REMEMBER. The Life Story of Ivy Northage edited by Brenda Marshall
A new title. Ivy's story is rich in interest, from her colourful childhood early in the century, through her unwilling introduction to the psychic world and a long, hard training by her guide, Chan, to the peak of professionalism. He promised that she would witness every kind of physical phenomena and her accounts of these séances are truly amazing. A book to be enjoyed on many levels.
£7.99 paperback, ISBN 0 903336 32 4

INSIGHT AND INTUITION by Julie Soskin
Julie's eagerly-awaited manual on psychic and spiritual development is virtually a do-it-yourself manual on cosmic consciousness. Exercises in each chapter help to internalise the essence of what we have read and integrate it into our daily lives.
£9.99 paperback, ISBN 0 903336 14 6

TRANSFORMATION by Julie Soskin
The fourth channelled work by Julie Soskin reveals the enormous shift now occurring in the evolution of humanity and the changes this will bring in our lives.
£6.99 paperback, ISBN 0 903336 24 3

IN TOUCH WITH RAYNOR C. JOHNSON
by Sheila Gwillam
With a foreword by Paul Beard. Wisdom and spiritual insight from a renowned scientist, author and spiritual philosopher
£8.99 paperback, ISBN 0 903336 15 4

THE NEW SCIENCE OF THE SPIRIT by David A. Ashe
An exciting new approach providing a framework for the universe in which the laws of physics and the laws of the spirit become one.
£9.95 hardback, ISBN 0 903336 56 1
£6.99 paperback, ISBN 0 903336 55 3

PRINCIPLES OF THE UNIVERSE by Keith Casburn
Communications from a source beyond the time frame of our solar system; the multidimensional nature of being; how to become the spiritual beings we really are.
£6.99 paperback, ISBN 0 903336 28 6

IZARIS by Keith Casburn

Communications from Izar, one of the second magnitude stars in our universe, tells us how we relate vibrationally to stars and galaxies, and the demands this makes on us mentally, emotionally and physically.

£8.99 paperback, ISBN 0 903336 12 X

SOUL TREK by Julie Gale

A channelled book tracing the soul's evolution from the Source, through physical incarnation and beyond. Sheds new light on subjects such as group souls, twin souls and reincarnation.

£8.99 paperback, ISBN 0 903336 26 X

SOULWORK: FOUNDATIONS FOR SPIRITUAL GROWTH
by Sue Minns

The College's answer to those unable to attend CPS classes. This 166-page tabulated workbook and the six audio cassettes are based on Sue Minns' Foundation Course at the College of Psychic Studies. They offer step-by-step guidance for your own inner unfoldment, providing direction along the way. Graduated lessons cover: Breathing, Meditation, The Aura, Chakras, Healing, Psychic Energy, Body/Mind, Inner Child and Soul, Karma and Reincarnation.

£39.99 Workbook & six audio-cassettes, ISBN 0 903336 16

The College of Psychic Studies
16 Queensberry Place
South Kensington
London SW7 2EB
Telephone: 0171 589 3292/3
Fax: 0171 589 2824
E-mail: cpstudies@aol.com
Website: www.psychic-studies.org.uk